SACRED SEED
AND
LIVING BREAD

DR. T. D. STUBBLEFIELD

Brett:
   May God bless you always
with the seed of his truth
and the bread of his favor.
      T. D. Stubblefield
         7/9/14

Cover Design by Proximitee Design

Printed in the United States by
Mira Digital Publishing
Chesterfield, Missouri 63005

CONTENTS

Old Testament Reflections

New Testament Reflections

FOREWARD

And so the journey began on February 6, 2000 in suburban Chesterfield, Missouri, some twenty-five miles west of the spiraling Arch in downtown St. Louis that welcomes travelers to the city and to the Midwest. Now in its fifteenth year, this journey has proven to be a providential union between Pastor and people that has transformed both. Joseph Fort Newton in his splendid sermon *"In the Vestry"* described this profound possibility very well when he wrote, "Preachers shape Churches — that is one half of the truth: Churches also mold preachers — that is the other side; and when the Church honors the pulpit the pulpit will honor it."

Over the years of preaching and pastoral ministry, I have been helpfully teased by Isaiah's affirmation of God's provision in Chapter 55 of his profound and sweeping prophetic anal. He said,

> *"For as the rain cometh down, and the snow from heaven, and returneth not thither, but watereth the earth, and maketh it bring forth and bud, that it may give seed to the sower, and bread to the eater"*
> *(Isaiah 55:10 KJV) [emphasis mine].*

In the stream of the prophet's magnificent attestation, each Sunday before preaching, I appeal to God to "Give seed to the sower and bread to the eater." The prayer is a humbling reminder to me and to the congregation that all of our help comes from the Lord! Years ago, an inspiring devotional from Charles Spurgeon's book <u>Daily Help</u> etched this awareness indelibly in my spirit. Spurgeon shared this timeless insight:

> *"Whenever we are privileged to eat of the bread which Jesus gives, we are satisfied with the full and sweet repast. When Jesus is the host, no guest goes away*

empty from the table. Our head is satisfied with the precious truth which Christ reveals; our heart content with Jesus, our hope satisfied, for whom have we in heaven but Jesus? And our desire is satiated for what can we wish for more than to 'know Christ' and to be found in him? Jesus fills our conscience, till it is at perfect peace; our judgment with the certainty of his teachings; our memory with recollections of what he has done, our imagination with the prospects of what he is yet to do".

What preacher-pastor would not desire these types of treasured and transforming transactions in the minds and hearts of the people to whom we minister in the glorious name of our Lord and Savior Jesus Christ? The articles that I now share with a larger audience are aimed at somehow attempting to scale this prodigious mountain and pursue this high, ambitious and sometimes daunting goal.

Sacred Seed and Living Bread is the accretion of one pastor's sincere desire to fulfill a sacred calling and unavoidable stewardship. These articles, inherently pastoral, represent expositional espousals from a pastor who shares the Apostle Paul's perspective and passion for the local church: "For I am jealous over you with godly jealousy: for I have espoused you to one husband, that I may present you as a chaste virgin to Christ" (II Corinthians 11:2).

The compilation and publishing of these articles have been deferred and dormant for years, but have been suddenly driven out of remission by the author's growing awareness of his own mortality. There is an urgent sense of unshakeable debt and undeniable responsibility to the larger body of Christ that continues to well up within me, greater than any protestation or expectation that the publishing of these articles might be perceived as vain or vacuous. To the end that even one of these excursive explorations into the Word of God might encourage, nurture, inform or inspire faith in some other in the body of Christ, I will be eternally grateful and my sense of indebtedness satisfied and assuaged.

I have found much needed encouragement and inspiration for this project in Eugene Peterson's moving paraphrase of the vaulted and vibrant vocals of the psalmist who said,

> *"I scrub my hands with purest soap, then join hands with the others in the great circle, dancing around your altar, God, Singing God-songs at the top of my lungs, telling God-stories. God, I love living with you; your house glows with your glory" (Psalms 26:6 - The Message).*

Sacred Seed and Living Bread is the collection of my God-stories. It mirrors not only the collusion and consequence of a pastor's concern for the flock of God which he has been called to serve, but is as well the ongoing narrative of the constructive and compelling collision of ideas and insights at the intersection of his own spirit and heart. These perspectives are still being inspired by the currents and confluence of biblical exegesis, theological reflection, and the experiential engagement between pastor and people, shepherd and sheep, bishop and believers.

The imperishable seed God provides to this sower, while vital and vibrant with regard to substance and verity (truth), is undoubtedly diverse in regards to its source. Nature in all her matchless beauty, majesty, volatility, and untamed fierceness, human life in all its vitality, variety, and even viciousness, and the Word of God, incomparable in wealth and wisdom have all collectively conspired as sacred seed to encourage, indeed compel reflection in the heart of the preacher and reiteration as living bread in the lives of God's people. I pray that you, too, will be touched.

ACKNOWLEDGEMENTS

This meager offering is the accretion of a thirty-seven year personal, professional and spiritual pilgrimage. Thirty one of those years I have served as the pastor-teacher of two historic congregations — the First Baptist Church of Georgetown, Kentucky (1983-1999) and the First Baptist Church of Chesterfield, Missouri (2000-present). Our shared experience of ministry is the seedbed where many of the principles, priorities and perspectives chronicled in this book find their genesis. For our striving together to earnestly contend for the faith and do the work of the Christian ministry, I am truly grateful.

I am indebted as well to the great cloud of mentors and ministers who, through their writing, speaking , preaching or example, have touched both my head and heart and indelibly impacted my perspectives about God, the Bible, the church, preaching and Christian ministry. Their ranks are too luminous and numerous to number or name here (for fear of any unintended yet likely omission), but their example has inspired me to strive to be a blessing to others as they have been a blessing to me.

I will always be indebted to the compelling spirit and tenured tenacity of my mother, Irene Foster, our family's matriarch and "peaceful warrior" who communicated to me and my eight siblings by precept and example the value of hard work, the importance of family, and devotion to God and the church.

My wife Judy, the mother of our four children and my "journey companion", is my pearl of great price. Her true love, devotion, dedication, support and constant encouragement over the years allowed me to pursue excellence in ministry and fulfill my calling as a pastor, preacher and Christian leader. My journey companion, more than any other, has consistently sounded the trumpet that summoned me to this task. Finally, our children - Darius, Jakeeta, Charlton and Kacy, now all grown up and raising our grandchildren, but will always be never-ending and refreshing springs of incentive, insight and inspiration for their Dad.

To these and so many others the Lord used to touch my life, I say thank you and to God be the Glory!

Old Testament Reflections

Designer Men and Women

**"And God said, Let us make man in our image, after our
likeness: and let them have dominion over the fish of the sea,
and over the fowl of the air, and over the cattle, and over all
the earth, and over every creeping thing that creepeth upon the
earth. So God created man in his own image, in the image of
God created he him; male and female created he them."**

(Genesis 1:26-27)

In the world of high fashion where change is as frequent and
frantic as shifts in the wind or weather, to ascribe to a garment or
an accessory the label "designer" is to invest it with a value and
quality that transcends the ordinary. Designer and discount are
on different ends of the fashion spectrum. Smart shoppers know
the "designer brands" and are either drawn by them or repelled
by them depending on experience, taste, budget or any number
of other factors, both small or great.

Real fathers are committed to doing everything they can as
both providers and protectors to help our children navigate the
generational rapids that begin in infancy and end at adulthood.
It is at this critical bend on the river of life that we pray our
"babies" grow up, and experience and express the physical,
mental, emotional and most importantly spiritual maturity of
adulthood. One sure indicator of this is financial independence.
Fathers and mothers alike celebrate that point and place in life
when our kids get jobs, move out, start paying their bills and
become financially self-sustaining. Hallelujah! I knew we were
getting close to that marvelous (and painfully for some parents),
"illusive" moment with one of our daughters when she informed
my wife (who subsequently informed me with great chagrin)
that she had recently purchased a "Coach purse." My initial
response betrayed my dire and desperate lack of knowledge of
designer labels. I basically said, "What's the big deal?" However,
my aptitude and awareness skyrocketed when I received a quick
tutorial that correlated the "Coach" label with dollars and cents.

It was at that moment that I knew in my heart we were nearing that point with this daughter where the cash cow was dying and the brook would soon dry up!

It occurs to me that by making us in His image, God has placed upon both men and women His "designer label." The Word of God reminds us of this stupendous truth, for it says, "And God said, 'Let us make man in our image, after our likeness; and let them have dominion over the fish of the sea and over the fowl of the air, and over the cattle, and over all the earth …' So God created man in his own image, in the image of God created he him, male and female created he them" (Genesis 1:26-27). A few centuries later, David, the sweet songwriter of Israel, would ask the question, "When I consider thy heavens, the works of thy fingers, the moon and stars, which thou hast ordained, what is man that thou art mindful of him and the son of man, that thou visitest him?" (Psalm 8:3-4). The answer to this question commences with an understanding of our uniqueness in creation as the "image bearers" of God but consummates in the reality of a priceless redemption, for God loves and values us so much that He came to this planet as a human being and died for our sins.

Designer men and women are valued, vital, virtuous and victorious because God has placed His own personal and powerful imprint or label on us. We have been "bought with a price"! The Wisdom writer observes that not only has God made us but has literally "planted eternity in the human heart", assuring that our ultimate and deepest desires can only find fulfillment and true expression in a relationship with Him (Ecclesiastes 3:11). Are you wearing God's designer label?

Made In God's Image

"And God said, Let us make man in our image, after our likeness: and let them have dominion over the fish of the sea, and over the fowl of the air, and over the cattle, and over all the earth, and over every creeping thing that creepeth upon the earth. So God created man in his own image, in the image of God created he him; male and female created he them."

(Genesis 1:26-27)

What does the Bible say about the essence and nature of man? David, perched beneath the radiance and sublime incandescence of a starlit sky, asked the searching question, "What is man, that thou art mindful of him? And the son of man, that thou visitest him?" (Psalm 8:4). Philosophers, scientists, educators, sociologists and psychologists have wrestled with this question down through the centuries in order to define and delineate some cogent and comprehensive response to David's query.

The study of man is called anthropology. I believe that biblical anthropology provides the clearest, most concise and most compelling response to the question David raises. First, the Bible teaches us that we are <u>God's image bearers</u>. The creation narrative in Chapters 1 – 2 reveals that we are made in the image of God. We are made for relationship and fellowship with God, with minds to know God, hearts to love God and wills to obey God. The African Bishop of Hippo, the sainted Augustine, was expressing this primitive and primary desire when he wrote, and I paraphrase, "Lord, Thou hast made us for Thyself and my heart is restless until it finds its rest in Thee."

The Bible also suggests at many points that we are <u>God's image boosters</u>. We are here to concretize and communicate the essence of God to a broken world. We are God's ambassadors; we are involved in the ministry of reconciliation, proclaiming to those who are lost that "God was in Christ reconciling the world to Himself" (II Corinthians 5:19a). In the Sermon on the Mount, Jesus said to the disciples and us, "Let your light so shine before men, that they may see your good works and glorify your Father which is in heaven" (Matthew 5:16). While God is quite capable to (and will at the end of history) vindicate Himself, we are living and breathing commercials, testifying to the greatness and goodness of God.

Finally, we are <u>God's</u> <u>image</u> <u>beneficiaries</u>. The late Dr. Lewis Sperry Chafer, Professor of Systematic Theology for years at Dallas Seminary, argued convincingly that we receive over thirty five irrevocable blessings at the moment of salvation, election and adoption into the family of God, and indwelling of the Holy Spirit. Most of all, every believer shares the eternal life of God, and while our relationship with God has a beginning, it has no ending. The Bible then provides the definitive response to David's question, "What is man that thou art mindful of him?" God loved and loves us so much that He became human, died for our sins, was raised for our justification, sits at the right hand of the Father and intercedes for us, and will one day return in glory to receive us into His eternal Kingdom!

Created for Relationship

"And God said, Let us make man in our image, after our likeness: and let them have dominion over the fish of the sea, and over the fowl of the air, and over the cattle, and over all the earth, and over every creeping thing that creepeth upon the earth. So God created man in his own image, in the image of God created he him; male and female created he them."

(Genesis 1:26-27)

Genesis 1:26-27 affirms our creation in the image and likeness of God. The Church Fathers called this *imago deus*. God created mankind and womankind for relationship and fellowship with Himself. This is an awe-inspiring truth! God, who is flawless in character, limitless in power and knowledge, who transcends time and space and is unsearchable in love and mercy, desires a relationship with us. No wonder the Psalmist declared, "0 Lord, how excellent is thy name" (Psalm 8:1). Consequently, there is continuity and correspondence between God's nature and our own. God is a Person who has manifested Himself as Father, Son and Holy Spirit. God has created us with minds to know Him, hearts to love Him and wills to obey Him. The distinguished African bishop and Church Father Saint Augustine said, "Thou hast made us for thyself and our hearts are restless until they find their rest in Thee." The poet William Wordsworth exclaimed, "...there is a presence that disturbs me with the joy of elevated thoughts, a sense sublime of something far more deeply interfused..." We know that presence is none other than the Person of the God and Father of our Lord Jesus Christ, who indwells every believer through the Holy Spirit.

Who is this God that wants to have a relationship with you and with me? He is the Creator of the universe and the Redeemer of all humanity. In the person of Jesus Christ, God came to this planet and laid down His perfect humanity on the cross as a sacrifice for the sins of the whole world. He is above all, in all and through all, and in Him we live and move and have our very being. No wonder, when Jesus rode triumphant at the outset of

Passion Week into Jerusalem, the crowds cried out, "Hosanna, Hosanna!" Jesus reminded them that if they muffled their praise, even the rocks would worship His holy and righteous name. The prophet Isaiah reminded his beleaguered audience of the true basis of hope. "For ye shall go out with joy, and be led forth with peace: the mountains and the hills shall break forth before you into singing, and all the trees of the field shall clap their hands" (Isaiah 55: 12). Let us join all the hosts of heaven in worshipping Him who is, who was and who is to come.

The Priority of Relationship

**"And the LORD God said,
It is not good that the man should be alone;
I will make him an help meet for him."**

(Genesis 2:18)

An interesting and arresting headline in a recent edition of the USA TODAY caught my attention. It said, "After 19 years in the dark, coma victim's first word: Mom." The subsequent article recounted the miraculous experience of 39 year old Terry Wallis of Mountain View, Arkansas who, after being injured in a car crash in 1984, had been in a coma for nineteen years. Terry awakened from that coma on June 12, 2003 and his first word was "Mom."

This story reminded me of Ravi Zacharias's assertion in his insightful book <u>Can</u> <u>Man</u> <u>Live</u> <u>Without</u> <u>God?</u> He says that the secret to life is relationships. Healthy relationships are the mirrors from which we see ourselves and the windows through which we view the things that ultimately concern us. God accentuated the importance of relationships when in the perfection of the Garden He declared, "It is not good for man to be alone." After nineteen years in a coma, Terry Wallis' first spoken word was "Mom." His reference point was a primary relationship. He didn't say, "Car," "House," "Television," or "Bank," but he said, "Mom."

Relationship is primary in the spiritual life as well. Christianity is fundamentally a relationship with the living God who has been ultimately revealed to us in the person of the Lord Jesus Christ. Our fellowship with the Lord compels our fellowship with others in the body of Christ. At the point of salvation, when the Spirit of God awakened us from the coma of spiritual death, we were baptized by the Spirit into the body of Christ where we experience the dynamic unity of faith and the rich diversity of community.

Beyond Dislocation

"And the LORD God called unto Adam, and said unto him, Where art thou? And he said, I heard thy voice in the garden, and I was afraid, because I was naked; and I hid myself."

(Genesis 3:9-10)

God has eternally decreed that His sovereignty and human free will exist in this universe. Therefore, everything that happens is an expression of either God's direct, permissive, or overruling will. In the Model Prayer, we say, "Thy will be done on earth as it is in heaven." Blessing accrues to those whose wills align with God's will. This occurs in three basic areas.

God wants us to think the thoughts of God. (See Isaiah 55:8-9.) This is the *viewpoint* will of God. Those thoughts, God's magnificent truths, are recorded in the Word of God. God wants us to fulfill our calling in life as well. This is our niche orientation and represents the *occupational* will of God for our lives. (See Ephesians 2:10; 4:1.) Finally, there is a specific place of blessing. Many of us miss our blessing because we are spiritually displaced. Jonah's blessing was in Nineveh, but he fled disobediently to Joppa. The place of blessing is the *geographical* will of God.

Original sin in the Garden was characterized fundamentally by dislocation. The Lord Jesus Christ came walking through the Garden and called unto Adam, "Where art thou?" (Genesis 3:9). Beyond our spiritual dislocation, there is a loving God who finds us wherever we are.

Overcoming Dislocation

"And the LORD God called unto Adam, and said unto him, Where art thou? And he said, I heard thy voice in the garden, and I was afraid, because I was naked; and I hid myself."

(Genesis 3:9-10)

Today, I continue preaching from the Prophets with a sermon rooted in the life of the prophet Jonah. This short but profound prophetic chronicle is a reminder to me and you that a fundamental problem in life is dislocation. Jonah suffered excruciating misery before experiencing the mercy of God because he was displaced and misplaced by his own selfishness, self-centeredness and disobedience to the revealed will of God. Jonah fled from the presence of God and disregarded the Word of God with grievous consequences ensuing.

In essence, sin is fundamentally a matter of missing the mark. This is the basic meaning of the Greek word translated "sin" in the New Testament. The Apostle Paul affirms the universality of this problem by reminding us that "all have sinned [missed the mark] and come short of the glory of God." (See Romans 3:23.) From the pulpit to the pew and on to the parking lot, there are none who are exempt. The fall of man and woman in the Garden culminated tragically in their displacement and dislocation. God in the person of the Lord Jesus Christ comes walking through the garden in the cool of the day and asks the searching question, "Where art thou?" (Genesis 3:9b). This question was not raised by the Divine for information but was a question of interrogation. Adam and Eve had moved; their sin and iniquity had separated them from God (compare Isaiah 59:2).

There is no better place to be in life than in the "center" of God's will. Jonah's plight and deliverance is a reminder that when we find ourselves spiritually "off center" or "out of sorts" that there is a way back to God. And the good news is that God takes the initiative to bring us back. Resonating even now in my heart as I write these words are the lyrics of the well know gospel song, "Take Me Back!" The song says "... take me back dear Lord to the place where I first believed." It is my fervent prayer today that whatever you are struggling with or whatever you are going through that not only will you find your way to God but that you will be assured that God will find you and will give you and me mercy for our misery, blessing for our brokenness, healing for our hurts and forgiveness for our failures.

Giving Up Isaac

**"And Abraham stretched forth his hand
and took the knife to slay his son."**

(Genesis 22:10)

I have observed that education is not merely the accumulation of facts, figures, data and details, nor just the ability to recite or regurgitate them on cue. Real education encompasses the ability, insight and discernment to ask the right questions in order to get to the heart of an issue. In this regard, questions can be as revealing as answers. A mother shared with me some time ago how her seven year old daughter, rocking and reeling from the teasing and taunting of another child at school, asked her a probing and profound question: "Mommy, why does God allow people to be mean?"

One of the remarkable aspects of Jesus' ministry in the Gospels was His ability to get to the heart of the matter in his dealings with people. So often he did this with questions rather than providing answers or information. The woman at the well of Samaria who wanted to dip and dab in a discussion of religious ritual was rocked to her core when the Lord said to her, "Go, call thy husband and come here" (John 4:17). This request launched a marvelous and momentous spiritual transformation in this woman's heart and subsequently infected an entire city when she ran back and boldly shared her testimony, "Come see a man which told me all things that I ever did."

While the outcome was not as encouraging, the application is still consistent in my next example. Approached by a rich young ruler who inquired as to the requirements for inheriting eternal life, Jesus moved to the heart of the matter when he challenged this young man, who had been faithful in observing the Law, to "sell whatever you have and give it to the poor" (Mark 10:21). Unable to part with that which he prized the most, this would-be disciple went away sorrowful because "he had great possessions."

This is exactly what happened to Abraham in Genesis 22. Having blessed him and Sarah with a first born son and long awaited heir, God said to him, "Take now thy son, thine only son Isaac, whom thou lovest, and get thee into the land of Moriah; and offer him there for a burnt offering upon one of the mountains which I tell thee of" (Genesis 22:2). The Bible records that Abraham without hesitation obeyed this order and prepared to offer his only son. Before he could thrust the death blow with the knife, God intervened and a ram caught in a thicket was offered instead of young Isaac. Abraham named the place Jehovah-jireh because of his renewed faith that God sees us and provides our needs. God wanted to know if Abraham placed Him first and foremost.

God indeed sees and knows our hearts and will test our faith and love for Him within the promptings of His powerful and purposeful Providence. Is there some Isaac today that is keeping you or me from being all that God would have us to be? If so, it is time to "give up Isaac" and be reminded anew that the Lord will provide.

Recollections — Digging Again the Wells

**"And Isaac digged again the wells of water,
which they had digged in the days of Abraham his father;
for the Philistines had stopped them after
the death of Abraham: and he called their names
after the names by which his father had called them."**

(Genesis 26:18)

Let's consider today what the words <u>faith</u>, <u>foundation</u>, <u>family</u>, <u>father</u> and <u>future</u> have in common? Is there a shared thread and theme that connects them, or are they just arbitrary selections from some word list? The truth of the matter is that all these words rushed into my consciousness as I contemplated writing this article for Father's Day. The realities these words communicate were prompted and prodded primarily by my own personal recollections and reflections. Perhaps you have had a similar experience. I am not much different than Isaac of old who revived the wells that his father Abraham had dug. (See Genesis 26:12-25.)

My faith in God, others and self rest solidly on a foundation erected in a Christian family where the father (in this case my grandfather) demonstrated both by precept and example unconditional love and commitment. While I was not quite eleven years old when my grandfather died, the impact he had on my life and my future was vast and immeasurable. His legacy still looms large in my life and he completes the picture in my mind of what a "real man" looks like.

A few months ago, I was at a seminar and the question was asked by the facilitator, "What person in past or recent history would you like to spend a day conversing with if you could?" Many prominent personages paraded down the corridors of my mind, but the one that registered and resonated most was my maternal grandfather. This remarkable man ousted C. S. Lewis, Martin Luther King, Jr., Eugene Peterson, Abraham Lincoln, Manuel Scott, Sr. and W.E. B. Dubois hands down and with no contest at all. There is so much I would like to say to him and so many things I would love to ask him. I would ask him a number of things: "Granddaddy, you married my grandmother when you were fifteen years old (she was thirteen), stayed married for over fifty years, raised seven of your own children, five of your siblings when your parents died, made a living on a farm that you owned and never finished fifth grade. Granddaddy, you never owned a car but walked to church twice on Sunday and made sure that your family was there. What were you doing when you would leave the house and say that I'm going to my old praying ground? Granddaddy, what made you so strong?"

What a time we would have! In a future luminous with possibility, I look forward to having this conversation with my grandfather. I have no doubt that he is with the Lord and is part of that cloud of witnesses spoken of in Hebrews 12:1. His faith and fortitude still encourage me as I run the race that is set before me. I'm thankful that God gave him to me and to my family; for apart from his presence in my life, I would be devoid of the experience of knowing what a father really is and should be. When my mother chides something I do or say by saying that I'm just like her father, it is always a treasured commendation. I treasure his memory today and am thankful that God providentially placed him in my way.

Never Alone

"And Jacob was left alone; and there wrestled a man with him until the breaking of the day."

(Genesis 32:24)

An unknown author penned the words that are now the moving stanzas in the great hymn "Never Alone." The third stanza says,

> *"When in affliction valley*
> *I tread the road of care,*
> *My Savior helps me carry*
> *The cross so heavy to bear,*
> *Tho all around me is darkness*
> *And earthly joys are flown,*
> *He promised never to leave me*
> *Never to leave me alone."*

How wonderfully these words reflect the assurance every believer has that God will never leave or forsake us. There are solitary points on the "road of care" we all travel where we are gripped by pangs of isolation and loneliness. These are the times when the chilling echoes of "I'm all by myself," "No one cares" or "No one understands what I'm going through" reverberate through the heart and mind. These moments can become perilous slopes of vulnerability as well where the enemy attacks our faith and seeks to steal our joy. However painful it may be, God often uses the disillusion, disappointment and despair that attend even our most treasured relationships to reveal the priceless and unrivalled glory of our union with Him. During these times, we recognize and rejoice over the constancy of His care. The late Dr. Paul Tillich, preacher and theologian, said it very well: "Language has created the word loneliness to express the pain of being alone, and the word solitude to express the glory of being alone."

Stripped of all earthly support, Jacob was left alone by the Brook Jabbok; but it was here that God redeemed his past, secured the present and leveraged the future. The word "Jabbok" means "luxuriant river" in the Hebrew. (See Genesis 32:24-32.) If you are experiencing a season of loneliness, be encouraged today that while you may be lonely, as a child of the King and as a beneficiary of an inexhaustible spiritual estate, you can never be alone. For the believer, loneliness only stirs and stimulates our homesickness for God. That isolated island in our souls that is awakened by loneliness and estrangement can only be occupied by God.

The Heart of the Preaching Matter

"And Jacob was left alone; and there wrestled a man with him until the breaking of the day."

(Genesis 32:24)

In Genesis 32:24, Jacob, while fleeing from his uncle Laban, faced the approaching armies of his offended brother Esau. At the River Jabbok he wrestled with the Angel of the Lord all night long. Wrestling with one's self in the presence of God is a challenge to anyone involved in ministry. Such humbling horizon-tality (God's way up is down!) and vertical vigilance and vision is the singular and solitary means of facing our own Esau - the shadows of our past and present - and experiencing redemption from the inherent duplicity of our sinful natures before the face of God.

For the preacher-pastor, meeting God at Jabbok before meeting our people is the essential basis of a substantive ministry. In the privacy of our priesthood with God, the preacher is transformed and transfigured by the renewing of the mind. At the river of life where the preacher wrestles with self and sin, God arrests us. God touches the preacher in deep places, leaving the messenger with a limp that is both an emblem of reconciliation and the lingering currency of dependency.

Is this not the secret of preaching in the power and demonstration of the Sprit of God? The heart of the preaching matter is the matter of the preacher's heart. It is significant that the Apostle Paul, while acknowledging the frailty of the human conduit with these words, "But we have this treasure in earthen vessels that the excellency of the power may be of God, and not of us," reminded his readers of a far greater reality. He said, "For God, who commanded the light to shine out of darkness, hath shined in our hearts, to give the light of the knowledge of the glory of God in the face of Jesus Christ" (II Corinthians 4:6-7). Into this light every preacher must enter humbly and faithfully. It is this revealing and redeeming light that radiates through the Lord's servants in compassionate and effective ministry to others.

Your Name, Please?

**"And he said unto him, What is thy name?
And he said, Jacob."**

(Genesis 32:27)

In a pre-incarnate appearance in the Old Testament, the Lord
Jesus Christ as the Angel of Jehovah wrestled with Jacob all night
by the River Jabbok according to Genesis 32:24-28. In the throes
of the Angel, Jacob finally died to self and decided to live for God.
The Lord asked him, "What is thy name?" (v. 27) The first time
Jacob was asked this question, he lied to his father as part of a
scheme to steal the birthright from his brother Esau. (See Genesis
27:18.)

God wants to know my and your name today. Not the name
that we go by, but who we really are in the secret places of our
hearts. Being honest with God about ourselves and our sins is a
prerequisite to blessing and prosperity. God gave Jacob a new
name, but left him with a limp as a perpetual reminder that apart
from God he could do nothing.

Transforming Trajectory

**"But as for you, ye thought evil against me;
but God meant it unto good, to bring to pass,
as it is this day, to save much people alive."**

(Genesis 50:20)

While on vacation, I toured the US aircraft carrier Midway while attending the National Pastor's Conference in San Diego, CA. Over nine hundred feet long, this valiant and vast vestige of the World War II era was capable of unprecedented offensive strike capability and was home to over 4,500 officers and seamen. In the sub deck of the ship were massive furnaces that transformed water into the steam which powered the huge turbines that propelled this behemoth on its way. This image stuck starkly in my mind as I recalled a line in a prayer that acknowledged to God our tendency to hold on to "the bitterness of loss that we have not turned into sacrifice."

One of the real challenges in the Christian life is maintaining what I call a "transforming trajectory." We must aim and live at such an altitude that we can truly say "our problems come to make us strong". Not to do this is to become ensnared in the lowlands, sub terrains and on the frozen tundra of the spiritual life. Like the water on the Midway, God heats up the crucibles of our lives by allowing us to experience situations and people that stretch and even stress us. Compressed and compacted by his compassion, these trying experiences have remarkable potential to become the substance of new insights, new revelation and new depth in our relationship with God and others. I believe this is the source of the wonderful exhortation by James, the Lord's brother, to "count it all joy when ye fall into divers temptations; knowing that the trying of your faith worketh patience" (James 1:2a).

When life gives us a lemon, we can either bemoan or begrudge its acidity and bitterness, or we can squeeze it and, through God's grace and the "splendor" of His love, transform the juice into sweet and refreshing lemonade. The ability to do this has everything to do with viewpoint and trajectory. Joseph embraced this truth and, although despised and betrayed by his brothers and sold as a slave in Egypt, he could say "what you meant for evil, God meant for good" (Genesis 50:20).

I learned on my tour of the Midway that an aircraft carrier before launching its jets and planes for battle must turn into the wind. We too must face the wind of our tried and straitened experiences. We must, by faith, not fly from them but into them. Only then can we launch from the turbulent decks of despair, disappointment and discouragement and climb on lofty wings into the embrace of our God who works in us to will and do of His good pleasure.

New Beginnings

"And the LORD spake unto Moses and Aaron in
the land of Egypt, saying,
'This month shall be unto you the beginning of months:
it shall be the first month of the year to you.'"

(Exodus 12:1-2)

So began the instruction that God gave His servant Moses as preparations were made for Israel's miraculous liberation after four hundred thirty years of Egyptian bondage. This date, this beginning of months would become the defining moment and memory in the historic consciousness and pilgrimage of God's chosen people. The Passover and the Feast of Unleavened Bread would endure in Israel's tumultuous history as perpetual reminders of Yahweh's saving grace and the means by which He redeemed them from the bondage of tyranny, oppression, sin and suffering.

While writing to the Corinthians, the Apostle Paul challenged them with the following words: "Purge out therefore the old heaven, that ye may be a new lump, as ye are unleavened. For even Christ our Passover is sacrificed for us" (I Corinthians 5:7). Like Israel, during this period that marks a New Year and a new beginning, every member of God's church must be serious in considering the true basis of our salvation and spiritual freedom. Anything that is sinful (thought, word or deed - the old leaven), we should confess and seek the cleansing that can come only from the Christ who became sin for us that we might be made the righteousness of God which is in Him. (See I John 1:9; II Corinthians 5:21.) We must thank God today for being the God of new beginnings who is not only the Author but the great Finisher of our faith. As Israel waited for the hand of the Lord to affect their release, we too with sincere and joyous anticipation must wait in the days to come for the release of God's presence, power and purpose into our personal and collective lives. God is faithful and will see us through.

Christian! Engage!

"Now therefore give me this mountain,
whereof the LORD spake in that day;
for thou heardest in that day how the Anakims were there,
and that the cities were great and fenced:
if so be the LORD will be with me,
then I shall be able to drive them out, as the LORD said."

(Joshua 14:12)

I've spent much of the past week reflecting on what it means to be on mission for Jesus. According to Mark 10:45, the quintessential center and core of Jesus' ministry was service and not self. He said," The Son of man came not to be ministered to but to minister and give his life a ransom for many." Jesus was committed to this mission and nothing, not the misunderstanding of loved ones, the abandonment and betrayal of friends, the bitter attacks of His enemies, the loneliness and isolation of His calling or even the excruciating agony of death by crucifixion, could deter Him from fulfilling the mission God had given to Him.

Jesus models the kind of commitment that is sorely lacking in the church today. So many who call themselves Christians today are timid, tepid and tentative, content to reside on the fringes of ministry rather than "offer themselves as living sacrifices unto the Lord" (Romans 12:1). It reminds me of the movie *Top Gun* starring Tom Cruise as Maverick, a jet pilot who is training to be a member of the Navy's most elite fighter squadron. Because of the haunting effects of the tragic death of a friend and co-pilot, he fails to engage during a crucial battle. At this critical junction, after retreating from the battle and leaving his fellow pilots at risk, the command from his superior officer at the control center was clear and compelling: "Maverick, engage!" I can just hear our Lord and Savior Jesus Christ saying today to the church in North America, "Church, engage!" It is time to take the Great Commission seriously. It is time to take the stewardship of tithe, time, talent, treasure and temple seriously. This call to commitment is an urgent summons not only to the church as a whole but to every individual Christian.

This type of commitment is costly. One cannot be truly committed to being on mission for Jesus without being willing to give up something. Business as usual, being comfortable or just being liked may have to be sacrificed in order for us to be faithful. The costliness of commitment, however, is far outweighed by the rewards of serving the Lord. Whatever we sacrifice in the service of the Lord is a seed sown in the soil of His providence that will produce a harvest of blessing. David understood this and, while looking back over his life, both the track of his fears and the trail of his tears, he could only say, "I have been young, and now am old; yet have I not seen the righteous forsaken or his seed begging bread" (Psalm 37:25). Caleb understood this truth, too, and even though he was eighty-five years old and well into the sunset of his life, asked Joshua to "give me this mountain" (Joshua 14:12a). Caleb was looking for another conquest. He was not dialing down his commitment but dialing it up, because "he wholly followed the Lord God of Israel" (Joshua 14:14b).

What are you prepared to do for the Lord today? Jesus reminds us that the true path to greatness is serving Christ and others and not self. This is the path that leads us into the joy of the Lord.

Postscript to Victory

"Then sang Moses and the children of Israel
this song unto the LORD, and spake, saying,
I will sing unto the LORD, for he hath triumphed gloriously:
the horse and his rider hath he thrown into the sea."

(Exodus 15:1)

Shortly after their astounding victory and deliverance over Pharaoh's army at the Red Sea, Miriam, the sister of Moses, led the women of Israel in celebrative worship, dancing with praise and thanksgiving and singing unto the Lord "for he hath triumphed gloriously; the horse and the rider hath he thrown into the sea" (Exodus 15:1b). One week removed from the radiance and resonance of Resurrection Sunday, what must our conduct be as beneficiaries and celebrants of the finished work of the Cross and the coronation of the Savior who was raised from the dead for our justification?

Undoubtedly, we too <u>should</u> <u>worship</u> <u>and</u> <u>both</u> <u>praise</u> <u>and</u> <u>thank</u> <u>God</u> in the beauty of His holiness, and for love's sake celebrate the completed victory that has assured our passage from bondage to blessing. Jesus died so that we might live, and He lives today so that we might never die, giving us not only life but "life more abundantly." Our post- deliverance worship is multi-faceted and multi-dimensional and, if authentic, involves knowing God with our minds, loving Him with our hearts, and obeying Him with our wills.

Secondly, we live out the victory and deliverance Jesus secured for us by <u>being living</u> <u>witnesses</u> of His grace and goodness. Moses, Miriam and the masses were eyewitnesses of God's favor and power demonstrated at the Red Sea. Pharaoh's army was met by an exceedingly greater force as God enlisted the wind and the waves as chaperones and champions who escorted the Israelites through treacherous waters on dry ground. The early church witnessed the resurrection, and when endued with power from on high, the reality of this event moved them by witnessing from the innermost of their being to the outermost of the world.

Finally, the truth of the resurrection and the reality of our deliverance encourage every believer <u>to</u> <u>walk</u> <u>by</u> <u>faith</u>, remembering always that the God who made a road through the sea of our trials and tribulations will go with and before us into the promised land of possibility and spiritual prosperity. It is this truth that God reminded Joshua of as he assumed leadership of the Israelites after the death of Moses: "Every place that the sole of your foot shall tread upon, that have I given unto you, as I said unto Moses" (Joshua 1:3). As we worship God today, witness for and about Him at every opportunity; and as we walk by resurrection faith on the dry ground of our problems and perils, we too must sing as Israel did: "Thou in mercy hast led forth thy people which thou hast redeemed; thou hast guided them in thy strength unto thy holy habitation" (Exodus 15:13).

Fresh Starts and New Beginnings

**"And Samson called unto the LORD, and said, O Lord GOD,
remember me, I pray thee, and strengthen me, I pray thee,
only this once, O God, that I may be at once avenged
of the Philistines for my two eyes."**

(Judges 16:28)

The end of the old year and the start of the new are for many
people a time of reflection, inspection and evaluation. The New
Year represents a fresh start and a new beginning. Commitments
and resolutions mirror a sincere determination to achieve goals
and actualize dreams; to get it right or do it better this time. So
often though as the minutes turn into hours, the hour's days, and
the days turn into weeks and months, these rock solid intentions
turn into pretentious putty and shifting sand. They become the
source of much frustration and disappointment

The apostle Paul recognized the futility of human will and
effort apart from the grace and sufficiency of God. He wrote these
words to the believers at Rome: "I do not understand what I do.
For what I want to do I do not do, but what I hate I do" (Romans
7:15). Some would condemn this statement as tragic pessimism,
but Paul insightfully and humbly assents to the helplessness and
hopelessness of those who place their confidence in the flesh.
Centuries earlier the prophet Jeremiah voiced a similar concern.
He said, "Thus saith the Lord, Cursed by the man that trusteth in
man and makes flesh his arm and whose heart departeth from the
Lord" (Jeremiah 17:5).

The presence of indwelling sin in our lives derails the best laid
plan and the most sincere intention. Whatever we aspire or desire
to do we must base our resolve and commitment on God's power
and not our own. Samson, the judge and defender of ancient
Israel, was blessed with incredible strength but squandered his
opportunity to lead because he lacked self-discipline and humility.
In the end, blinded and humiliated, he got it right! He prayed,
"O Sovereign Lord, remember me, O God, please strengthen just
once more" (Judges 16:28a).

Obedience

"And Samuel said, Hath the LORD as great delight in burnt offerings and sacrifices, as in obeying the voice of the LORD? Behold, to obey is better than sacrifice, and to hearken than the fat of rams."

(I Samuel 15:22)

Obedience involves our initial response to God's call and claim on us in the salvation experience, but a life of perpetual, unrelenting surrender as well. We must constantly say to God, "Have thine own way, Lord, have thine own way!" Because human personality is embodied existence, both the spirit and the body must be disciplined and trained to obey God. (See I Corinthians 6:19.) God is glorified when body and spirit honors and obeys Him. Dallas Willard in his book, The Disciplines of the Spirit notes, "The vitality and power of Christianity is lost when we fail to integrate our bodies into its practice by intelligent, conscious and steadfast intent. It is with our bodies we receive the new life that comes as we enter the Kingdom" (p. 20).

Holy obedience is the ambitious aspiration to glorify God in body and spirit. In order for this to happen, the inner life must be transformed. In order for God to do something with us and through us, God must first do a work within us. At this point, what begins in grace and is sustained by grace requires submissive action on the part of the believer to assure continued spiritual transformation. (See Romans 12:1-2; Ephesians 4:20-24.) Our holy obedience is the cause and the consequence of transformation, renewal and maturation in the Christian life.

Obedience is the foundation for effective Christian ministry. While salvation endues us with the spiritual capacity to reach out to God and through God to others, sin and corruption resists and impedes this response. The flesh must be brought under subjection in order for God's unique destiny to be actualized in our experience. This requires not only the submission of the believer to God's plan and purposes but the sanctifying power of the Holy Spirit as well.

An Attitude of Ingratitude

"And Nabal answered David's servants, and said,
Who is David? and who is the son of Jesse?
there be many servants now a days that break away every man
from his master. Shall I then take my bread, and my water,
and my flesh that I have killed for my shearers,
and give it unto men, whom I know not whence they be?"

(I Samuel 25:10-11)

The name Nabal has tragic notoriety in the Old Testament. The Hebrew word translated "Nabal" means "fool". His story is told in I Samuel 25:2-44. One cannot read this passage without recognizing the folly of this man's stewardship. Nabal was selfish and shortsighted in large part because he failed to recognize that even he was not a "self-made" man, but owed his prosperity to the goodwill of others. David and his mighty men had acted favorably on his and his family's behalf, guarding and protecting his flocks and herds. He was crippled by an attitude of ingratitude. What can we learn from the sad and tragic tale of this man's life?

First every believer should practice the arithmetic of thanksgiving. This is exactly what the writer of Psalm 103 does. Each day he was determined to "bless the Lord" in light of the remembrance or recognition of "all his benefits". A stanza in one of my favorite hymns says, "Count your many blessings - name them one by one, and it will surprise you what the Lord hath done." Our days should be shrouded with perpetual praise as we reflect on just how good God has been.

Secondly, we must realize the truth and significance of what Dr. Martin Luther King, Jr. said: "We are bound together in an inescapable network of mutuality tied to a garment of destiny." Dr. King was simply reminding us that we need each other, and action and attitudes do not occur in isolation or in a vacuum. Nabal was too narrow- minded and self-centered to recognize that others had contributed to his success and prosperity as well.

Trusting God During Trying Times

**"And she went and did according to the saying of Elijah:
and she, and he, and her house, did eat many days.
And the barrel of meal wasted not,
neither did the cruse of oil fail,
according to the word of the LORD,
which he spake by Elijah."**

(I Kings 17:15-16)

Trusting God during trying times is one of the major challenges facing any Christian. I begin this preaching assignment with a strong sense of Divine direction that God wants to speak to each of us and the wider audience who will listen to these messages at our point of need. How do we trust God when we face circumstances that seem to be beyond our control? What do we do when we get that call at two o'clock in the morning that turns our lives upside down? What do we do when a routine visit to the doctor's office turns into something much more serious and life threatening, or when one's job ends with hardly any notice after years of faithful and dedicated service? What do we do when the darkness overtakes the light and when hope flickers like a burning candle?

None would deny that these are trying times that we live in. We live in a time when so much of what can happen and does happen is beyond our control. Our present plight is aggravated and exacerbated by suffocating uncertainty. Nothing is sure or guaranteed anymore, except our faith in God and God's faithfulness to us. But this truth and reality becomes the very arena of testing and trial when we face difficulty and distress. How do we hold on to our faith when we are just trying to hold on? This is the crisis that many have faced, face now or will face as we seek to live our lives to the glory of God. The late G. K. Chesterton, a noted Christian thinker, once said, ""The Christian ideal has not been tried and found wanting; it has been found difficult and left untried." In essence, he reminds us that our advance to maturity of faith is not "problem-free" but includes the possibility of pain and suffering that can disrupt, disarm and diminish our faith in God.

The good news is that the Bible is full of stories of persons just like us who faced trying circumstances and overcame them through faith in God. The first sermon in this series will take a close look at someone who did just that. Rather than retreat from or surrender to circumstances, the impoverished widow who became a hostess to the prophet Elijah trusted God and experienced miraculous blessing. I pray that her story will become your and my story, and that whatever we are going through, we will find strength and comfort in the God who promises to sustain us and who will never suffer the righteous to be moved.

Constants and Contradictions

"Now Naaman, captain of the host of the king of Syria,
was a great man with his master, and honourable,
because by him the LORD had given deliverance unto Syria:
he was also a mighty man in valour, but he was a leper."

(II Kings 5:1)

Recently, while I was reading this passage as part of a daily devotion, the phrase *but a leper* leaped off the pages into my head and heart. I thought that despite Naaman's considerable accomplishments, he was still flawed by the dreaded disease of leprosy. God the Holy Spirit is teaching us an important truth in this passage. Like Naaman, each of us is characterized both by constants and contradictions. While our constants are commendable and the source and catalyst of great success and prosperity in life, it is the contradictions that allow us to truly celebrate the grace and mercy of God. Through the constancy of his character, capability and commitment to country and king, Naaman had experienced great victory, success and notoriety. However, it was the leprosy [a symbol of sin in the Bible] that drove him from the comfort of his success into the presence of God and God's prophet. Read Judges 5:1-19.

His desire to be healed from the disease of leprosy encouraged, indeed necessitated that Naaman depend on God and trust God's word as mediated by the prophet Elisha. There was no self-cure for leprosy. Only by dipping in the waters of the Jordan seven times according to the word of the prophet could Naaman experience healing. The lesson for me and for you today is that God will never allow us to become so comfortable with our own accomplishments or success in life or in ministry to the extent that we glory in what "we have done." Rather, the needling and nagging experience of some flaw, some inadequacy, some need will be permitted so that we might be encouraged to ultimately trust God for strength and deliverance. In the annals of Scripture and in the history of the church, this has been the case time and time again. Most of the prominent biblical characters that were used mightily of God were at their very best, like Naaman, flawed. Noah got drunk, Abraham lied, Jacob cheated and stole, David sinned and murdered, Peter cursed and denied, and Paul was haunted throughout his ministry because he persecuted the church. Yet, God used each of them in a marvelous and mighty way to advance His kingdom. Despite the "buts" in our lives, the haunting and hobbling contradictions, God can use you and me, too. Say to him today, "Have thine own way, Lord; have Thine own way!"

When Life Comes Crashing In

"And Hezekiah received the letter of the hand of the messengers, and read it: and Hezekiah went up into the house of the LORD, and spread it before the LORD. And Hezekiah prayed before the LORD, and said, O LORD God of Israel, which dwellest between the cherubims, thou art the God, even thou alone, of all the kingdoms of the earth; thou hast made heaven and earth. LORD, bow down thine ear, and hear: open, LORD, thine eyes, and see... "

(II Kings 19:14-16a)

Every time I hear the television commercial about Ford trucks - "Ford trucks are built to last"- or the Chevrolet counterpart - "Like a rock!"- I think about how unlike trucks human beings are. Our lives, relationships, hopes and dreams are fragile and fleeting things. Not only are we haunted daily by the sinister seductiveness of our own corrupt natures, but we are vulnerable to and victimized by the contingent nature of human experience. In a moment's notice, our lives can be turned upside down; and this can happen at no fault of our own. Anyone who thinks they are really in control and are in the driver's seat in the journey of life is seriously confused and deluded about the true nature of our existence.

What then are we to do? I was hoping you would ask. We must trust in God who is the "Rock" and whose staying power is eternal. When life comes crashing in on us starkly reminding us of the plethora of uncertainties that characterize our experience, we must cast our burdens on the Lord and leave them there. This is exactly what the good king Hezekiah did. When his well-intentioned reforms and hopes for the nation were being held hostage by the threats and siege of the Assyrian army, he went into the house of the Lord and prayed to God who "dwells between the cherubim" and who is sovereign over all nations and all things. (See II Kings 19:14-19.) God miraculously delivered Judah and her faithful king from the hands of the Assyrians. He can and will do the same for you and me today!

Limits

**"Seeing his days are determined,
the number of his months are with thee,
thou hast appointed his bounds that he cannot pass."**

(Job 14:5)

What would our lives be if there were no limits to what we could do, say, or think? While the thought might be momentarily tempting and tantalizing to some, the consequences would be tragic and traumatic. A wise person once said, "Freedom without authority is anarchy and authority without freedom is tyranny." Jesus said, "Ye shall know the truth and the truth shall set you free" (John 8:32). God has placed limits and boundaries on our existence if for no other reason than to remind us that we are not God and are never truly the "masters of our own fate."

In addition, we experience limits and boundaries because of decisions others have made, of which we had absolutely no input. For example, none of us had a choice in the family that we were born into. The legacy and lineage of our family of origin establish boundaries and limits that we must face for better or for worse for the rest of our lives. Then, there are the choices that we make ourselves. While some of those decisions create self-limiting restraints because of commitments to others, there are decisions that we make from positions of weakness when we succumb to the solicitations of our sin natures or choose to disobey the clear mandates and teachings of God's Word. I'm sure there are not too many of us here today who have not at some point in time as we reflected on our lives asked the question, "What if?"

The good news today is that no matter what limits or restraints we face, or whatever bondage we might be experiencing, God can lift us up, out and beyond our circumstances. In fact, God can turn the cursing of bad choices and decisions into blessing so that "all things truly work together for good for those who love Him and are called according to His purpose" (Romans 8:28). God can transform impossibilities into possibilities that stretch the limits of our horizon so that we can only joyfully resonate as did the Apostle Paul who said, "Now unto him that is able to do exceeding abundantly above all that we ask or think, according to the power that worketh in us, Unto him be glory in the church by Christ Jesus throughout all ages, world without end. Amen" (Ephesians 3:20).

I thank God that through the grace mediated by a glorious Gospel that we can live "beyond our limits." Even death, the greatest limitation of all, has been swallowed up in victory because Jesus did not only die for our sins but was raised with power and majesty for our glorification.

Moonstruck with Majesty

"O LORD our Lord, how excellent is thy name in all the earth! who hast set thy glory above the heavens. Out of the mouth of babes and sucklings hast thou ordained strength because of thine enemies, that thou mightest still the enemy and the avenger. When I consider thy heavens, the work of thy fingers, the moon and the stars, which thou hast ordained; What is man, that thou art mindful of him? and the son of man, that thou visitest him? For thou hast made him a little lower than the angels, and hast crowned him with glory and honour."

(Psalms 8:1-5)

In Psalm 8:4, David asked a profound question. "What is man, that thou art mindful of him and the son of man that thou visitest him?" The magnificent musings in this classic psalm were probably prompted by David's glimpse of the star cluttered galactic grandeur that overwhelmed him with a humbling awareness of God's majesty. He was gripped as well with a nagging, needling sense of man's apparent insignificance in the whole scheme of the created order. Yet, further reflection chronicled in this psalm reveals that David moves to higher ground in his assessment of humanity's worth and value to God.

First, David affirms that God has made us. Man and woman are created in the image of God and are designed to reflect God's glory or essence in what we feel (emotion), what we know (mentality) and what we do (volition). The great reformer Martin Luther said it well: "Thou has made us for Thyself and our hearts are restless until they find their rest in Thee." In rank, we have been made just a little lower than the angelic creation but, unlike them, we have been crowned with glory and honor.

God has also given us dominion or authority over God's good creation. Paulo Friere in his book, The Pedagogy of the Oppressed, insists that what makes us truly and authentically human is the God given right to name our creation. Like Adam, we are authorized to name the world around us and the world in us. And our naming should and must reflect the claiming of a privileged position in the created order. Not only has God made us, but God has redeemed us with His own precious blood. He has established for time and eternity the true value of every human life; for He ransomed us through His vicarious suffering and death on the cross. The ultimate answer to the question David raises in Psalm 8 is found not in the rudiments of a biblical anthropology (the doctrine of man), but rather in the glorious radiance of the Gospel of the Lord Jesus Christ who became sin for us that we might become the righteousness of God in Him (II Corinthians 5:21)

Authentically Human

**"When I consider thy heavens, the work of thy fingers,
the moon and the stars, which thou hast ordained;
What is man, that thou art mindful of him?
and the son of man, that thou visitest him?"**

(Psalms 8:3-4)

What does it mean to be authentically human? The Word of God reveals that every human being is made in the image of God. Each person is unique and created for relationship and fellowship with God. When reading the Genesis narrative, it is quite apparent that Adam was created with a super-intellect. He exercised this vast knowledge by naming all the creatures that were brought before him. Even today, God allows us to participate in naming our creation. For example, we have the opportunity to look at what is going on within us or around us and view those events from either a divine or human perspective. A wise man once commented, "When some people smell flowers they immediately look for coffins." What are you seeing in the world within and around you? Some people always choose to see the bad and the ugly! There is enough of that to occupy you and me for a long while. If you want to find problems with yourself, in your marriage, with your children or your church, believe me, there will be enough to go around.

However, because of the birth of Christ, His sinless life, vicarious death, glorious ascension and imminent return, we can also choose to focus on the good knowing that God has not abdicated His throne and that He is absolutely committed to saving each of us. What a wonderful gift: the knowledge that we are created in God's image. Therefore, we have the capacity, indeed the divinely ordained ability, to look at life from the viewpoint and perspective of the One who causes all things to work together for the good of those that love Him and are the called according to His purpose.

Holy Obedience

"LORD, who shall abide in thy tabernacle?
who shall dwell in thy holy hill?
He that walketh uprightly, and worketh righteousness,
and speaketh the truth in his heart."

(Psalms 15:1-2)

Obedience is the foundation on which the super-structure of ministry is constructed. The prophet Samuel warned King Saul, "Behold, to obey is better than sacrifice, and to hearken than the fat of rams. For rebellion is as the sin of witchcraft, and stubbornness is as iniquity and idolatry. Because thou hast rejected the word of the LORD, he hath also rejected thee from being king" (I Samuel 15:22). Our obedience to God's will, Word and way is not spontaneous but necessitates a disciplined resolve. The harsh reality is that the sin and corruption which is an inherent part of human existence resists and impedes our response. The Apostle Paul said, "…when I would do good, evil is present with me." The flesh must be brought under subjection in order that the unique destiny established by God for us can be fulfilled in our lives.

Yes, while the spirit is willing, so often the flesh is weak. Our failures and shortcomings often lead us to despair. But the good news is that God's grace draws us into His holy presence creating a consciousness of sin that is both acute and recoiling. The late Andrew Murray said, "It is the sinner dwelling in the full light of God's holy, redeeming love; in the experience of that full indwelling of divine love, which comes through Christ and the Holy Spirit, who cannot but be humble. Not to be occupied with thy sin, but to be occupied with God, brings deliverance from self."

Consciousness of imperfection begins the fight against "them". St. Francis de Sales, author of the classic devotional <u>Introduction to the Devout Life</u>, raises a searching question regarding our failures and flaws: "How can we fight against them unless we see them, or overcome them unless we face them? Our victory does not consist of being unconscious of them but in not consenting to them, and not to consent to them is to be displeased with them." Holy obedience is displeasure with self and sin that finds healing, hope and help in pleasure with God.

A Declaration of Worship

**"The heavens declare the glory of God;
and the firmament sheweth his handywork."**

(Psalms 19:1)

One of the tragic signs and traumatic symptoms of our times is "wars and rumors of wars." Around the globe, in Iraq, Afghanistan, Israel, Lebanon, in Africa and in so many other places, conflicts rage, innocents suffer and lives are lost. And then there are the wars that erupt in the human soul; these conflicts see under the surface of our lives but are all the more deadly and dangerous, destroying marriages, families, homes and even churches. All of this of course is the result of sin and corruption of the human nature, and the violation of the boundaries that God has set in nature and in His Word that govern our relationships on a personal, interpersonal and ultra-personal level.

How wonderful and marvelous, I thought, if rather than confronting the haunting horror of war and conflict around this planet (both declared and undeclared), we were riveted with the news of a "declaration of worship". This is the essence of Psalm 19. It is a declaration to worship that begins in the "uttermost" (the heavens), and reaches to the innermost (the meditation of the heart). This is the true destiny of mankind and womankind: to join in concert with all of creation in a worshipful declaration of the "glory of God and to shew forth His handywork."

As we continue today the sermon series on **"The Blessings and Barriers of Meaningful Worship,"** let us commit to calling for and praying for a cease-fire on unproductive and unfruitful conflict on any level, and rather consecrate ourselves to a "declaration of worship". The New Testament church has a primary and pressing responsibility in the area of worship. Someone said, "To know God is our greatest treasure and to worship God is our greatest treasure." The world should be able to look at us and see the peaceful cessation of divisive and destructive conflict as well as the redeeming reconciliation of relationships through the grace and power of God who gives us peace. Like the Samaritan woman, when the barriers that hobble and hinder our relationship to God and to others are removed, it should lead us to meaningful worship.

Believe to See

**"I had fainted, unless I had believed to see
the goodness of the LORD in the land of the living."**

(Psalms 27:13)

Psalm 27 very beautifully punctuates and illustrates the life of faith as one that moves between confidence and calamity, celebration and anxiety, excitement and discouragement. It is believed that King David wrote this psalm while fleeing from his son Absalom who had fermented rebellion against his father and was seeking to take his life. The confidence and faith that David exudes in this psalm reminds us that it is during times of crisis and testing that our faith is transformed from the abstract to the concrete; from profession to practice. "The Lord is my light and salvation … "speaks with timeless relevance to every generation of believers as a basis for our authentic experience of God. Although our existence is tentative and uncertain, we can be assured of the abiding presence of God who will "… in a time of trouble hide us in His pavilion."

While this psalm is not directly quoted in the New Testament, the principles it communicates find vital expression there. The passionate confidence of the psalmist can be compared to the Apostle Paul's victorious spirit in Romans 8:28ff. The same positive mental attitude is portrayed in I John 4:4. The encouragement to "sing praises" unto the Lord despite our circumstances is a reminder that our relationship to God ultimately informs the quality, character and intensity of our worship in spirit and truth (John 4:24). We can worship God no matter what is happening for we are not captives to our circumstances but rather children of God who have received precious promises to "wait on the Lord and be of good courage."

So, no matter what you are going through today, trust God's faithfulness. The Psalmist encourages us to "believe to see the goodness of the Lord in the land of the living." This means that our faith perception must always precede the experience in life of the visible and tangible reality of our hopes, dreams and prayers. Hold on, relax and believe that whatever you need according to His will and perfect plan for your and my life, God will provide.

Sorry For Not Being Sorry

**"Blessed is he whose transgression is forgiven,
whose sin is covered. Blessed is the man unto whom
the LORD imputeth not iniquity,
and in whose spirit there is no guile."**

(Psalms 32:1-2)

"Are you sorry?", the wise, old pastor asked the dying man who, although a Christian, had lived a decadent and disgraceful life. "No", was the response from the man as death's shadow crept closer and closer. But the sagacious minister sensed that this response was more despair than defiance and so he asked the man another question, "Are you sorry that you are not sorry?" Tears formed in eyes that mirrored the deadening toll of sickness without and sin within, and the man said in a quiet voice of contrition, "Yes." This cry for help from deep within the caverns of this man's soul was enough for the sensitive and sagacious pastor to pray for God's grace and mercy.

Guilt and shame are the dark and distant cousins of humanity that remind us that there is a moral conscience in us and a moral law in this universe that holds us accountable. Adam and Eve experienced this when their transgression coupled nakedness with shame. Their only recourse was to cover themselves with fig leaves as they made their retreat from innocence and hid in the Garden. It has been said that guilt comes when we acknowledge that we made a mistake, but shame is much more devastating because we are admitting that we are a mistake.

Undeniably, sin when unconfessed can place us on a costly track that will lead to resignation and despair. But when we refuse to rationalize, make excuses or blame others for our sin and sins, confession will propel us in an opposite direction on that same track to a safe place where we can experience forgiveness, restoration and renewal. Judas, overwrought with the dire and dastardly results of his betrayal of our Lord and the unbearable weight of guilt his act precipitated within, went out into the night and hung himself. Guilt and shame are not permanent parking places, but exit ramps on the interstate of life where we slow down in order to merge with God's grace and mercy. These enemies of our faith and spiritual life become cruel friends when they force us into the arms of God and the experience of His unfailing compassions.

An anonymous poet wrote these moving words: "If I could shut the gate against my thoughts, and keep out sorrow from this room within, or memory could cancel all the notes of my misdeeds, and I unthink my sin; How free, how clear, how clean my soul should lie, discharged of such a loathsome company." With a matching mood, the old hymn asks the question, "What can wash away my sin?" The choral response is, "Nothing but the blood of Jesus!" "What can make me whole again?" Again the refrain rang, "Nothing but the blood of Jesus!" And then the celebrative words, "O, precious is that flow that makes me white as snow. No other fount I know, nothing but the blood of Jesus." Don't be gagged by guilt today or held hostage by shame. Take your burdens to the Lord and leave them there. "Blessed is he whose transgressions are forgiven, whose sins are covered" (Psalm 32:1).

Evening Then Morning

"For his anger endureth but a moment;
in his favour is life:
weeping may endure for a night,
but joy cometh in the morning."

(Psalms 30:5)

In the Book of Genesis Chapter One, God who created everything that is out of nothing looked at the primitive chaos and began saying, "Let there be!" And at God's command, the earth, formless, void and shrouded in dense darkness was awakened and roused from its primordial slumber to pristine life and light in all its compelling and colorful variety. In this crescent scene, each stretch and stroke of God's creative power and provision was punctuated by the inspired narrator of these holy happenings with the phrase, "and the evening and the morning ..." (1:5, 8, 13, 19, 23, 31). This phrase occurs six times in the first chapter of the Bible and is the broad stroke that brackets God's activity during the first six days of creation. This type of repetition, recurrence and redundancy certainly has a Divine purpose.

Upon reflection, the number of occurrences of this phrase is significant because "six" in the Bible represents imperfection or incompleteness. The Apostle Paul hints at the provisional nature of the present created order marked and marred by sin when he writes to the church at Rome, "For we know that the whole creation groaneth and travaileth in pain together until now" (Romans 8:22). God's work is not complete until our hope is fulfilled by the glorious coming of the One who will usher in a "new heaven and a new earth, for the first heaven and the first earth were passed away" (Revelation 21:1).

More significantly for me, however, is the fact that this phrase seems to defy the natural way of thinking about and experiencing time when it places "evening" before "morning". We tend to think of the days of our lives as sunrise (dawn/morning) then sunset (dusk/evening). But in God's economy, evening always predates morning. It's night first and then the morning. This pattern is repeated throughout the Scriptures. One of the most remarkable occurrences is Psalm 30:5 where the writer says, "Weeping may endure for a night, but joy cometh in the morning." The application of this tremendous truth for all of us is the recognition that night and darkness are the other side of day and light. Moreover, our experience of night and darkness in any of its forms (circumstantial or chronological) is but the precipice and porch that leads to the dawning of a new day and the entrance of light. You and I can make it through our nights because morning will surely come.

Tuning In When Life Is Tuning Out

"I will bless the LORD at all times:
his praise shall continually be in my mouth."

(Psalms 34:1)

As I was preparing to write this article, my mind somehow drifted into an episode of the classic sitcom "Andy of Mayberry" I saw some years ago. In this particular episode, the City of Mayberry's community chorus was rehearsing for the annual state competition. The problem was that Deputy Barney Fife wanted the lead for the musical selection they had chosen. But when Barney sang, he always sang "off key". There was someone much more capable than Barney who the members wanted to sing the lead. Sheriff Andy and the other members of the Mayberry Chorus were searching for a way to break the news to Barney without hurting his feelings.

The phrase "off key" resonates in my mind and heart as I think of the journey called life. Upon further reflection, I suspect that for many of us the trials and temptations we face seem to be "off key" from the primary chords and melodies that make up our lives. These discordant notes are irritating and distracting, cutting against the very grain of what we perceive as authentic being and genuine blessing. Life's musical is not always pleasant, and the selections the Lord either chooses or allows for us are far from symphonic. Shakespeare was at least partially right when he said, "Life is full of sound and fury, signifying nothing."

Yet, when God is the symphony conductor of our lives, in due season the chords do come together and we begin to see that transcending the discordant notes of our tried experiences is a beautiful melody that rings and resonates in our souls to the praise and thanksgiving of God who does all things well. God even takes the "off key" experiences and rewrites the music in such a way that "all things work together for the good of them that love God, to them who are the called according to His purpose" (Romans 8:28). God in providential wisdom establishes the key and meter of life and turns the wistful, weary songs of the night into the jubilant anthems of morning joy. Faced with the pain of his own "off key" experience, the patriarch Job acknowledged this reality when he said, "Where is God my maker, who giveth songs in the night?" (Job 35:10). So if there is a note or chord that you are struggling with that just doesn't seem to fit what you've chosen or anticipated in life, give it over to God and He can and will work it out. Therefore, we must bless the Lord at all times and His praise must be continually in our mouths. (Psalm 34:1)

Damaged Goods

**"Why art thou cast down, O my soul?
and why art thou disquieted in me? hope thou in God:
for I shall yet praise him for the help of his countenance."**

(Psalms 42:5)

A recent issue of U.S. News & World Report caught my attention with the caption, **"Miracles of Brain Repair ...** Daring surgery brings hope for victims of stroke, Parkinson's and depression." The related article was an informative overview of the advances in medical science in this area that has provided hope, help and healing to patients and their families suffering from damage, dysfunction and disease. The human brain is fragile, powerful and complex, a remarkable reminder that we are "fearfully and wonderfully made" (Psalm 139:14). In a similar fashion, the soul and spirit in us that makes us God's image bearers is vulnerable and susceptible to disease, disruption and damage.

I have for some time now gained encouragement and insight form a wonderful little book in my personal library titled <u>Healing for Damaged Emotions</u> by David Seamands. At the very beginning, he recognizes the reality of emotional disease and distress in the body of Christ. He says, "Understanding that salvation does not give instant emotional health offers us important insight into the doctrine of sanctification. It is impossible to know how Christian a person is, merely on the basis of his (or her) outward behavior" (p. 13). Seamands is in symphony with the Psalmist who in a kind of imaginary dialogue with his own soul said, "Why are thou cast down, O my soul? And why art thou disquieted in me" (Psalm 42:5a)?

How wonderful it is to know that whatever ails us deep in the secret places of our hearts, we can bring it to God and, in the grip of His grace, find healing and restoration. "Trouble don't last always". The Psalmist recognized this and encouraged himself beyond the disequilibrium in his own soul and spirit with these words: "Hope thou in God, for I shall yet praise him for the help of his countenance" Psalm 42:5b). With the scalpel of His omniscience, God can penetrate the deep places of soul and spirit and transform sadness into joy, midnight into morning and depression into delight. You and I don't have to be stroked out by strife or stained by stress; we can take our burdens to the Lord and leave them there.

While I learned that the whole field of brain repair is at best "science in progress," I know with certainty that God has perfected the processes that allow us by faith and through His amazing grace to recover from the problems, the past and the pitfalls that perpetuate our pain.

Dealing with Disappointment

"Why art thou cast down, O my soul?
and why art thou disquieted in me? hope thou in God:
for I shall yet praise him for the help of his countenance."

(Psalms 42:5)

The only sure and certain way to avoid the experience of disappointment is to live our lives devoid and destitute of any expectations or hopes. In the sitcom "Hogan's Heroes", Sergeant Schultz (the jovial, yet sometimes cynical prison guard) often said, "I know nothing and I see nothing." This was his patent response when asked a question about the latest ruse at the camp. If you or I know nothing, see nothing, desire nothing and expect nothing, then we might be able to dodge or dance around disappointment. Unfortunately, however, under those circumstances our lives will be bland and insignificant. The late Alexander Pope said, "Blessed is he who expects nothing for he shall never be disappointed."

Disappointment is part and parcel of the experience of being human. One cannot read the Gospels without recognizing implicitly and explicitly that there were times when Jesus was disappointed by the perception and performance of the disciples. I believe when he wept at the tomb of Lazarus, he did so not because of any sense of grief but rather disappointment in Mary and Martha's lack of faith.

Our involvement in relationships with others will necessarily expose and exacerbate our vulnerability to disappointment. Love is not only a passionate flower of possibility, but it can also be a pernicious portal of disappointment. When we love and care for others, our destinies become intertwined with theirs. The prophet Isaiah experienced deafening disappointment when the great King Uzziah died because he felt that the health and wealth of the nation of Judah rested on the laurels of the king's nobility, integrity, and ability.

Perhaps you are wrestling with disappointment today; disappointment in yourself, in a relationship, or circumstances you are experiencing presently. Be encouraged that disappointment and despair are not the last words. We can minister effectively and serve Christ through our disappointment if we hold on and hold out. Disappointment is often the catalyst that God uses to help us regain our spiritual focus. The Apostle Paul said it best: "And let us not be weary in well-doing, for in due season we shall reap, if we faint not" (Galatians 6:9).

Look Out for Lock Outs

**"Cast me not away from thy presence;
and take not thy holy spirit from me.
Restore unto me the joy of thy salvation;
and uphold me with thy free spirit."**

(Psalms 51:11-12)

Recently, while serving as volunteer chaplain for our police department, I accompanied one of our local police officers while responding to a "lockout." A motorist had locked his keys inside his car and could not gain access to the vehicle. In this particular instance, the owner could have opened the vehicle without the keys but had also forgotten the external key pad combination. There are times in our spiritual journey when we too experience "lockout." Our spiritual advance in Christ and access to the riches and resources of this redeeming relationship is hampered and hindered because we have lost possession of the "spiritual keys" that are the basis of victorious Christian living.

What are these spiritual keys?" Upon reflection, I believe the critical keys that assure our advance in the plan of God are prayer, Bible study, worship, fellowship and ministry to others. Each of these keys opens up infinite possibilities in our walk with Christ and our relationship to those around us. Without them, our lives will become stagnant, sterile and stationary. Although heirs of a glorious spiritual vehicle that is designed for blessing and prosperity, we will find ourselves stalled and stymied on the road of life. Sin is the primary cause of spiritual "lockout". It can happen as the result of an inappropriate mental attitude such as pride or jealousy, the harmful and hurtful activity of the tongue such as lying and maligning, or overtly through inappropriate behaviors such as stealing or sexual sinning. David was experiencing "spiritual lockout" when he asked God to "Restore unto me the joy of thy salvation and uphold me with thy free spirit" (Psalm 51:12). Jesus was seeking to remedy and remove the Apostle Peter's experience of "spiritual lockout" when he asked Peter, "Simon, son of Jonas, lovest thou me more than these?" (John 21:15).

How wonderful to know today that we don't have to live in a lockout situation. The motorist called "911" and the police responded. You and I can call on the name of Jesus and He will answer. And when Jesus comes, He will restore to us the keys of the Kingdom. After our response call, the police officer radioed dispatch with these words, "Entrance gained." I learned that this is law enforcement jargon used when a lockout situation has been resolved. Praise God that on a hill called Calvary, Jesus resolved the ultimate lockout situation and, when His redeeming work was done, he declared, "It is finished!" Entrance has now been gained into His eternal Kingdom for all that believe because of His death, burial and resurrection.

God Can Handle It!

"Cast thy burden upon the LORD, and he shall sustain thee: he shall never suffer the righteous to be moved."

(Psalms 55:22)

We gather today as a worshipping and faith community amidst the departing radiance of the old year and the ascending glory of the coming year. This New Year looms on our horizon like a glorious sunrise glistening brightly on the ocean of our possibility and the sea of our potential. This affirmation does not disregard nor diminish the dark clouds that shroud our world in a vale of suffering, violence, terror, hatred and war. Nor does it ignore the increasing volatility of our economy that swells the ranks of the unemployed and disenfranchised and the alarming loss of moral virtue and value that threatens to leave our society spiritually anemic and bankrupt. It does recognize, however, our belief that God is in charge and whatever happens, God can handle it. I also believe that the times in which we live afford wonderful and rare opportunities to share the Gospel of the Lord Jesus Christ to those who are searching for consistent and coherent answers to life's ultimate questions of origin, meaning, morality, history and destiny.

Through the prophet Isaiah, God encouraged another generation of believers who faced similar challenges with these words: "Fear thou not, for I am with thee, be not dismayed; for I am thy God. I will strengthen thee; yea, I will help thee; yea I will uphold thee with the right hand of my righteousness" (Isaiah 41:10). Like Israel of old, our hope is not ultimately rooted in some misguided sense of our own ability, nor in the machinations of men, but rather in the goodness and righteousness of God who promises not to leave us to ourselves or to our circumstances. God continues to assure Isaiah and the people with these words, "I will open rivers in high places, and fountains in the midst of the valleys; I will make the wilderness a pool of water, and the dry land springs of water." (Isaiah 41:18)

Be encouraged today that whatever challenges you face, whatever uncertainty or insecurity you have, whatever problems you or I must endure in the days ahead, God will see us through. The Psalmist was bolstered by this hope and wrote, "Cast thy burden upon the LORD, and he shall sustain thee; he shall never suffer the righteous to be moved" (Psalm 55:22). This is true because God backs up His promises with a power that knows no limitations and a presence that is personal and persistent. God alone can irrigate the dry places of our lives and cause fountains to break forth in the midst of our valleys. God can handle it!

Wanted Witnesses!

"God be merciful unto us, and bless us;
and cause his face to shine upon us; Selah.
That thy way may be known upon earth,
thy saving health among all nations."

(Psalms 67:1-2)

The word translated "witness" in the New Testament comes from the Greek word which is the basis for our English "martyr". How interesting this is. Christians who bore witness of the life changing, soul saving message of the Gospel during the period of the early church did so at risk to their own lives. Anyone who shared this message with the lost could be tormented, imprisoned or even killed. This is exactly what happened to Stephen, one of the first deacons of the early church, who witnessed to his own countrymen about Jesus and was subsequently stoned to death.

The implication of this reality speaks volumes to each of us today. While many believers in Third World countries, many Islamic cultures and countries ruled by oppressive regimes are suffering for their testimony and faith, those of us who live in America can share the Gospel with others without fear of reprisal. Yet, as one of my seminary professors was often fond of saying, "Jesus Christ is the church's best kept secret." Those who earnestly desire to share the Gospel with others must be willing to experience a different kind of martyrdom. We must die to self so that we can completely live to God and for God. More importantly, when we force "self" to abdicate the throne of our lives, then Christ can truly dwell in us and work through us to His praise and glory. When this happens, the church will make known to all of creation the manifold wisdom of God as it has been revealed in the Gospel.

I am by no means suggesting that such an abdication is easy. It does however represent one of the perennial challenges of the Christian life and is the essential prerequisite to authentic witnessing. Paul expresses this truth quite eloquently in Galatians 2:20. "I am crucified with Christ: nevertheless I live; yet not I, but

Christ liveth in me: and the life which I now live in the flesh I live by the faith of the Son of God, who loved me, and gave himself for me." Yes, the Lord has need of witnesses today but "true witnesses" will lay their life down for the truth. What are you prepared to do?

The Sinister Seduction of Submersion

**"Until I went into the sanctuary of God;
then understood I their end.
Surely thou didst set them in slippery places:
thou castedst them down into destruction."**

(Psalms 73:17-18)

Whenever flying, I still marvel at how dramatically different is the view on the ground when the plane is taxiing to the runway and the view of the landscape at cruising height. Many times when this level is attained, the clouds that hid the sunlight from view on the ground are now beneath the plane and the sun shines ever so radiantly. These changes are all the result of altitude. The higher one climbs in the plane, the clearer the view. In fact, at cruising altitude, we are able to see sight- encompassing details and landmarks that one could never see on the ground. This is true in the spiritual realm as well. So often we find ourselves succumbing to what I call the "sinister seduction of submersion". We are so submerged in what we are doing or in what is going on around us that we cannot see the big picture or see clearly. Clouds of despair, disillusionment and disappointment hide the sunlight from our view. Darkness and shadows shade and shield us from truth. It is only when we change our altitude that we are able to change our attitude. This can occur spiritually in any number of ways. Meditation upon the Word of God can catapult us into another conceptual domain and perspective. No wonder the Psalmist said, "Thy word is a lamp unto my feet, and a light unto my path"(Psalm 119:105).

Authentic and genuine worship can move us into an entirely new realm of sensing, seeing and serving. This is the clear teaching of Psalm 73:17 where the biblical writer declares, "When I tried to understand all this, it was oppressive to me till I entered the sanctuary of God; then I understood their final destiny"(NIV). Another altitude shifter is prayer. Prayer is extraterrestrial conversation and communication that places the believer in contact with the transcendent ground of our being. In other words, when we pray we book a flight into the very bosom of God's Being. Such flight is never coach seating, but always first class. When praying, the plane of our existence and experience climbs to an entirely new level. This is important to remember because on the ground, we suffer sometimes from the infestation of the rats and rodents of sin and suffering in the cargo holds of our lives. We must remember to pull back the lever of faith and move to the heights above us where those pests and predators will die of oxygen deficiency.

George Matheson, the blind Scottish preacher of another era whose writings inspire me, understood this truth ever so well and wrote, **"O joy that seekest me through pain, I cannot close my heart to thee; I climb the rainbow in the rain and feel the promise is not vain that morn shall tearless be."** There is a tearless morning and a clear sky beyond the veil of our pain and problems. But we must climb the rainbow of God's promise, provision and power to arrive there.

Valuing the Victory

**"Mercy and truth are met together;
righteousness and peace have kissed each other."**

(Psalms 85:10)

The Cross stands at the apex of human history; at the veritable crossroads of civilization. At the Cross, all that is good in God merged with all that is evil in man. At the Cross, the suffering wrought by sin, shame and death wedded the sufficiency of God in the Person of Christ whose sinless humanity became the atoning sacrifice for the sins of the world. At the Cross, hope became the boundless and blessed balm that heals our hobbling hurts.

All human history moves toward this moment. The Cross is the moment that is the "high noon" of revelation and the place where the shadows cannot be seen anymore; only the bright light of His glory illuminates. It is undoubtedly the place that the Psalmist spoke of: "Mercy and truth are met together; righteousness and peace have kissed each other. Truth shall spring out of the earth; and righteousness shall look down from heaven" (Psalm 85:10).

The Cross was the place where the only begotten Son was "made ... to be sin for us, who knew no sin; that we might be made the righteousness of God in him" (II Corinthians 5:21). Here the last and most formidable stronghold was broken, its walls scaled as Jesus took away the sting from death and the victory from the grave.

We gather at the Table of the Lord today to commemorate this resounding strategic victory. We are no longer engaged in a struggle with an uncertain outcome. Because He lives we can face every tomorrow and every challenge that life brings. Because He lives all fears dissipate into the ocean of His faithfulness. The death, burial and resurrection of the Lord Jesus Christ has interpenetrated history with what C. S. Lewis called a "good infection". You and I can catch this good infection "near the Cross" and near the Person whose blood became the propitiation (mercy seat) for not only our sins but the sins of the whole world

(I John 2:1-2). In relationship with Christ we are formed and transformed into His image and likeness. We who already bear the imprimatur of His essence from creation can now reflect and mirror His spiritual likeness as reflections and reflectors of His glory.

This is the victory Christ offers to us; this is the true victory of the Cross! It is the hope that we can be changed moment by moment into the likeness of the One Who has no beginning and no ending. The Apostle Paul lauded and leveraged this possibility to the believers at Colossae when he wrote, "To whom God would make known what is the riches of the glory of this mystery among the Gentiles; which is Christ in you, the hope of glory" (Colossians 1:27).

Cloudy Pillars

**"He spake unto them in the cloudy pillar:
they kept his testimonies,
and the ordinance that he gave them."**

(Psalms 99:7)

The Lord communicates to His servants in every generation. (See Hebrews 1:1-3.) The absence of light, the presence of uncertainty or the lack of assurance in any situation is no indication that God is not speaking or concerned. He has promised never to leave us or forsake us and that nothing can separate us from the love of God which is in Christ Jesus.

This text reminds us that the God who is both Creator and infinitely creative speaks from the "cloudy pillar". God's concern and compassion does not radiate merely in the sun shiny days of our experiences, but in the darkness and the hovering clouds as well. God is not limited and, therefore, uses every sound, sight, scene and situation to communicate His love, concern and providential goodwill to those who enter into covenant (relationship) with Him. The cloudy pillar, the evidence to the nation of Israel of God's presence, hovered above the Tabernacle in the wilderness. This constant reminder of God's presence and faithfulness was an incentive to Israel to keep His laws and the ordinances that had been given through divine inspiration. The cloud reminds us of the darkness that looms at every sunset and nightfall of life's experience and beyond every horizon of our hopes. However, the fact that it was a "pillar" is a striking reminder to us of God's strength and ability to deliver us not only *from* the storms of life, but *in* the storms as well.

What cloudy pillar has dampened your joy and disabled your confidence? Don't forget that God is the Creator of both darkness and light, and He can use either for your and my edification and God's own glorification as He speaks to us from the cloudy pillars of life.

Precious Memories

"Bless the LORD, O my soul:
and all that is within me, bless his holy name.
Bless the LORD, O my soul,
and forget not all his benefits."

(Psalms 103:1-2)

One function of the mentality of the soul is memory. In our memory center resides the recollections of our life pilgrimage. Memories can be good or bad, upsetting or energizing. There is a relationship between our worship and our memory. Worship pulsates and pivots between the polarities of praise and thanksgiving. We praise God for who He is. We give thanks to God for what He has done.

The author of Psalm 103 exhorted his own soul to bless the Lord, to positively blame the Lord for the spiritual and material benefits experienced in life. Psychologists call this autosuggestion, but the spiritual principle is much more profound. As we accumulate spiritual data in the mentality of the soul through Bible study, meditation, reflection on our life experiences and prayer, the capacity is developed within to erupt in anthems of praise and thanksgiving to and for God. Indeed these are the precious memories that linger.

Biblical Revelation

"Thy word is a lamp unto my feet, and a light unto my path."
(Psalms 119:105)

Biblical revelation addresses our fundamental uniqueness as creatures made in the image of God. We are both children of this world (dust) and children of God (Spirit). Revelation manifests that which concerns us ultimately. The Word of God addresses both our contingent and transcendent natures. Dietrich Bonheoffer was right: "God is not the limits of life but the center."

In revelation, God has drawn back the venetian blinds of His essence and invaded the human coordinate with "good news", offering life everlasting that is not only pregnant with possibility but inexhaustible in mystery. God's initiative requires a faith response on our part. This is much more than the formality of assent to a doctrine or the superficiality of church membership alone, but rather the attitude of confessed insufficiency that is met by the awesome sufficiency of God that can only be experienced in personal relationship.

Can You Hear Me Now?

"The LORD shall preserve thy going out and thy coming in from this time forth, and even for evermore."

(Psalms 121:8)

The well known Verizon wireless telephone commercial with the rather austere man moving from locale to locale and asking, "Can you hear me now?" reminds me of how important it is in life to stay connected to God in every situation and circumstance. There is absolutely no part of our lives where we can be blessed apart from God's guidance. The moment we lose our connection with this reality, we are in dire straits. God has promised in His word to go before us, to watch our "going out and our coming in (Psalm 121:8b).

We all know that in some areas wireless telephone services are subverted by signal interference or signal blackout. This is never true of the Lord who has placed within and around every believer not only the seal and insignia of our special relationship to Him, but a special guidance system that orders our steps. Bob Mumford in his book Take Another Look at Guidance tells of a certain harbor in Italy which can only be reached by sailing up a narrow channel between dangerous rocks and treacherous shoals. Many ships have wrecked here and navigation is difficult. In order to guide the ships safely into port, someone mounted three lights on three huge poles in the harbor. When the lights are perfectly lined up and seen as one, then ships can safely proceed up the narrow channel without incident. On the other hand, if more than one light is seen, then the ship's captain knows that he's off course and in danger.

God has provided three navigational beacons that gives guidance and direction to the believer. The Word of God is our objective guide. "Thy word is a lamp unto my feet, and a light unto my path" (Psalm 119:105). The Spirit of God is our subjective (interior) guide. Jesus said of the Spirit, "... He shall teach you all things, and bring all things to your remembrance whatsoever I have said unto you" (John 14:26). Finally, the experiences of life can become our <u>reflective</u> <u>guide</u> as we by faith perceive God's powerful and providential presence working in our lives. "The steps of a good man are ordered by the Lord and He delighteth his way" (Psalm 37:23). When these beacons align in our experience, we know that God will lead us safely along the way. When we follow God's light, we never need to ask Him, "Can you hear me now?"

F.A.M.I.L.Y.

**"Except the LORD build the house,
they labour in vain that build it:
except the LORD keep the city,
the watchman waketh but in vain."**

(Psalms 127:1)

I've spent many moments during the past week thinking about the importance of family and friends. The word "family" etched itself on my consciousness and I began playing a kind of word game associating different concepts with the letters in the word. I asked, "What realities are prompted and projected by these letters? The letter **"F"** communicates **"foundation"**. Strong families (and marriages) are not only the foundation of the church but our society. In many ways it is true, "so goes the family, so goes our society." Perhaps it was family that the Psalmist had in mind when he wrote, "If the foundation be destroyed, what can the righteous do?" (Psalm 11:3).

The letter **"A"** stands for **"acceptance."**. The family is (and definitely should be) the one place where we can find acceptance and affirmation. It is a safe and warm place in the midst of a world that is growing increasingly cold, callous and critical. It is the place where prodigals can return home to the warm, loving and forgiving embrace of unconditional love. The letter **"M."** stands for **"maturity"**. The family is the place where behavior is formed and the environment where maturity is expected and experienced. In his family of origin, exposed to the love and discipline of a mother and grandmother, Timothy grew to maturity. The Apostle Paul assumed as much when he challenged him by saying, "God hath not given us the spirit of fear, but of power, and of love and of a sound (mature) mind" (II Timothy 1:7).

"I" stands for **"inspiration."**. The dictionary defines inspiration as "an aspiring or being inspired mentally or emotionally; any stimulus to creative thought or action." The family was designed by God as the place of stimulus where our children, teens and young adults are inspired and encouraged to reach their full potential. Every child is a bundle of possibility and the family is the incubator! The Bible says, "Lo, children are an heritage of the Lord; and the fruit of the womb is his reward." (See Psalm 127:3.) I imagine often when reading Hebrews 12:1 that family members who have gone on to be with the Lord are celestial cheerleaders who encourage our race of faith. "Wherefore seeing we also are compassed about with so great a cloud of witnesses, let us lay aside every weight, and the sin which doth so easily beset us, and let us run with patience the race that is set before us."

The letter **"L."** was easy for me. Surely this stands for **"love."**. Not just any type of love but the agape love of the Bible. This is the love that embraces the Beloved unconditionally. This is the love that God has for his children and indeed had for an estranged world. This is the love that prompted the greatest gift of all according to John 3:16. This is the love that carries a mother to death's door in order to give birth to

her child. It is the love that took our Savior to the Cross to give birth to our spiritual life and destiny.

Finally, the letter **"Y"** stands for **"Yes."**. Why "Yes?" The church is compelled today at a time when marriage and family is being attacked and assailed by those who are attempting and succeeding in changing God's Divine Design to say an unconditional "yes" to the Family. Say "yes" because marriage between a man and a woman is the only biblical basis for the family. Any other alternative or arrangement will ultimately incur God's wrath and deteriorate and destroy the moral foundation of this nation which was founded on biblical and spiritual principles. We must say "yes" today and do all we can in our power to exude and exemplify to a broken world that God's way is right.

Divine Interruptions

"Except the LORD build the house,
they labour in vain that build it:
except the LORD keep the city,
the watchman waketh but in vain.
It is vain for you to rise up early,
to sit up late, to eat the bread of sorrows:
for so he giveth his beloved sleep."
(Psalms 127:1-2)

When I was a child, I was taught never to interrupt adults when they were talking. Failure to observe this unwritten commandment could result in swift retribution and painful reprisal. I learned quickly that this admonition fell squarely within the category of "respecting one's elders". Upon further reflection, my mind moves quickly to John Mansfield's definition of life. He said that "life is a series of uninvited interruptions." I agree and should note further that those interruptions are either Divinely caused or Divinely permitted. God has the sovereign right to interrupt our plans and our agendas. God neither needs nor seeks our permission. To ignore this reality is to disregard the clear teaching of the 127th Psalm which reminds us that all our human efforts apart from God are pointless and purposeless.

"Unless the LORD builds the house, its builders labor in vain. Unless the LORD watches over the city, the watchmen stand guard in vain. In vain you rise early and stay up late, toiling for food to eat— for he grants sleep to those he loves" (Psalm 127:1-2 – NIV).

While building our spiritual houses, God sometimes speaks to us through "Divine interruptions." These "speed bumps" along the road of life are providentially positioned to deepen our faith and encourage our transformation into God's likeness. The late C. S. Lewis in his book The Problem of Pain says, "God whispers to us in our pleasures, speaks in our conscience, but shouts in our pains; it is His megaphone to rouse a deaf world." Perhaps you are dealing with a difficult interruption today. If so, trust the providence of God and don't allow circumstances or lack of faith to provoke you into interrupting God as He speaks. Trust that God will provide provision, power, purpose and pardon for the interruptions.

Passing Tests and Permanent Triumphs

"If thou, LORD, shouldest mark iniquities,
O Lord, who shall stand?
But there is forgiveness with thee,
that thou mayest be feared."

(Psalms 130:3-4)

Failure is not a welcomed word or welcomed visitor! In a culture permeated with the idolatry of self and which pays perpetual homage to the gods of human achievement and success, we are conditioned, coaxed and coached from a very early age to succeed no matter what. An impassionate and callous culture has a very low tolerance for failure. Students who fail are ostracized, marginalized and stigmatized in the classroom. Employees who fail to meet expectations, who miss the mark are penalized and traumatized with the prospect of job separation or termination. College and professional coaches who fail to win experience the ire of fans and swift retribution from the schools and the teams that employ them. Even the church has been accused of being "the only army that shoots its wounded".

I am grateful today that God truly looks beyond our faults and sees our needs. While God will not wink at or ignore our sins ,we can be confident that God will never give up on us! How encouraging the words of the great hymn by Lucie Campbell: "But if you try and fail in your trying, hands sore and scarred from the work you've begun, take up your cross, run quickly to meet Him, He'll understand. He'll say 'Well done.'" Charles Swindoll makes an interesting observation regarding failure. He says, "Great accomplishments are often attempted but only occasionally reached. Those who reach them are usually those who missed many times before. Failures are only temporary tests to prepare us for permanent triumphs." The greatest accomplishment of all is to live a life pleasing to God. Because we are not a perfect people and because we do not live in a perfect world, we will experience failure. Spiritually, morally, occupationally and experientially, we will miss the mark.

Be encouraged today that God meets us at the very depths of failure. The late Dr. Reinhold Niebuhr, noted theologian, said, "Accept the fact that we have been accepted." It is still true that nothing can separate us from the love of God which is in Christ Jesus. During the despair and disappointment of failure the Psalmist cried out, "If thou Lord shouldest mark iniquities, O Lord who shall stand? But there is forgiveness with thee, that thou mayest be feared" (Psalm 130:3-4). The crooked corridor of failure can often lead to the blessed doorway of a new intimacy and dependency on God, who is intent on rescuing us from the success syndrome.

The Eternally Present God

"Whither shall I go from thy spirit?
or whither shall I flee from thy presence?
If I ascend up into heaven, thou art there:
if I make my bed in hell, behold, thou art there.
If I take the wings of the morning,
and dwell in the uttermost parts of the sea;
Even there shall thy hand lead me,
and thy right hand shall hold me.
If I say, Surely the darkness shall cover me;
even the night shall be light about me."

(Psalms 139:7-11)

Any thoughtful reflection on the reality of God as revealed in the Bible must assent that God is a Person who desires relationship and to be eternally present with those He has created and redeemed. To this glorious end, God is unrelenting. The Bible portrays this truth in a number of colorful and compelling ways. In the Book of Exodus, the presence of God goes before Israel as a pillar of fire at night and a cloud during the day. When Israel paused during her journeys, the Shekinah Glory of God rested above the Tabernacle.

Ezekiel saw a vision of God by the River Chebar and described God's presence as a "wheel in the middle of a wheel." The prophet Hosea became a living metaphor for the presence of God as he reached out to redeem and restore an adulterous wife. Even when we transgress God's commandment, God is poised to forgive and cleanse us. Be encouraged today that no matter what you are facing, God is present in the midst of those circumstances and is prepared to command a blessing on your behalf. Draw nigh to God and God will draw nigh to you.

Making a Difference

**"My son, hear the instruction of thy father,
and forsake not the law of thy mother."**

(Proverbs 1:8)

I remember vividly how I felt when my first child was born, our oldest daughter. When I saw her for the first time, the doctor was holding her up in the window of the delivery room. At that moment, looking at her while her tiny eyes were darting about the room, seemingly infatuated with curiosity for the new world she had entered, I felt such a tremendous, almost frightening weight of responsibility. It occurred to me in that fleeting but unforgettable moment that this beautiful little girl, a fragile bundle of joy and potential, was wholly dependent on me and her mother for everything. Apart from my recognition as a young preacher that God is faithful and would provide everything I needed to be a husband to my wife and a father to our precious firstborn, the sheer magnitude of it all would have diminished the joyful celebration of that precious and priceless moment. I remembered the words of the Psalmist, "Lo, children are a heritage of the Lord and the fruit of the womb is his reward. As arrows are in the hand of a mighty man, so are children of the youth" (Psalm 127:3-4).

There have been many times in the past few years when in the corridors of my mind I have revisited the sights, scenes, sounds and sighs of that virgin and vital moment. Now a father of four, guardian of two and grandfather of one, I can only marvel at the sufficient grace of God who "hath given unto us all things that pertain unto life and godliness, through the knowledge of him that hath called us to glory and virtue" (II Peter 1:4b). While I am in no way a perfect father or husband or a perennial paragon of parenting, I can truly say that I have, through the grace of God, done the very best I can by precept and example to make a difference in my children's lives and to be a strong tower for my family.

My son, a Baptist preacher and a divinity student at Southeastern Baptist Seminary in Wake Forest, North Carolina, has been asked to speak this morning at his church there about "what his father means to him." Two of my daughters and my granddaughter will be present as well. I have no idea what he plans to say and I really wish I could eavesdrop on that service. Whatever else he says, I pray that he will say that I loved him and took care of him, his siblings and his mother, making a positive difference in their lives. And I hope he knows that since the night his sister was born, God has truly carried me as I have tried to carry the awesome weight of responsibility for my family.

The Urgency of Saving Souls

**"The fruit of the righteous is a tree of life;
and he that winneth souls is wise."**

(Proverbs 11:30)

The words "casual" and "urgency" are worlds apart with regard to meaning and intensity. Yet, in many of our churches today they coexist. They are odd partners, cohabiting in our ministries in an alarming and disheartening way. In many ways, these words represent both the way things are and the way they should be. The disfigured union of these two words and the realities they represent is a sad signal of the state of the contemporary church today.

I am reminded of the warning and exhortation of the Old Testament prophet Amos to rebellious and apostate Israel. He said, "Woe to them that are at ease in Zion, and trust in the mountain of Samaria, which are named chief of the nations, to whom the house of Israel came! "(Amos 6:1). Amos, the farmer who became a prophet-preacher, lashes out at the sins of his people with an urgent and visual pronouncement of coming judgment. He desired to mobilize the nation to repentance and the recovery of their commission to be a light and witness for God to the nations. Yet, Israel, like a basket of rotting fruit, was ripe for judgment because of hypocrisy and indifference.

There is nothing as urgent as the salvation of lost souls. This is the primary mission and essential ministry of the New Testament church. The local church and every believer salts, seasons and saturates the lives of others as we reflect the glory of God in Jesus Christ. This requires more than a brief interlude of worship on Sunday morning and then business as usual the rest of the week. It demands a sense of urgency and passionate, willful submission to the Spirit of the Lord who desires nothing less than to change us into the glorious image of Christ. When Jesus determined to go to Jerusalem and fulfill the Father's plan by dying on the cross for the sins of the whole world, there was something so intense about His demeanor that villages along the way were afraid to receive Him. (Luke 9:51-53) How intense and passionate are you and I today about the saving of lost souls and the fulfillment of our commission to take the Gospel to the ends of the world?

A Righteous Remnant

**"Righteousness exalts a nation
but sin is a reproach to any people."**

(Proverbs 14:34)

The wisdom writer makes a profound statement in Proverbs 14:34. "Righteousness exalts a nation but sin is a reproach to any people." These words introduce an important spiritual concept recorded in the Word of God. I call it the doctrine of the <u>spiritual pivot</u>. (See Genesis 18:23-26; Ezekiel 22:23-31 and Matthew 5:13-16 as well.)

The real test of any society is not the extent to which evil and sin prevail; but rather the presence of a righteous remnant, which is the active and influential existence of the people of God who are led by the Spirit of God and living faithfully to the Word of God. Someone once said that the only thing worse than the evil that bad people do is when good people stand aside and say or do nothing. Biblical history reveals that even in the most desperate and despicable of environments, the presence of those whom God deems righteous can be the difference between deliverance and destruction, between restoration and judgment.

God desires that every local church function as a pivot that will encourage men, women, boys and girls to turn their hearts to God. In order for this to happen, we must maintain our saltiness through the study of the Word, believing prayer, authentic Christian fellowship and a burning desire to reach others for Christ.

Caring Words

"A word fitly spoken is like
apples of gold in pictures of silver."
(Proverbs 25:11)

A few years ago, the Federal Reserve Board raised the prime interest rate. In a policy statement related to this key adjustment in the financial markets, six words were mistakenly omitted. Those words were **"longer-term inflation is well contained."** The omission of those words in the initial policy statement created quite a fervor on Wall Street. The stock exchanges and commodities markets were literally reeling from the ambiguity in the report and the lack of a clear statement about the Board's assessment of inflationary trends. Only when these six words were added and the statement revised did the markets rebound and close with a gain.

My first thoughts upon hearing this story had to do with how significant words are in our culture and society. I thought as well about the tenured Oklahoma University baseball coach who lost his job after a storied career because of the derogatory and racist remarks he made while attempting to characterize one of his African-American players. Yes indeed, words do make a difference. The wisdom writer said, "A word fitly spoken is like apples of gold in pictures of silver" (Proverbs 25:11).

So many of us have been encouraged or chastened for our good by the nurturing and caring words of mothers whose loving ministrations have indeed made the high places of our lives low and the rough places smooth. The lack of that encouragement, support and motherly admonition would have sent our lives reeling in a different direction. We thank God for mothers who cared enough to say the right thing, at the right time, in the right way, and for the right reasons.

Finally, when I heard this story about the omission of six words in the Federal Reserve Board's statement, I thought about how God has the power—no matter what we are going through

— to add an addendum to the circumstances of life. His words matter as none others! When He speaks, storms are stilled, blind folk see, crippled folk walk, and sick people are healed. When God speaks, the dead are raised and sins are forgiven. When God's words invade our situations and circumstances, foundations shift, tides change, directions are reversed and we discover that we can do all things through Christ who strengthens us.

Inner Beauty

**"Favour is deceitful, and beauty is vain:
but a woman that feareth the LORD, she shall be praised."**

(Proverbs 31:30)

Always when the Bible speaks of the beauty of a woman, it does so from the perspective of her interior (or internal) beauty or integrity. The wisdom writer says, "Favor is deceitful, and beauty is vain but a woman that feareth the Lord, she shall be praised" (Proverbs 31:30). Paul directed Timothy to exhort the women of Ephesus with these words, "I also want women to dress modestly, with decency and propriety, not with braided hair or gold or pearls or expensive clothes, but with good deeds, appropriate for women who profess to worship God" (I Timothy 2:9-10 – NIV).

This is certainly not an admonition or rebuke to women who pay attention to their outward beauty and appearance. Rather, it is a sober reminder that the greatest asset a woman possesses is a devout and godly life. Selfless devotion to God and others may very well enhance the outward appearance. Therefore, a woman's measure is not so much what she puts on, but the loving service and devotion she gives out.

The End of the Beginning and the Beginning of the End

**"To every thing there is a season,
and a time to every purpose under the heaven."**

(Ecclesiastes 3:1)

Recently, I heard a speaker contrast the "end of the beginning" with the "beginning of the end." It occurred to me upon hearing the explanation that perception and perspective are intimately and inextricably intertwined and interrelated. Contrast the observation that "the glass is either half empty or half full." In both cases, the quantity of the liquid in the glass is the same but the difference is perception and consequently perspective. The old axiom that "beauty is in the eye of the beholder" is part and parcel of this principle and pattern.

I believe it is a unique perceptive pattern that drives the perspective of the wisdom writer who wrote, "To everything there is a season, and a time to every purpose under the heaven" (Ecclesiastes 3:1). The author was aware of a transcendent Person and Presence who he felt predetermined the events of life. He would later write in this same chapter, "He [God] hath made everything beautiful in his time; also he hath set the world in their heart, so that no man can find out the work that God maketh from the beginning to the end" (Ecclesiastes 3:11). The <u>Message</u> paraphrases this passage: "God made everything beautiful in itself and it its time—but he's left us in the dark, so we can never know what God is up to, whether he's coming or going."

The application of this principle at the outset of this New Year is that it is critically important as believers that we maintain the right perspective regarding the things around us and the things within us. However, the pessimism of the wisdom writer reflected in the aforementioned verses must be seasoned with awareness that through meditation, study, fellowship with other believers, prayer and worship we can discern and know the will of God for our lives.

One of my commitments (*not resolutions*) during the coming year is to be more consistent in spending personal and private time with the Lord so that I can listen and hear that "still small voice" that resounds and resonates louder than earthquake, wind or fire. This desire is fueled by the perspective that God has a plan and purpose for my life (*and yours, too*) and that God wants me to know what it is! How else could the Apostle Paul say, "For it is God which worketh in you both to will and to do of his good pleasure" (Philippians 2:13). The prophet Jeremiah was in concert with Paul when he wrote, "For I know the thoughts that I think toward you, saith the LORD, thoughts of peace, and not of evil, to give you an expected end" (Jeremiah 29:11).

I encourage you, too, as we face another New Year that will surely be fraught and filled with seasons of uncertainty, that you earnestly seek to know God's will for your life so that you may view whatever experiences or challenges you face from God's view and vantage point and not your own. This is the secret to true happiness and blessing. It is the difference between the "beginning of the end" and the "end of the beginning."

Voices and Choices

"Remember now thy Creator in the days of thy youth, while the evil days come not, nor the years draw nigh, when thou shalt say, I have no pleasure in them."

(Ecclesiastes 12:1)

While facing the prospect of succeeding his father David as king, Solomon asked God to grant him wisdom. God granted his request and so much more. The Books of Ecclesiastes, Proverbs and Song of Solomon are rightly called "wisdom literature". Solomon's wisdom was not just the expression of God's favor but also the results of applying divine truth to his own experiences in life. All of us should be quick to hear the man who had the financial resources and status to experience every human and sensual pleasure in life, and yet reached the conclusion that life without God is not worth living and is merely "vanity of vanities."

Our youth today are bombarded with choices and inundated with voices that suggest money, sex, worldly success and pleasure is everything. "If it feels good, do it!" is the prevailing maxim of the day! This viewpoint fails to recognize the dignity of human existence and the reality that God has made us for relationship and fellowship with Himself. This is not only our greatest treasure but our greatest pleasure as well. Solomon encouraged his readers to remember their "Creator."

God is the one whose image we bear and in Whom is the secret of lasting joy and prosperity. Solomon's exhortation is seasoned with urgency for this predisposition: to know, love and serve God is a duty best executed during our youth, because evil days will surely come. Only those who build their lives on the solid foundation of faith in God, who is revealed as both Creator and Redeemer in the Bible, can endure the test of time, enjoying the promise, presence and power of God through all the seasons of life.

Confronting Guilt

**"Come now, and let us reason together, saith the LORD:
though your sins be as scarlet, they shall be as white as snow;
though they be red like crimson, they shall be as wool."**

(Isaiah 1:18)

An interesting headline in The Wall Street Journal grabbed my attention. It read, "Breaking a Taboo, Army Confronts Guilt After Combat." The article reported on the research of a West Point professor in the area of the morality of killing in combat. Because of our armed forces present engagement in Afghanistan and Iraq, and the number of soldiers returning home traumatized by their combat experience, the military is taking a closer look at this problem. They have discovered that even soldiers who are trained to kill in combat and to defend their own lives and the lives of their fellow soldiers experience significant guilt from taking the life of another human being.

This article validates the truth of the Apostle Paul's teaching in the Book of Romans. He said, "For when the Gentiles, which have not the law, do by nature the things contained in the law, these having not the law, are a law unto themselves, which shew the work of the law written in their hearts, their conscience also bearing witness, and their thoughts the mean while accusing or else excusing one another" (Romans 1:14-15). The knowledge of right and wrong is enmeshed in the human conscience. C. S. Lewis builds a case for the moral God of Christianity in his classic book <u>Mere Christianity</u> by beginning with a discussion of natural law. The universal sense of good and evil points to a moral absolute; something or Someone outside of us. When good has been violated and conscience corrupted then it leaves a residue of guilt and shame in the human soul. Even conditioning and a pre-justification rationale as in the case of the soldiers in the article cannot remove the nagging sense that some unintended violation has occurred when a human life has been taken.

The healing of guilt and shame in the human heart is the balm that the Gospel provides and the supreme business of the church. For people who are hurting deep inside because of guilt ("I made a mistake") or shame ("I am a mistake"), Jesus is the answer. Our ancestors asked the question, "What can wash away our sins?" The refrain provided the redemptive response, "Nothing but the blood of Jesus." There is salvation for our souls, mercy for our misery, sacrifice for our sins, forgiveness for our failures , healing for our hurts and hope for our habits because Jesus is our mercy seat, the Person and place where God's grace meets us in a time of need. Even in the Christian army there are soldiers scarred and marred by the blight of unresolved guilt and shame.

Beyond Encounter

"Also I heard the voice of the Lord, saying, Whom shall I send, and who will go for us? Then said I, Here am I; send me."

(Isaiah 6:8)

Mission is the essential and non-negotiable consequence of the Christian Gospel. The phenomenal message of the cross makes it an imperative indicative; a reality so transforming that it compels the Christian witness to the world. "For the reaching of the cross is to them that perish foolishness; but unto us which are saved it is the power of God" (I Corinthians 1:18). This dynamic has precedents beyond the ascended Lord's Great Commission to the church recorded in Matthew 28:18-20. In the local church there is a compelling continuum that begins with the supernatural datum recorded in the Scriptures. The truth claims of the Christian faith are absolute and exclusive in their declarations, but inviting and inclusive in their implications and participation. What begins with message moves to the maturation of those the Lord adds to the church, and inevitability embraces the discovery, development and deployment of their specific ministries and gifts. The final thrust and propulsion on this continuum is the local church's global mission to the world.

Our mission as a congregation is related to *spiritual density*. This is the reflected glory of God in the lives of those who are occupied with His Word, worship, work and witness. The development of motivational virtue within the context of our vertical relationship with God (priesthood) will result in functional virtue in our horizontal relationship with the world (ambassadorship). In this regard, Isaiah's *temple encounter* with God recorded in Isaiah 6:1ff is instructive. The prophet-to-be was experiencing personal trauma and the nation's corporate upheaval because of the demise and death of the great King Uzziah. The sequence of encounters in this passage involves confrontation of the transcendent holiness of God, confession of personal and corporate sin, cleansing by God's grace, and finally, commissioning for service and mission.

Christian missions emerge out of a vision of God's holiness. Worship such as what we experience today energizes, enables and qualifies our witness to the world.

Failure to Print

"Also I heard the voice of the Lord, saying, Whom shall I send, and who will go for us? Then said I, Here am I; send me."

(Isaiah 6:8)

Twice I sent the document to the printer and twice it failed to print! Becoming frustrated and quickly approaching a deadline I thought, "Do I need to adjust the print properties again or alter the print command?" Then, almost embarrassing, I discovered what was wrong. In my haste, after adjusting the print properties and returning to the main print screen, I had simply forgotten to click "ok" and give the computer the permission to send the document to the printer. This was why both documents failed to print.

Soon afterwards, the spiritual implications of this experience began to crowd into my mind. God wants to use us and to bless us but it requires our unconditional obedience and ready response. An unwillingness to say "yes" or "ok" to God or His commands is one of the primary reasons that we fail in the spiritual life. The possibility of failure is heightened by the fact that there is often more than one voice seeking our obedience and surrender. The landscape is charred with the negative consequences that come from making bad choices. The Gospel artist Sandra Crouch sings a song that says,

Yes, Lord, Yes, Lord From the bottom of my heart, To the depths of my soul Yes, Lord, completely yes; My soul says Yes!

When we say "Yes Lord!" it is like right clicking "ok" on the computer when you are ready to print a document. When we say "Yes" we are giving God permission to print the ink of His essence on the pages of our heart. Is this not what Isaiah does during his temple encounter with God and in response to God's question, "Whom shall I send, and who will go for Us?" (Isaiah 6:8). The prophet said, "Here am I! Send me." This constituted an "ok" exempting Isaiah from the possibility that the document of his message and ministry would fail to print into the lives of the people God had called and sent him to serve.

To exploit the computer analogy even further, "ok" is the right click for any child of God who truly desires the blessing that comes from obedience and surrender to the will of God. Saul, Israel's first king, at the scene of his most notable failure was told by the prophet Samuel, "Hath the LORD as great delight in burnt offerings and sacrifices, as in obeying the voice of the LORD? Behold, to obey is better than sacrifice, and to hearken than the fat of rams" (1 Samuel 15:22). Obedience is better than sacrifice. So the next time God speaks to you in His Word or through His Spirit, don't fail to print, just click "ok" and be prepared to experience the delight of the One who delights in your and my obedience.

Exclusively Inclusive

"For unto us a child is born, unto us a son is given:
and the government shall be upon his shoulder:
and his name shall be called Wonderful, Counsellor,
The mighty God, The everlasting Father, The Prince of Peace."

(Isaiah 9:6)

The incarnation of the humanity of Christ is the subject of the majestic prologue of John's Gospel. (See John 1:1- 14.) Jesus Christ, while born in Bethlehem, has been from everlasting to everlasting the beloved Son of God. (See Isaiah 9:6.) It was essential that Jesus enter into this vale of suffering and tears so that he might redeem all of humanity from our sin. (See Hebrews 1:3; I John 2:1.) Jesus Christ is the atoning sacrifice (mercy seat, propitiation) for the sins of the whole world.

The Bible claims that the message and ministry of Jesus is exclusively inclusive as regards salvation. Jesus himself said, "I am the way, the truth and the life: no man cometh unto the Father but by me" (John 14:6).

Jesus is not *one* of many ways to salvation but the *only* way. (See Acts 4:12.) Therefore, it is essential amidst the commercializing hoopla of these days that believers maintain a spiritual perspective and prayerfully seize every opportunity to tell others about the *real reason for the season.*

On the first Christmas morning, the humanity of Christ was born in Bethlehem. The angelic hosts understood the significance of the new arrival and sang, "Glory to God in the highest and on earth peace, good will toward men" (Luke 2:14). Jesus Christ is not only peace *from* God but the basis of peace *with* God and the unfathomable conduit of the peace *of* God to a broken and sinful world.

Our Focus and Our Foundation

**"Thou wilt keep him in perfect peace, whose mind is stayed
on thee: because he trusteth in thee. Trust ye in the LORD for
ever: for in the LORD JEHOVAH is everlasting strength."**

(Isaiah 26:3-4)

Prayer has been described as conversation and communication
with an "ideal companion". Prayer is the most intimate application
of the priesthood of the believer. According to Matthew 7:7, we
are encouraged to "ask, seek and knock." Prayer is the natural
consequence of the redeeming relationship that is established
at the point of salvation. Therefore, the lack of or disinterest in
prayer is symptomatic of disease and disruption in the most
important relationship of all. The Apostle James said that we
"have not because we ask not." (James 4:2).

Prayer is not primarily an expression of a sensed need, but
rather the affirmation of our utter dependence on God. In prayer,
we communicate to God that what is primary and essential for
our well being comes only from HIM. We acknowledge with
broken hearts and bent knees that we simply cannot live by bread
alone, but by every word that proceed out of the mouth of God.
(See Matthew 4:4.) Prayer *is* a discipline of the Spirit and requires
preparation and intention. Amidst busy schedules and the hectic
pace of our lives we must set aside time to have conversation and
fellowship with God. Failure to do so will leave us spiritually
anemic and weak in the face of the continuous, unrelenting assault
of the demonic forces that seek to rob our joy and bankrupt our
peace of mind.

The prophet Isaiah provides the elixir, the antidote for every
generation of believer. He said, "Thou wilt keep him in perfect
peace, whose mind is stayed on Thee; because he trusteth in
Thee" (Isaiah 26:1). When our focus is on the Lord in prayer, our
foundation is stable and sure and we will not be shaken by the
inevitable difficulties of our days.

The Rocks in the Stream

"In those days was Hezekiah sick unto death.
And Isaiah the prophet the son of Amoz came unto him,
and said unto him, Thus saith the LORD,
Set thine house in order: for thou shalt die, and not live."

(Isaiah 38:1)

It has been said that, "It is the rocks in the bed of the stream that give the stream its sound and melody." James said in his epistle, "Consider it pure joy, my brothers, whenever you face trials of many kinds, because you know that the testing of your faith develops perseverance. Perseverance must finish its work so that you may be mature and complete, not lacking anything" (James 1:2-4 NIV). None of us would enlist voluntarily for trouble and trial, but these things are a part of the fabric of life. Our candidacy for suffering is established the moment we are born. Job, a man intimately familiar with broken-ness exclaimed, "Man that is born of a woman is of few days, and full of trouble. He cometh forth like a flower, and is cut down: he fleeth also as a shadow, and continueth not" (Job 14:1).

How do we deal with the inevitable breaks in life? Since we can't hide from them or escape them, we must recognize and reaffirm by faith that God is present in every storm. There is never a time when God is not with us. This is difficult to grasp when facing excruciating trials and straitening circumstances. Yet, when we view our circumstances from God's vantage and viewpoint, we can assuredly hope for "a break" in the "breaks" of life. God weaves providentially through the tapestry of our lives the variegated threads of our circumstances in such a way that "... all things work together for good to them that love God, to them who are the called according to his purpose" (Romans 8:28b). When you or I experience our "break," be encouraged today by the words of the hymn that says, "Be not dismayed whatever betide, God will (and God can) take care of you, through every storm and over all the way."

The Sovereignty of God

"Remember the former things of old:
for I am God, and there is none else;
I am God, and there is none like me,
Declaring the end from the beginning,
and from ancient times the things that are not yet done,
saying, My counsel shall stand,
and I will do all my pleasure."

(Isaiah 46:9-10)

The sovereignty of God has to do with God's control and direction of the events of both angelic and human history. God is sovereign because God is God! There is none like God in essential nature. God is eternal, spirit, immutable, omnipotent, omnipresent, omniscient, holy truth and love. All three Persons of the Godhead share these attributes. The sovereignty of God in history is expressed in God's unlimited knowledge in eternity past of all actual and possible thought and activity in both the angelic and human realm. In a moment that we call eternity, God decreed that everything that happens would happen.

Therefore, there is nothing that catches God by surprise. Each new day pregnant with potential is a day that the LORD has truly made. Because all that God decreed or purposed in eternity past is for His pleasure and glory and our ultimate blessing, we should rejoice in every day. God's faithfulness is as the rising of the sun and the setting of the same. His mercy and truth endures to all generations.

Many are gripped with anxiety and concern because of the present war in Iraq and the overall conditions of our society and world. However, a healthy faith and positive outlook can only be bolstered on the Word of God which assures us that God is in control. On behalf of Sovereign God, the prophet Isaiah encouraged another generation of believers faced with national disintegration and international strife with these words.

"Remember the former things of old; for I am God, and there is none else; for I am God, and there is none like me... My counsel shall stand, and I will do all my pleasure" (Isaiah 46:9-10).

Who or what are you trusting in these difficult days that we find ourselves. I don't know about you but I share the exultation of the hymn writer who declared, "On Christ the solid rock I stand, all other ground is sinking sand, all other ground is sinking sand!" Jesus Christ is in control of history and He does not waver but is the same yesterday, today and forevermore.

The Silence of God

"He was oppressed, and he was afflicted,
yet he opened not his mouth:
he is brought as a lamb to the slaughter,
and as a sheep before her shearers is dumb,
so he openeth not his mouth."

(Isaiah 53:7)

The prophets were uniquely called of God to speak to God's covenant people during times of distress and difficulty. God's ultimate advocate and arbiter of His grace and mercy was the servant who suffered silently. This is the profound and compelling message of Isaiah 53:7: "He was oppressed, and he was afflicted, yet he opened not his mouth: he is brought as a lamb to the slaughter, and as a sheep before her shearers is dumb, so he openeth not his mouth."

The most recent sermon anchored in this text was titled **"The Silence of the Savior."** I shared with you that God's silence takes on at least three forms in the Word of God and in the history of his dealings with Israel and the Church. First, there is the experiential silence of God that proves His sufficiency. This is the silence that the disciples found so unsettling on a stormy sea that prompted their plaintive cry and call, "Master, carest thou not that we perish." Many of us in our walk with the Lord have experienced seasons where it seems as if the Lord has engaged the spiritual and relational "mute" button. Secondly, there is the eschatological silence of God that punctuates His sovereignty. In Revelation 8:1, we find these words, "And when he had opened the seventh seal, there was silence in heaven about the space of half an hour." In context, this occurs after the Lamb (Jesus Christ) is enthroned at the right hand of God the Father (Revelation 7:17). God's final, consummate and exhaustive word to creature and creation is His Son. The silence in Isaiah 53:7 is the elective silence of God that parallels His suffering. Jesus, our Passover, suffered "as a lamb" and "as a sheep" before His oppressors and accusers. He elected this path knowing that this was the means through and by which redemption would be secured for all of humanity.

In our lives there will inevitably be seasons of straitening and straining silence. But be encouraged that we will also experience the overwhelming peace of the God of comfort and hope during times of stress, hardship, fear and uncertainty. Isaiah reminded his generation of this wondrous truth in Isaiah 12:2-3: "Behold, God is my salvation; I will trust, and not be afraid: for the LORD JEHOVAH is my strength and my song; he also is become my salvation. Therefore with joy shall ye draw water out of the wells of salvation." We drink from a fountain that will never run dry and, even when God is silent, those refreshing streams irrigate the desert places of our experience.

The Spoils of Victory

"Therefore will I divide him a portion with the great,
and he shall divide the spoil with the strong;
because he hath poured out his soul unto death:
and he was numbered with the transgressors;
and he bare the sin of many,
and made intercession for the transgressors."

(Isaiah 53:12)

The death of the Lord Jesus Christ on the cross secured a strategic victory in the cosmic conflict between good and evil. According to Romans 1:4, Jesus was declared to be the Son of God with power, according to the spirit of holiness by the resurrection from the dead. The last enemies, death and the grave, were defeated soundly when Jesus rose from the grave. As we commemorate His death today during the observance of the Lord's Supper, we must remember that we celebrate as joint-heirs with Christ the spoils of a victory that was announced in the wake of the devastation of the original sin in the Garden of Eden. (See Isaiah 53:12.) In the Garden of Eden, the Lord God said to the serpent, "And I will put enmity between thee and the woman, and between thy seed and her seed; it shall bruise thy head, and thou shalt bruise his heel" (Genesis 3:15).

The Bible does not attempt to rationalize or psychologize evil, but very plainly acknowledges the presence of evil and the demonic in both the angelic creation and the pre-fall innocence of the perfect environment of Eden. From the fatal failure and tragic transgression of the first man and woman, the Bible reveals how God has been at work to eradicate evil, redeem men and women from sin and eternal damnation, and restore both creature and creation to its original condition. The Lord Jesus Christ, the "only begotten of God," secured for all mankind a victory so complete and compelling that now, whosoever shall call on the name of the Lord shall be saved. While still capable of deception and destruction, the demonic forces under Satan's command are in disarray and recognize perhaps more astutely than we do that their demise has been determined and their domination broken in the lives of those who trust in the Lord Jesus Christ. Be encouraged today that we are already victorious in Christ and that we are "more than conquerors through him that loved us" (Roman 8:37).

The Preacher's Call

**"Before I formed thee in the belly I knew thee;
and before thou camest forth
out of the womb I sanctified thee,
and I ordained thee a prophet unto the nations."**

(Jeremiah 1:5)

This is a classic passage considered by many to be the call of Jeremiah to the prophetic ministry. God reminds the prophet-to-be that his call has both post- natal and pre-natal implications. It has been said that "you don't pick preaching up; preaching picks you up!" The preacher must be borne and bolstered aloft to the exalted vocation of preaching by an abiding, unshakeable sense of divine call. However, this is actuated in the preacher's experience; it is a pressing prerequisite to proclaiming the Word of God. The preacher is accosted and arrested by God in the inner self. The consciousness of divine calling gives birth to a resoluteness and tenacious passion to proclaim good news. This is well attested by the Apostle Paul who characterized his own resolve with these words: "For though I preach the gospel, I have nothing to glory of; necessity is laid upon me; yea, woe is unto me, if I preach not the gospel!" (I Corinthians 9:16).

God always takes the initiative. The preacher only answers God in obedience and submission. None is worthy and God is not so impoverished that He needs human instruments to do His will. Therefore, at the very outset, the call to preach is shrouded in contradiction. Those who preach must approach this holy vocation with a humbling awareness of their spiritual bankruptcy and glaring unworthiness. Spiritually impoverished yet, by amazing grace, God's messengers are blessed to possess the keys to the Kingdom of heaven. This awareness and resulting humility is the starting point for spiritual vitality and production in the minister's life. This is not only true of the preacher but of every believer. Our sense of nothingness is the prelude for the experience of God's Almightiness. The earthiness and unworthiness of the vessel brings into bold and brilliant relief the extravagance of the treasure it bears. "But we have this treasure in earthen vessels that the excellency of the power may be of God and not of us" (II Corinthians 4:7).

Desperately Wicked

**"The heart is deceitful above all things,
and desperately wicked: who can know it?"**

(Jeremiah 17:9)

The word of God says, "The heart is deceitful above all things, and desperately wicked: who can know it?" (Jeremiah 17:9). I thought of this passage while reading recently about the arrest of an alleged serial killer in Wichita, Kansas who the police believe has tortured and killed at least eleven people over the years. The suspect was very active as a church leader and even directed a group of Cub Scouts. How could this be? How could a person who professes to being a Christian maim, torture and kill another human being and taunt the police regarding his actions. If the allegations are true, how could these two extremes of behavior reside in the same person? The prophet Jeremiah provides the appropriate and only response to such evil. It's the heart! Jesus affirmed this same truth in the Gospels when he rebuked the religious leaders for their preoccupation with external rituals. He said, "… that which cometh out of the man, that defileth the man. For from within, out of the heart of men, proceed evil thoughts, adulteries, fornications, murders, thefts, covetousness, wickedness, deceit, lasciviousness, an evil eye, blasphemy, pride, foolishness: All these evil things come from within, and defile the man" (Mark 7:20b-23.

I believe a person whose heart has truly been changed, while under the control of the Holy Spirit, could never do the things this individual has been accused of doing. However, under the control of the old sin nature and its destructive trends, we are capable of anything. Remember, it was King David, the man that God said was "a man after His own heart," who committed adultery and then premeditated murder. Remember Saul, soon to be Paul the apostle, stood by while Stephen was stoned to death. No wonder he made repeated references to grace in his epistles, for he recognized as must each of us, "by the grace of God I am that I am." We all reside somewhere spiritually between "Lord have mercy on me" and "Glory Hallelujah."

The breaking story of the alleged serial killer and his church and community involvement reminded me anew that we dare not look on the outside and judge a man or woman for good or for bad. Someone said, "There is some good in the worst of us and some bad in the best of us." Only God really knows the heart. Sin is so dire and despicable that our only true recourse is to cast ourselves as did David at the mercy of God and ask him: "Search me, O God, and know my heart: try me, and know my thoughts: and see if there be any wicked way in me, and lead me in the way everlasting" (Psalm 139:23-24). I find it deeply moving that God, knowing the very worst in our hearts and knowing all that we would do and could do, still chose to commend His love to us while we were yet sinners and give Christ to die for us.

Ground Zero

"The heart is deceitful above all things,
and desperately wicked: who can know it?
I the LORD search the heart, I try the reins,
even to give every man according to his ways,
and according to the fruit of his doings."

(Jeremiah 17:9-10)

Ground Zero is a term that is associated with the devastation, carnage and loss of human life resulting from the terrorist attack at the World Trade Center on September 11, 2001. Those who have personally visited the scene leave forever changed. I can relate to their experience after visiting the site of the Oklahoma City bombing one year after the attack there. These two dark and tragic moments in our nation's history are constant reminders of the evil that lurks in the human heart. The prophet Jeremiah said it best: "The heart is deceitful above all things, and desperately wicked: who can know it? (Jeremiah 17:9).

But the phrase "ground zero" encourages another image in my head and heart related to the character of Christian ministry. Ground zero is the point where authentic ministry is transacted amidst the ruins wrought by sin and suffering. Here, the unsearchable riches of Christ and the "good news" - that is the Christian Gospel - engage the poverty and plight of those "who have sinned and come short of the glory of God" (Romans 3:23). Ground zero is not an ivory tower or a rosy bed of ease but the place where the cries of those who are hurting, hopeless, hobbled and haunted by the terror of sin and the incessant onslaught of evil are heard. Ground zero is the place where our common humanity makes us equals; here all men and women are fractured, finite and frail.

Yet, at the heart of the Gospel is the wonderful truth that God has not left us alone amidst the ruins of tattered dreams and shipwrecked hopes. God is neither insensitive to our pain, unconcerned about our suffering, nor disinterested in our plight. God loved and loves us so much that He left His throne in glory and came to earth—ground zero— in order to bring us from ruin to riches. The Apostle Paul reminded the church at Corinth, "For ye know that the grace of our Lord Jesus Christ, that though he was rich, yet for your sakes he became poor, that ye through his poverty might be rich"(II Corinthians 8:9). Our responsibility as believers is to courageously and compassionately join the Lord at ground zero and help build up the waste places.

Life Support

**"It is of the LORD'S mercies that we are not consumed,
because his compassions fail not.
They are new every morning: great is thy faithfulness."**

(Lamentations 3:22- 23)

The basis of financial prosperity is rooted in the very heart of God who has valued and vested His creation. In Genesis 1:26-27, the Bible records that God determined to make us in God's own image for both fellowship and relationship. God made us living souls with minds to know God, hearts to love God and wills to obey God. In Psalm 8, the author asks, "What is man that thou art mindful of him?" (vs. 4a). The politician, the scientist and the sociologist would all respond to this question differently. However, the Bible reminds us that God has valued us so much that He gave the very best He had in order to redeem us from everlasting doom and destruction. (See John 3:16.)

God desires to bless us. But in order to bless us, God cannot compromise His perfect righteousness. Therefore, our blessing is bound up with our obedience. In Deuteronomy Chapter 28, Moses, the servant of the Lord, set before the children of Israel both blessing and cursing. God's promises were compelling, and embraced both the spiritual and material welfare of the nation. Obedience would result in bountiful blessing. Disobedience to God's commandment would result in death and demise.

God's grace keeps giving. God not only saves but provides the life support we need in order to advance us in the Plan of God that stretches from time into eternity. Jeremiah reminded Israel that the Lord's compassions fail not and great is God's faithfulness.

Powerful Preaching

**"So I prophesied as I was commanded:
and as I prophesied, there was a noise, and behold a shaking,
and the bones came together, bone to his bone."**

(Ezekiel 37:7)

Powerful preaching in the African-American context is launched from a hermeneutic that affirms the ethic of Jesus Christ as the definitive elixir for what Howard Thurman calls the "hounds of hell that dog the footsteps of the poor, the dispossessed and the disinherited" (in Jesus and the Disinherited, 1976, page 36). This unholy trinity includes fear, deception and hatred. Preaching predicated on critical, creative and compelling exegesis of the text and the times (the experiential coordinates of the audience) aims both to illuminate and liberate.

When this type of preaching occurs, crippling and catastrophic fear is submerged in the ocean of a renewed self-esteem that is the birthright that Jesus gives to all that are oppressed. Deception is transformed into a simple yet profound authenticity that disarms the oppressor, empowers the oppressed and hobbles both pretense and advantage. Hatred is transfigured into a love so sincere and searching that those otherwise superficial boundaries are eradicated. Then the pulse of universality and the thread of commonality which makes all human beings brothers and sisters are rediscovered and redefined. Of course the possibility of such universality presumes consistency to and concert with the Gospel of the Lord Jesus Christ, that old, old but eternally redeeming story of His death, burial and resurrection. (See I Corinthians 15:1-4.)

The best in Black preaching has always presumed that ultimate truth is revealed in a Person. That Person, the Lord Jesus Christ, is uniquely revealed in His Passion. That passion (His death, burial and resurrection) is the basis of the Gospel proclamation through preaching. (See I Corinthians 1:18-21.) And that powerful proclamation is the means of receiving God's power and God's provision. The Apostle Paul said, "For I am not ashamed of the gospel of Christ: for it is the power of God unto salvation to every one that believeth; to the Jew first, and also to the Greek. For therein is the righteousness of God revealed from faith to faith: as it is written, the just shall live by faith" (Romans 1:16-17).

Stretch or Stress

"Although the fig tree shall not blossom,
neither shall fruit be in the vines;
the labour of the olive shall fail,
and the fields shall yield no meat;
the flock shall be cut off from the fold,
and there shall be no herd in the stalls:
Yet I will rejoice in the LORD,
I will joy in the God of my salvation."

(Habakkuk 3:17-18)

Habakkuk is one of the truly remarkable prophets in the Old Testament. His name in the Hebrew language means "to embrace" or the "one who clings". Some believe he was a musician/theologian and a member of the temple choir. He was a contemporary of the prophet Jeremiah. His prophecy is set and situated in the difficult and dire days of the Kingdom of Judah. It is early 7th century B.C and Babylon is the uncontested world power. Jehoiakim, the son of Josiah and a poor image of his father, was King; a godless king who terrorized the prophets, promoted idolatry and led the nation down the path of destruction (cf. II Kings 23:34-24:5).

Habakkuk did not confront the people, but **CONFRONTED GOD** as he wrestled with the problem of evil and suffering around him. Theologians call this problem theodicy. The reality of pain and suffering is one of the primary arguments that atheists use to attack the Christian faith. An analysis of this unique book of the Bible will reveal some key themes. In Chapter 1 we find Faith Perplexing; Chapter 2 – Faith Perceiving; Chapter 3 – Faith Praising. In Chapter 1, Habakkuk is sighing; in Chapter 2 – he is seeing; and in Chapter 3 – he is singing. As he posted, positioned and postured himself for God's response (Chapter 1 -2), God's final word was "the just shall live by faith." This important verse is quoted three times in the New Testament (Hebrews 10:38; Romans 1:17; Galatians 3:17).

When I read of Habakkuk's struggles I think about how the new NFL season began full blown last Sunday. It hardly escapes my notice during the NFL pre-game shows on FOX & ESPN that the players arrive at the stadium early and engage in a disciplined regimen and ritual of stretching. These well-conditioned, professional athletes know how absolutely necessary this pre-game discipline is in order to reduce the possibility of injury in competition. We, too, when in the throes of our difficulties and disappointments, must stretch as well if we are to truly learn how to trust God during trying times. The truth of the matter is <u>either we stretch</u> <u>or</u> <u>we</u> <u>will</u> <u>stress</u>. We stretch out on God and for God through purposeful witnessing, patient waiting, and passionate worshipping. When these activities are primary in our lives, then God will see us through our struggles.

More practically, when we study our Bibles, pray, fast, fellowship with other Christians, support those in need and forgive our enemies, we are engaging in spiritual stretching. The Apostle Paul understood these truths. They encouraged him while he languished in a Roman prison. Because he knew how to stretch, he could write one of the most joy-filled of all his epistles from prison. I am excited returning to Philippians 4:10-14 so that we can learn more from Paul about how we can live above our circumstances. Like Habakkuk, he knew about the stretch that overcomes our stress.

Tithing—A Biblical Perspective

"Bring ye all the tithes into the storehouse,
that there may be meat in mine house,
and prove me now herewith, saith the LORD of hosts,
if I will not open you the windows of heaven,
and pour you out a blessing,
that there shall not be room enough to receive it.
And I will rebuke the devourer for your sakes,
and he shall not destroy the fruits of your ground;
neither shall your vine cast her fruit
before the time in the field, saith the LORD of hosts.
And all nations shall call you blessed:
for ye shall be a delightsome land,
saith the LORD of hosts."

(Malachi 3:10-12)

Some believers declare tithing (systematically giving God 10% of one's gross income) to be an integral part of the Christian life and therefore a requirement for all Christians. Others, however, oppose tithing because they say it is based on Old Testament legalism and leads to a self-righteous spirit. I believe there are sound, biblical reasons for tithing that ought to inspire everyone who truly loves the Lord to give to God and experience the true basis of spiritual blessing, wealth and prosperity.

Seven Biblical Reasons Why Every Christian Should Tithe

- Abraham, our spiritual father, paid tithes to Melchizedek, Priest-King of Salem, 430 years before the giving of the Law at Mt. Sinai (Genesis 14:20).

- Our Lord Jesus Christ, a High Priest after the order of Melchizedek, ever lives to receive our tithes (Hebrews 7:1-10).

- Jesus paid tithes, thus fulfilling the Law and declaring His proper relationship to the Law (Matthew 5:17).

- The privileges and responsibilities under grace far exceed the commands under the Law (Matthew 5:21-48).

- Jesus sanctioned the payment of the tithe (Matthew 23:23).

- The early church tithed and even exhibited unlimited generosity by exceeding the requirements of the Law (Acts 4:34, 37).

- No Christian <u>can</u> <u>afford</u> <u>not</u> <u>to</u> <u>tithe,</u> for 90 cents with God's blessing is always more than $1.00 without it! (See Malachi 3:8-12.)

Ultimate blessing and prosperity in life always come from aligning our attitudes and actions with the will of God. God's will not only includes His geographical will (where He wants us to be), vocational will (what He wants us to do), essential will (what He wants us to be), but also His viewpoint will (what He want us to think). Our giving must reflect the viewpoint of God as recorded in the Word of God. This is the basis of the appeal of the Apostle Paul who said, "Let this mind be in you, which was also in Christ Jesus" (Philippians 2:5). In I Corinthians, 2:15-16 he says, "But he that is spiritual judgeth all things, yet he himself is judged of no man. For who hath known the mind of the Lord, that he may instruct him? But we have the mind of Christ." Hallelujah, saints! We have in the inspired Word of God, the mind (viewpoint) of Christ that governs and guides us as we attempt to live out the Christian life. In the area of giving, God's perfect mind has designed a plan of giving: tithes and offerings that blessed the saints of old and will bless you and me as well— right now and right here—when we faithfully apply its principles to our lives.

New Testament
Reflections

His Name is Jesus

**"And she shall bring forth a son,
and thou shalt call his name JESUS:
for he shall save his people from their sins."**

(Matthew 1:21)

The angel Gabriel appeared to Joseph who was preparing to break his engagement with Mary. He told Joseph that Mary's pregnancy was "of the Holy Ghost" and that she would bring forth a son whose name would be "JESUS". He would save His people from sin. At the very beginning, the angelic message signaled what would be crucial and critical to the ministry of Christ, indeed, the very humanity of Jesus was fitted for the task before Him.

Jesus came to save His people from sin. Was He to be strictly a "Jewish" savior? The Gospels are clear that the ministry of Jesus would break down barriers and open new paths into the hearts of men and women. He defied Jewish tradition, reaching out to those who were considered outcasts and the off-scouring of the world, inviting them to the banquet of grace. He said, "They that are whole have no need of the physician, but they that are sick: I came not to call the righteous, but sinners to repentance" (Mark 2:17).

The mission of Jesus is evidence as well of the utter futility and devastation wrought by sin. Humanity is desperately lost and, apart from the sinless sacrifice of the humanity of Christ, would ever remain estranged from the life of God. There is no other way to God but Jesus Christ who said, "I am the way, the truth and the life; no man cometh to the Father but by me" (John 14:6)

God Has Not Left Us Alone

*"Now all this was done, that it might be fulfilled
which was spoken of the Lord by the prophet, saying, Behold,
a virgin shall be with child, and shall bring forth a son,
and they shall call his name Emmanuel,
which being interpreted is, God with us."*
(Matthew 1:22-23)

In response to the prayers of the Israelites who were suffering bondage and oppression in Egypt, God responds by reminding Moses, the instrument of God's deliverance, of the promise he had made to the patriarchs Abraham, Isaac and Jacob. He said that he would "come down to deliver them out of he hand of the Egyptians and to bring them up out of that land unto a good land" (Exodus 3:8a). At this critical junction in the life of the nation of Israel, God promises to enter into their situation in a unique and unprecedented way to bring about deliverance and prosperity. Contrary to those who believe that God created the world, set it in motion and then retreated with no concern or compassion for either creature or creation, this passage reminds us of God's continuing involvement with that which He has made. The Latin church fathers called this **creation ex continua**. God entered the "now" of Israel's experience of suffering with the hope of deliverance.

In a similar way, during this season we celebrate the wonderful reality of God, who came to this earth as the Lord Jesus Christ and who gave His life for the sins of the world. (See I John 1:1-2.) In the Gospel of Matthew the angel announced to Joseph that the birth of Jesus was the fulfillment of another prophecy. "Now all this was done that it might be fulfilled which was spoken of the Lord by the prophet saying, behold a virgin shall be with child and bring forth a son and they shall call his name Emmanuel, which being interpreted is, God with us" (Matthew 1:22-23). The Apostle Paul reminded the Philippians that Jesus "made himself of no reputation and took upon him the form of a servant and was made in the likeness of men" (Philippians 2:7).

It should be the source of great encouragement and joy to all of us today that God loved us so much that He came down and entered into life as the unique God- man of human history in order to liberate us from the bondage of sin. Even in a world filled with so much violence, strife and suffering, we must affirm as Christians that God has not left us alone or to ourselves. Because Jesus lived, died and rose again, everyone has the opportunity to enter into a promised land flowing with the milk and honey of love, hope and peace. Because of this wondrous reality, the shepherd's song of praise at the birth of Jesus should be our very own during this season: "Glory to God in the highest and on earth, peace, and good will toward men" (Luke 2:24).

The Adventure of Advent

"Now when Jesus was born in Bethlehem of Judaea
in the days of Herod the king, behold,
there came wise men from the east to Jerusalem, Saying,
Where is he that is born King of the Jews?
for we have seen his star in the east,
and are come to worship him."

(Matthew 2:1-2)

The word "advent" comes from the Latin word <u>adventus</u>, which means, "to arrive." On the Christian calendar, <u>Advent</u> is the season of devotion that includes the four Sundays before Christmas. While contemplating the meaning of the word and the season, it occurred to me that when you add the letters "ure" to "advent" you have the word adventure. Combining the two concepts, this season should be a time of great spiritual expectation and daring adventure for the believer. As we anticipate another celebration of the arrival of God in the person of the Lord Jesus Christ on this planet, the church should be gripped with the excitement and unparalleled uniqueness of this event. Because of His birth, life, death, burial, resurrection and imminent return, this season does not have to be "business as usual," but an exciting, daring adventure of faith and boundless expectation that God is ready to do a new thing in our lives!

So often this season is described as the "season of giving". What do we really mean when we say this? Many times the reference or inference is to the exchange of gifts that takes place between people who like or love each other. Often the reference is to the sporadic and intermittent spirit of charity that infects people during the holiday season, only to leave and not to be seen again for another twelve months.

When believers refer to the "season of giving" our immediate focus should be on the greatest gift of all. Christmas is the adventurous celebration of the birth of the Lord Jesus Christ, whose humanity was born in a stable in Bethlehem, but who has always been God and the second person of the blessed Trinity.

The prophet Isaiah described this paradox best when he said, "For unto us a child is born, unto us a son is given..." (Isaiah 9:6). While the child was born, the Son was given because the Son has always been. Thank God today for giving us the gift of God's own Self. Let us never forget to celebrate the <u>real</u> <u>reason</u> for the season of giving.

The Shadow Side of Christmas

"Then Herod,
when he saw that he was mocked of the wise men,
was exceeding wroth, and sent forth,
and slew all the children that were in Bethlehem,
and in all the coasts thereof, from two years old and under,
according to the time which he had
diligently enquired of the wise men."

(Matthew 2:16)

In the Gospel of Matthew there is a disturbing footnote about the slaughter of the children two years of age and under, victims of the egotistical rage and demented wrath of King Herod. This horrific violence directed toward innocent children born in Bethlehem and neighboring towns was Herod's maniacal response to what he perceived as mockery by the wise men, who had appeared at his court a few weeks after the birth of Jesus inquiring "Where is he that is born King of the Jews?" (Matthew 2:2). These wise men or Magi from the east who subsequently found the young child Jesus and presented him with gifts of gold, frankincense and myrrh, rather than reporting to the king his whereabouts, "departed into their country another way" (Matthew 2:12).

This tragic episode that is undeniably part and parcel of the Christmas story as revealed in the Gospels bristles and bleeds with unspeakable pain and suffering. In essence, it punctuates the reality that is often forgotten during this season: the first Christmas was the inescapable prerequisite and precondition for Calvary. In order to redeem humanity from the slave market of sin, it was necessary that God come to this planet in human form. In a classic passage in the Book of Philippians, the Apostle Paul writes, "Your attitude should be the kind that was shown us by Jesus Christ, who, though he was God, did not demand and cling to his rights as God, but laid aside his mighty power and glory, taking the disguise of a slave and becoming like men. And he humbled himself even further, going so far as actually to die a criminal's death on a cross" (Philippians 2:5-8 TLB). The writer of the Book of Hebrews is even more explicit regarding this truth. "What we do see is Jesus, made 'not quite as high as angels,' and then, through the experience of death, crowned so much higher than any angel, with a glory 'bright with Eden's dawn light.' In that death, by God's grace, he fully experienced death in every person's place" (Hebrews 2:9 MSG).

The light of the world shining ever so brightly and brilliantly on that first Christmas morning pierced and penetrated darkness, and the Bible says, "And the darkness comprehended it not" (John 1:5b). King Herod's vain, vicious and violent response to that true Light was but a painful prelude to the tide of events that would culminate in the death of Jesus on Calvary. Tragically, the shedding of the blood of innocent children became the sign and signification of His suffering death. The shining of light and the shadow of darkness are intertwining sides of the same reality. We can and must celebrate Christmas because despite the pain and suffering in our world today, "God now stands in the shadows watching above His own."

God's Originals

"Let your light so shine before men,
that they may see your good works,
and glorify your Father which is in heaven."

(Matthew 5:16)

Disciples equipped to penetrate the culture as salt and light and as God's "originals" will think critically about what we believe and why we believe it. This commitment to the pursuit of the truth or mystery of God must not be close-minded or narrow, but inclusive and affirming; recognizing that the truth that has its quintessential (ultimate) fulfillment in Jesus Christ, who is the "center" of the Christian faith (and for me the circumference as well), is also resident in nature and in the diverse experiences of persons made in the image of God. The down and dark side of denominationalism is that it closes our eyes, makes us mean and myopic and unable to see the bushes that are burning around us. God is present in the commonplace and the ordinary.

The stories of the Bible that happened (which revealed God's glory or Hebrew *kabod*), are now happening in the commonplace and crisis moments in the lives of people – birth, death, marriage, surfing and even suffering. Those willing to pay attention (or as Moses did on the backside of a desert – "turn aside") will find God present, powerful and pardoning. These places, points and portals are truly "Holy Ground". At these intersections, we must be willing and ready to celebrate the already "everywhere" presence and power of God.

An Intrusive Invitation

"Come unto me, all ye that labour and are heavy laden,
and I will give you rest. Take my yoke upon you,
and learn of me; for I am meek and lowly in heart:
and ye shall find rest unto your souls.
For my yoke is easy, and my burden is light."
(Matthew 11:28-30)

The primary word for labor in the new Testament is **kopiano**, which means, "growing weary" or "toiling". This is the word that Jesus uses in the compelling invitation of Matthew 11:28-30. "Come unto me, all ye that labour and are heavy laden, and I will give you rest. Take my yoke upon you, and learn of me; for I am meek and lowly in heart; and ye shall find rest for your soul. For my yoke is easy and my burden is light." Upon prayerful reflection, this passage yields a number of permanent principles and transcendent truths regarding the nature of life.

Human life is characteristically laborious and wearisome. This is the tragic legacy of the sin and disobedience of Adam and Eve. (See Genesis 3:1-19.) In an imperfect and corrupted creation, life is difficult, disconcerting and demanding. Consequently, men and women need rest. Not just the chronological rest afforded the first couple, but a rest of far grander and more enduring proportions.

The words of Jesus in this text signal unprecedented hope and compelling opportunity, a welcome intrusion and intervention into the weary days of our lives. Jesus invites the weary and those who are burdened by the cares and concerns of this world to come to Him and, in the context of a saving relationship with Him, experience supernatural rest. This invitation is sounded from the crucible of human suffering and need. It is the gracious summons of the Christ who entered into the very vortex of the human predicament, experiencing first hand our own privations and perils, yet infusing our mundane experience and our contingent existence with an aura of the divine and the eternal.

This invitation is intimate and personal, a timeless offering of spiritual repose and everlasting rest to the disinherited, the disenfranchised and the disillusioned. Only Jesus can lighten our loads and bolster our burdens. He does so by entering into our experience and laboring alongside of us. Our burdens, our despairs, and our disappointments become His own. In this relationship and only here, we find rest for our souls.

The Ambiguity of Faith

"He answered and said unto them,
He that soweth the good seed is the Son of man;
The field is the world;
the good seed are the children of the kingdom;
but the tares are the children of the wicked one;"

(Matthew 13:37-38)

The word "ambiguity" has taunted and teased me of late. It is an interesting word. The dictionary defines ambiguity as "the possibility of two or more meanings." It is derived from the Latin word *ambiguitas*. In the context of my musings and conceptual meanderings about this word, I recalled a sermon I read recently which searching title was *The Ambiguity of Heroes*. The focus of the message was the flawed fragility of those we consider heroes. This was certainly true of biblical giants such as Abraham, Moses, David, Jeremiah, Jonah, Simon Peter and the Apostle Paul. The preacher of this sermon inferred that it is the ambiguity (shades and shadows) in the lives of our heroes that both attract and detract us. Our response to them is ambiguous, for it engenders love and hate, admiration and disappointment.

Ambiguity is at the heart of the parable that Jesus tells in Matthew 13:24-30 regarding the "wheat and the tares". Just as reception of the Word of God is likened to the differences in soil quality and texture (Matthew 13:1-23), the Kingdom of God is comprised of both wheat and tares that grow together. This is certainly true and accurate of the church, which is the primary manifestation of God's kingdom at this point in time in history. Tares or "weeds" grow alongside the wheat. These tares, sown maliciously by an enemy, look so much like wheat that in the parable, the servants are instructed not to separate them but to allow them to grow unmolested. The danger is that the premature removal or extraction of the tares could cause damage to the wheat or the good seed.

This ambiguity is the source of what Richard J. Neuhuas in his book <u>Freedom for</u> <u>Ministry</u> calls the "not-yet-ness" of the church. No local church, regardless of history, denominational affiliation, location, doctrinal stance or membership composition, is exempt from this phenomenon. Often, what looks like wheat is nothing but tares. Tares grow alongside wheat in the field of God's favor and yet, sadly, will not survive the harvest where Divine reapers will separate one from the other in time and for all eternity. A tare among wheat is the ultimate and blasphemous ambiguity in the spiritual realm; messengers and ministers of Satan who masquerade as members of God's flock are, according to the Apostle John, "the spirit of the antichrist." He writes, "Little children, it is the last time; and as ye have heard that antichrist shall come, even now are there many anti-christs; whereby we know that it is the last time. They went out from us, but they were not of us; for if they had been of us, they would no doubt have continued with us, but they went out, that they might be made manifest that they were not all of us" (I John 1:18-19).

The antonym (opposite) for ambiguity is certainty. It is imperative that each of us examine our moods and our motives as members of the Lord's church. We must be sure that it is the voice of Him who leads the sheep beside the still waters of His essence and into the green pastures of His presence and His provision that is our ultimate center and certainty. There is ambiguity even in the midst of this wondrous possibility; another voice, a thief whose primary mission is to steal, and to kill and to destroy. True believers will beware!

Focusing our Faith

**"And he commanded the multitude
to sit down on the grass, and took the five loaves,
and the two fishes, and looking up to heaven,
he blessed, and brake, and gave the loaves to his disciples,
and the disciples to the multitude."**
(Matthew 14:19)

During a recent devotional time, I experienced an encounter with the Word of God, one of those rare but refreshing insights that occurs at the illuminative intersection of text and times. Of course, such compelling collisions are always prompted by the leading of God's Holy Spirit, the Supreme Author of the Scriptures. While reading the account of the feeding of the multitudes in Matthew 14:15-21, I was impacted by the fact that Jesus, after receiving from the disciples two fishes and five barley loaves (which they had confiscated in the crowd), and miraculously multiplying these to proportions that could feed five thousand men (not counting women and children), the text says, "And he gave the loaves to his disciples, and the disciples to the multitude" (v. 19b).

I find this remarkable in light of the fact that Jesus could have easily excluded or bypassed the disciples and distributed the food directly to the hungry people. Yet, the miraculous fish and loaves again passed through the hands of "his disciples" and ministers, and then to the masses. By including the disciples in the distribution of the miraculous increase, Jesus was <u>focusing and fortifying</u> their faith. This turn and twist of the text tickles, teases, taunts and tantalizes me! How encouraging that God gives back to us that which we have experienced as inadequate, insufficient and inconsequential. He takes our flawed and fragile offerings of tithe, time, talent, treasure, and temple, blesses them and then encourages us to share our blessing with others.

The very disciples whose skepticism and doubt had prompted them to say despairingly, "but what are they among so many?" (John 6:9b) now handled with their hands the miraculous meal the Lord prepared, sharing it with others who were in danger of fainting by the way. I encourage each of us today to give Jesus our "fish and loaves" — whatever they are — failure, disappointment, uncertainties, broken relationships, sorrow, and addictions. He can touch and transform them in such a way that, however meager, minor or miserable they appear to us, they can be used to His glory.

Disputed Sovereignty

**"And I say also unto thee, That thou art Peter,
and upon this rock I will build my church;
and the gates of hell shall not prevail against it."**

(Matthew 16:18)

We do not minister or serve God in a vacuum. We have arrived in the world's court before the true King has been crowned. According to Richard Neuhaus, we live in the age of *disputed sovereignty*. Every knee has not yet bowed, nor has every tongue confessed that Jesus Christ is Lord of lords and the King of kings. Therefore, the personal experience of the believer and the corporate existence of the church are transacted not only on holy ground but a battleground as well. Jesus signaled this reality when announcing His intent to build the church. "And I say also unto thee, That thou art Peter, and upon this rock I will build my church; and the gates of hell shall not prevail against it" (Matthew 16:18).

Christianity is a bastion of hope, a fortress of faith that has been placed, literally, behind enemy lines. The church of the Lord Jesus Christ is a subversive force operating in a world that is controlled momentarily by the powers of evil. Those forces are in retreat and disarray because of the strategic victory of Jesus Christ on the cross. The Bible does not apologize, but rather recognizes the power and purpose of the devil, the ancient adversary who like a roaring lion walketh about seeking whom he may devour. (See I Peter 5:8b.) The Apostle Paul reminded the church at Ephesus that, "We wrestle not against flesh and blood, but against principalities, against powers, against the rulers of the darkness of this world, against spiritual wickedness in high places" (Ephesians 6:12b).

The battle rages on many fronts. Today, Satan and his forces are fiercely attacking not only the individual soul, but all the institutions of Divine origin: marriage, family, the national entity and the church. As we seek to work out our faith with fear and trembling we will undoubtedly experience conflict and opposition. Sometimes these attacks come from the most unlikely places. These are not only times of testing but great opportunities as well to stand still and see what the Lord will and can do. Remember, the battle belongs to the Lord. We must be encouraged today that the One who is in us is greater than the one that is in the world. The prophet Isaiah said it best: "No weapon that is formed against thee shall prosper; and every tongue that shall rise against thee in judgment thou shalt condemn. This is the heritage of the servants of the Lord, and their righteousness is of me, saith the Lord" (Isaiah 54:17).

Yonder Mountain

*"And Jesus said unto them, Because of your unbelief:
for verily I say unto you,
If ye have faith as a grain of mustard seed,
ye shall say unto this mountain,
Remove hence to yonder place; and it shall remove;
and nothing shall be impossible unto you."*

(Matthew 17:20)

"Never say never," was the testimony of Erik Weihenmayer, who in May 2001 became the first blind person to climb the summit of Mt. Everest. His unshakeable resolve buoyed and bolstered his stamina and steadfastness while he faced frigid cold, fierce storms and traversed torturous icefalls for two months with other members of his team on their way to the top of Mt. Everest. Erik depended on the vocal directions and descriptions of his fellow climbers to guide him through fierce mountainous terrain and was patient when their oversights and mistakes put his life in jeopardy.

I was entranced the first time I encountered this story, moved not only by this testament to the indomitable courage of the human spirit, but considering as well the implications and applications this achievement has for those of us who walk by faith and not by sight. Life, too, can be like a mountain climb; the terrain constantly shifting, storms coming and going unpredictably, deafening avalanches, deep crevasses and seemingly insurmountable cliffs to scale in order to reach our destination. Yet, we are not alone; for it is the still voice of Him who speaks certainty in the midst of our uncertainty that comforts us and compels us to move on. It is His voice, the Holy Spirit, that guides us beyond reason to trust and obey and not to rely ultimately on our senses and abilities.

Blasé Pascal, the French scientist, philosopher and a late convert to Christianity said it well: "Faith has it reasons that reason does not know." In a world so bound by the propositions that only what we can touch, taste, feel, see, hear and smell is real and if you can't measure it, it doesn't matter, it is refreshing to know that biblical faith takes us beyond sense and sensibility to the glorious summit where "all things are possible." This is the ground that Ruth the Moabite maiden and ancestress of King David occupied when she told her mother-in-law Naomi, "Intreat me not to leave thee, or to return from following after thee; for whither thou goest, I will go; and where thou lodgest, I will lodge; thy people shall be my people and thy God my God" (Ruth 1:16). This is the high ground that Job scaled when, against reason and even rebuke from his friends he said, "Though he slay me, yet will I trust him; but I will maintain my own ways before him" (Job 13:15).

What do you do when you face obstacles that loom before you like mountain heights? What do we do when reason and rationale say you can't go on, but something deep within says not only "you can" but "you must!"? A blind man decided that "never" was not admissible in the court of his life, and through discipline and determination stood triumphantly on the summit of Mt. Everest. We can do no less and, indeed, even much more, those who by faith believe and affirm that "I can do all things through Christ which strengtheneth me" (Philippians 4:13).

He Went a Little Farther

**"And he went a little further, and fell on his face, and prayed,
saying, O my Father, if it be possible,
let this cup pass from me:
nevertheless not as I will, but as thou wilt."**

(Matthew 26:39)

In the Gospel of Matthew, after sharing the Lord's Supper with the disciples for the first time, Jesus led them to the Garden of Gethsemane. Leaving the disciples at the entrance of the garden, the Bible says, "And he went a little farther, and fell on his face and prayed" (Matthew 26:39a). This description of our Lord's activity at this critical point of His ministry has always intrigued me – "and he went a little farther." In many ways this is a synopsis of the marvelous and magnificent mission that had brought the Lord from the very bosom of the Father down through forty-two generations in order to save us from our sins. There in the garden, He would pray earnestly prior to His arrest, "O my Father, if it be possible, let this cup pass from me; nevertheless not as I will, but as thou wilt" (Matthew 26:39b). At the end of His earthly life, Jesus was committed to going farther in order to redeem us from the slave market of sin.

What a wonderful lesson for us! Our relationship with God should inspire us always to go farther. We must never relent or retreat, but stretch, struggle and strain (if we must) in order to please Him who is the center and the circumference of our joy. We must never be satisfied or self-sufficient, but always leaning on and learning from the Lord. While attending a leadership summit last week, I heard one of the presenters say, "Often we confuse the edge of the rut we are in with the next horizon." How easy it is for us to become complacent and contented in spiritual things. Yes, Jesus shows us here in this powerful passage that there is a vital relationship between onward and upward.

There are three reasons or motivators in this text that compelled Jesus to go "a little farther." First of all, He was committed to His Father's presence. The Lord desired intimacy with the Father.

Through prayer He experienced what the late Dr. George Buttrick described as "conversation with the ideal companion." This desire, which nothing on earth can satisfy, prompted the Psalmist to say, "As the hart panteth for the water brooks, so panteth my soul after thee, O God" (Psalm 42:1). Secondly, Jesus went farther because He was committed to His Father's plan. God has a plan and purpose for you and me. When we move to the "nevertheless point" in our lives and say, "Not my will but Thine be done," it will compel us to go farther. This is a colossal struggle for us because we like to have our own way and do our own thing. Finally, Jesus went farther because He was committed to His Father's people. According to the Gospel of John, Jesus had just prayed for the disciples. He identified them as those whom the Father had given to Him (John 17:6). He acknowledged that He had kept them in His Father's name. Knowing that the disciples would have to face the fact and fear of His separation from them, He went a little farther and prayed.

I thank God today for encouraging us during those difficult times when we want to resist, retreat or resign from going a little farther. We experience renewed strength and determination through His Word, the Holy Spirit, prayer, worship, faithful friends and other means that God supplies to us in the garden of His grace. It is still true: "Every round goes higher and higher."

A Detailed Plan or Dedicated Persons

"And Jesus came and spake unto them, saying,
All power is given unto me in heaven and in earth.
Go ye therefore, and teach all nations,
baptizing them in the name of the Father,
and of the Son, and of the Holy Ghost:
Teaching them to observe all things
whatsoever I have commanded you:
and, lo, I am with you alway,
even unto the end of the world.
Amen."

(Matthew 28:18-20)

The message and ministry of Jesus is the model for Christian missions in the New Testament. In the Gospels, mission themes are both implicit and explicit. The ministry of Jesus and the Gospel of the Kingdom were pertinent for all people. Jesus does not give the church a full-blown mission strategy but rather, through the ministry of those He had chosen as apostles, lays the foundation for the church's activity and agenda after His resurrection. The kingdom ministry of Jesus Christ involved both an expansive, redeeming image of God's people and an inclusive view of God's people, a positive view and hope for all humanity. In his life, death, burial and resurrection Jesus provides us with the primary model for Christian ministry and missions—not a detailed plan, but rather, dedicated persons.

Energized and transformed by his sudden conversion on the Damascus Road, the Apostle Paul became a tremendous force for mission endeavor in the early church. He was shaped by a number of converging currents: secular Roman history, his Jewish religious background, early Christian traditions and Greek culture. Through Paul's effort, the cosmic commission that the Lord had entrusted to the church took on a uniquely cosmopolitan form as the great apostle preached the gospel from city to city with great effectiveness and impact.

Needless to say, the Bible is a textbook for those seriously committed to Christian ministry and missions. Unlike other books, the Bible never becomes irrelevant or dated, but speaks with timeless relevance to our own situation. The Bible addresses us where we are. As we develop a greater ministry and mission focus (outreach) in our own congregation, it is important that our initiative be anchored in the principles of the Word of God. Therefore, discipleship and missions are interrelated and interdependent. As we become faithful learners, we will also be compelled to launch out into the deep and let our nets down.

Staying Connected

*"And immediately the Spirit driveth him into the wilderness.
And he was there in the wilderness forty days,
tempted of Satan; and was with the wild beasts;
and the angels ministered unto him."*

(Mark 1:12-13)

According to Mark 6:31, Jesus withdrew from active ministry into a dessert in order to "rest a while." Someone said recently, "If you are available all the time you will not be worth anything when you are available." Even God rested on the seventh day of creation after looking at all that He had made and declaring that it was good and very good. (See Genesis 2:2.) The Gospels are consistent in revealing how Jesus would often disengage from the busyness of His ministry for solitude and solace. During these times, He would not only experience physical and emotional renewal, but spiritual renewal as well. Interestingly, these excursions would often occur prior to major decisions or confrontations with those opposed to His message and ministry.

In his moving Confessions, Saint Augustine reflected on the uniqueness of his own humanity and said, "Thou hast made us for Thyself and our hearts are restless until they find their rest in thee." When we become too horizontal, we also become bland, burdened and bewildered. We all need to experience what I call "verticality" or the renewal of our connection with God. We need to see our situations and circumstances from God's viewpoint and not ours. In order to do so, at appropriate times we must move away from the distractions and detractions around us.

The fact that Jesus, the perfect God-Man, was intentional about staying truly connected to the Father is an enduring example for all of us. This concern embraces both the stewardship of our bodies (temple) and the stewardship of our time. It is remarkable that the first occurrence of such a withdrawal in the Gospel of Mark was when the Spirit of God literally drove Jesus into the wilderness to be tempted of the Devil. Our Lord endured temptation because He was in the geographical will of God and there, even in the wilderness, experienced Divine sustenance and support. (See Mark 1:12-13.) How much time will you allow in your busy schedule this week to be alone with God?

Committed to Change

"Now after that John was put in prison,
Jesus came into Galilee,
preaching the gospel of the kingdom of God, And saying,
The time is fulfilled, and the kingdom of God is at hand:
repent ye, and believe the gospel."
(Mark 1:14-15)

The local church is a living organism. Therefore, if it is not growing or changing, the church must be diseased or dying. Change and the management of change are crucial to the life of the congregation committed to actualizing its vision and mission within the context of the coming kingdom of God. Lasting change must be purposive, intentional and deliberate. It must be prayed change and based on sound biblical, theological and theoretical foundations. The essence of God is far greater that the essence of any situation or crisis. God is sovereign, omniscient, immutable, omnipotent and absolute truth. God is faithful and, through Jesus Christ the Head of the church, is moving the body of Christ on earth toward completion and consummation.

In his book The Minister as Proactive Agent of Change, Dr. Larry McSwain observes the following.

"The first discipline necessary for a change theorist is theological conviction. Change derives from a particular view of God's activity in the world. The proactive change agent believes in the transforming power of the Gospel. As Jesus came preaching the kingdom of God (Mark 1:14), He set forth a standard of transformation of the world. Telling and doing the kingdom of God is the task of the change agent. Like Jesus, the change agent proclaims the power of God from beyond human history" (p. 27).

The leadership of the local church and every member must be committed to change for the kingdom's sake. God wants to do a new thing in our personal and corporate experiences as the people of God. Change for change sake can be demonic and deadly. However, "if we live in the Spirit, we must also walk in the

Spirit" (Galatians: 5:25). Such a walk will inevitably lead us into new vistas of change and transformation. This then necessitates a faith that forgets those things that are behind, pressing on toward the mark of the high prize of the calling of Christ Jesus.

Overcoming the Strong Man

**"No man can enter into a strong man's house,
and spoil his goods, except he will first bind the strong man;
and then he will spoil his house."**

(Mark 3:27)

The account of the deranged man living in a cemetery recorded in Mark 5:1-20 is a tragic tale of bondage. An appropriate assessment of this text must consider Mark's purpose in writing. What ends shape his method and shade his meaning in this particular rendering of the Jesus story? Mark does not write from the lofty tower of theological detachment but, rather, engages his audiences where they eat, drink, think and live.

Very early in the Gospel, Mark records the heightening resistance to and outright rejection of the Lord's ministry and message by the Jewish religious establishment. When His powers are ascribed to Beelzebub, he hints strongly that He is on a search and destroy mission; one that will conclude with the binding of the strong man whose house he has already entered and whose possessions He will ransack. In the wilderness, Jesus served an eviction notice on this strong man who is elsewhere called "the prince of the power of the air" or what the Apostle Paul describes as "rulers, authorities, powers of the dark world and spiritual forces of evil in the heavenly realm." (See Ephesians 6:12.) Jesus characterizes the strong man's deceitful and diabolical carnage elsewhere as "the thief that comes only to steal and kill and destroy." On the other hand, the Lord has come that we might have life and have it more abundantly. (See John 10:10.)

Through the magnificent force of His wonderful words and wondrous works, Jesus overcame the strong man. He is the Lord of lords and the King of kings. He is the sovereign ruler of heaven and earth. He commands the sea to hush, to be still and lie down like a lap dog in obedience to its master. The church that follows Jesus in this cosmic conflict of liberation must be willing to sail uncertain seas and traverse new frontiers. Bountiful beneficiaries of the spoils of war distributed by our Victor Christ, we can now take back stolen property. We must be radically different from the world as we boldly share the Lord's compassion and the Gospel with those like the man called Legion; those who are dispossessed and disinherited in our world and in whose hearts blistering storms of doubt and confusion still assail.

Passing Over to the Other Side

**"And the same day, when the even was come,
he saith unto them, Let us pass over unto the other side."**

(Mark 4:35)

The late Dr. Howard Thurman believed fervently that Jesus had a special courtship with those who are oppressed. Thurman, an imminent theologian and preacher who served a distinguished tenure as Dean of the Marsh Chapel at Howard University, gave the book he wrote on the dynamics of prejudice and oppression the searching title <u>Jesus and the Disinherited</u>. The word "disinherited" describes the state of those who are disenfranchised by the forces of personal and corporate (systemic) evil. The demoniac in Mark 5:1-20 was such a person. While we might speculate about the causes of his tragic traumatic state and demented condition, this man mirrored the devastation and destruction of radical physical, emotional, and spiritual privation and disenfranchisement.

Bereft of family and friends, this man was homeless. Without training or skills, he was unemployable and, therefore, penniless. Possessed as he was by unclean spirits, an addictive bondage, he was unable to change his condition by his own power. He was at high risk to himself and others. Is this man really unlike us? Is he any different than those who are held hostage by devilish desires, hobbling habits, paralyzing perspectives, and crippling concerns?

Jesus exorcises the demons from this man, reminding us that not only can He still the storm at sea, but He can conquer and control the storms in the human heart. His compelling compassion still brings Him close to those who are radically dispossessed and disinherited by the strong man, the vicious and vile forces of personal and systemic evil in our world that oppress, destroy, subjugate and deny persons authentic humanity and dignity. This passage reminds us that Jesus is not only concerned about <u>where</u> people live but <u>how</u> people live. He still challenges the church to pass over to the other side, taking Him as He is and defying the tumultuous sea of uncertainty, fear, terror and doubt in order to offer to those who are disinherited the living presence and power of the Gospel.

Sublime Offerings

"And they feared exceedingly, and said one to another,
What manner of man is this,
that even the wind and the sea obey him? "

(Mark 4:41)

Jesus stills the storm at sea and the disciples respond with utter wonder and amazement by saying to one another, "What manner of man is this that even the wind and the sea obey him?" (Mark 4:41). Their fragile emotions were vacillating erratically on a pendulum that swung helplessly between nightmarish fears and a nascent faith. How could this Jesus who at once was asleep and seemingly unaware and unconcerned about the dire straits in which they had fallen now stand boldly and brashly before the tempest and command its silence?

Perhaps a similar sentiment drove the hymn writer William Cowper, a man who was tormented by a different kind of storm, to write the immortal words, "God works in a mysterious way, His wonders to perform; He plants his footsteps in the sea, and rides upon the storm." Ravi Zacharias drives to the heart of this issue in his signal work, <u>Can Man Live Without God</u>. He argues that a clue to the essence of human nature can be found in a child's propensity to wonder. He says, "From gazing into the eyes of its mother as the child is nursed in her arms to the ecstasy that is experienced when riveted to the twinkling light of a Christmas tree - a child gasps a dozen times a day, overwhelmed by life's sublime offerings" (p. 77). Each of us has experienced (some of us are more aware than others) those "sublime offerings." In the wake of them, we have been left with childish wonder and awe in the presence of what the late A. W. Tozer calls "the Holy." As the prophet Elijah discovered, these indentations, indications and incursions of the Divine are not always in the storm, the fire or the earthquake, but are sometimes in the "still small voice" that speaks atomically in our experience. (See I Kings 19:12.)

Solomon wrote, "To everything there is a season, and a time to every purpose under the heaven" (Ecclesiastes 3:1). But as if to discourage our tendency toward arrogance, he then said in verse 11, "He (God) assigned each to its proper time, but the mind of man, he has appointed mystery, that man may never fathom God's own purpose from beginning to end" (Moffatt Translation). In other words, God will never allow us the pleasure of saying under any circumstances that we have figured God out. Blasé Pascal, the French physicist who came to belief in Christ as an adult said, "Faith has its reasons that reason does not know." This is what the disciples discovered about Jesus on the stormy sea that night. He is not only incomparable but incomprehensible apart from the faith that allows us not only to celebrate and worship His majesty, but to embrace the mystery of His being and His workings in the world and, indeed, in our own lives.

A Crisis of Faith

"And straightway the father of the child cried out,
and said with tears, Lord, I believe;
help thou mine unbelief."

(Mark 9:24)

The story of the father and his epileptic son are recorded in Matthew, Mark and Luke. The account in Mark 9:14-29 is the most complete and comprehensive, owing most likely to Mark's dependence on Peter's eyewitness account. The focus in this passage is on faith. This text reminds us that faith is not always standing strong and erect on the promenade of life, ready, willing and able to spread its wings and take eternity in its grasp. More often than we would like, our faith is in crisis anxiously groping in the dark and dense mazes of life trying to make sense of our circumstances and clawing its way sometimes reluctantly to the Light.

Each participant and player in the narrative embodies some aspect of a faith crisis. The father's crisis of belief is unwilling; the son's—uncontrollable; the disciple's—unconscious; and the scribe's—mocking and willful. When the story is concluded, the father is comforted, the son is cured, the disciples are empowered and the scribes are silenced and rebuked. This passage also takes us from the zenith of a mountaintop experience with Jesus where He is transfigured before Peter, James and John in manifested and resplendent glory. We, too, would be dazzled like Peter and say under similar circumstances, "It's good to be here." Like the disciples, we would rather stay on the mountaintops of life, build tabernacles and tents there and not come down, but this desire is fleeting and fictitious, for come down we must. Life throws us into its valleys and vales and there we, like the disciples, are demoralized and demonized as we face sin, sickness and suffering – others' and our own. There, in seasons of distress and woe, we acknowledge our kinship with the father in this text who cried out, "I believe but help mine unbelief."

No matter how well paved the roads and scenic the route, life's journey is dangerous, demanding and difficult. Somehow, I'm reminded of this inescapable reality so often now when I'm driving on what appears to be a safe and secure stretch of highway or interstate and I see a cross; sometimes more than one that punctuates the scene of some tragic and fatal accident. This is the context where we must learn, as did the father in this narrative, to trust God during trying times, which is the theme of our special sermon series. Often our prayer mimics his profound despair when he cried out to our Lord with tears streaming, "I believe; help thou mine unbelief" (Mark 9:24b).

The Paradox of Faith

"And straightway the father of the child cried out,
and said with tears, Lord, I believe;
help thou mine unbelief."

(Mark 9:24)

Was this plaintive scream of a tortured soul the festering follicles of a crippled faith or, in the presence of the Savior, the disturbing exhibition of what is true in the experience of all those who believe? Our human faith is never purely faith, but always mixed with an element of mystery, ambivalence and consternation (conceptual, emotional or volitional). Faith takes us beyond the limiting constraints of our own understanding and perceptions, but never destroys the vestiges of unbelief in us. True faith necessitates a leap beyond our own corrupted comprehension and paralyzing preoccupations. Yes, I believe, but help my unbelief! The dark legacy of sin lingers and, like a suffocating shroud, even limits our ability to trust and obey.

Nonetheless, authentic (not perfect) faith compels us to cross the borders of our own fractured, frail, and finite humanity and stretch the horizons of experience to embrace the reality of the One who cannot be exhausted by either the rational or the sensory. In fact, many times "faith simply doesn't make sense," but in the presence of the Holy, and when sinking under the strain of our own suffering, we simply cry out, "I believe, but help my unbelief!" The power for help, hope and healing is not ultimately in the operation of our faith, but rather in the superlative and perfect object of our faith, who is Jesus Christ. Therefore, faith is a non- meritorious system of knowing. We can't earn it, nor do we deserve it, but by faith we enjoy the pleasure and provision of God. (See Hebrews 11:6.)

What are you trusting God for today that has made you join the somber troupe who cry out, "I believe, but help my unbelief?" Even our faith must one day evolve beyond this veil of time and tears. The Apostle Paul said it best: "For now we see through a glass darkly; but then face to face: now I know in part, but then shall I know even as also I am known." (See I Corinthians 13:12.)

Standing Tall On Our Knees

**"And he said unto them,
This kind can come forth by nothing, but by prayer and fasting."
(Mark 9:29)**

The Transfiguration of our Lord and Savior Jesus Christ is recorded in all of the Synoptic Gospels: Matthew, Mark and Luke. Luke's account is distinctive in that he reminds us that Jesus did not ascend the mountain to be transfigured but, "… He took Peter and John and James, and went up into a mountain to pray" (Luke 9:28). Is this not a tremendous object lesson for those of us who desire to be true servants of God and experience power and glory for blessing and ministry? Prayer is not ultimately a descent but an ascent into the very presence of God. We stand tallest when we are on our knees. After praying and being transfigured in the presence of His disciples, Jesus descended from the mountain where He healed a young child who had an unclean spirit. He would later tell the disciples who were unable to heal the child that "This kind come forth by nothing, but prayer and fasting" (Mark 9:29).

Isn't it interesting that Jesus ascended the mountain to pray, and while there was transfigured? He descended the mountain after being transfigured during prayer, to transform the life of a young child and his father. In the valley of life, we are faced with many challenges. In order to manage these circumstances to the praise of the glory of God, to literally be transfigured and transformed in the very presence of difficulty and distress, sin and suffering, it is imperative that we take the high ground. Jesus, the perfect Son of God, gives to us the key to power and preeminence in spiritual things. We stand tall on our knees! In the divine economy, the high ground is always the low ground of prayer and communion with God.

Prayer is the portal and passport to the spiritual world, and faith is the currency we use to purchase divine assets needed to make it through our valley experiences. What Peter, James and

John experienced on the Mount of Transfiguration is a possibility for all that fervently and earnestly enter into the presence of God through prayer.

But to Minister

**"And whosoever of you will be the chiefest,
shall be servant of all.
For even the Son of man came not to be ministered unto,
but to minister, and to give his life a ransom for many."**

(Mark 10:44-45)

This biblical text provides strong clues to the uniqueness of Jesus Christ and His mission on earth. First of all, the term **"Son of man."** is used approximately seventy one (71) times in the four Gospels (fourteen times in the Gospel of Mark alone) as a title for Jesus. This phrase refers primarily to His humanity and His suffering. The early church fathers from Ignatius to Augustine saw in this phrase a reference to the human aspect of Jesus' origins. Jesus is the unique God-man of history. He is as much man as He is God and as much God as He is man. These two natures exist in one person. While the humanity of Jesus was born in Bethlehem, Jesus is the only begotten of the Father and has always existed eternally as one with the Father and the Holy Spirit. This is the clear teaching of Isaiah 9:6,: "For unto us a child is born, unto us a son is given: and the government shall be upon his shoulder: and his name shall be called Wonderful, Counselor, The mighty God, The everlasting Father, and The Prince of Peace." Indeed, the child was born, but the Son is given.

The word **"came."** in the text emphasizes the mission of Jesus. He came from Heaven to earth. He came down through forty two generations and was born as a child in Bethlehem. He came from the very throne of God. He came because there was no other way to redeem us from our sins. Look at the parallel text in Luke 19:10: "For the Son of man is come to seek and to save that which was lost." The Lord Jesus Christ is God-incarnate; the "human face of God". He angered the religious leadership of His day with unprecedented claims. "Jesus saith unto him, have I been so long time with you, and yet hast thou not known me, Philip? He that hath seen me hath seen the Father" (John 14:9a). Jesus came; and because He did, we moved from sin crouching at the door in Genesis 4:7 to a Savior knocking at the door in Revelation 3:20.

Finally, **Jesus' focus was not Self but Service**. He came not to be ministered to, but to minister. The word translated "minister" in Mark 10:45 is the word from which we get our word <u>deacon</u>. It is one of the words translated **"servant."** in our New Testament. The original word means to "hasten after or pursue; to run through the dust." This word views a servant primarily in relationship to his or her work. This is a fresh and empowering word to a culture and society that is excessively self-centered and self-absorbed. Unfortunately for many, the primary issue is "What's in it for me?" Jesus' words here are in contrast to the self -seeking of James and John in the larger text. We are all in the service of the Lord. On a humorous note, a little boy strolling through the church with his father inquired about the pictures of former members that were hanging on the wall along the corridor. He asked, "Father, who are these people?" His father responded that they were members of the church who died in the service of the Lord. The little boy without hesitation responded, which service, Father, because I don't want to attend that one!" Jesus gave His life as a ransom for sin. What are you (and I) prepared to give and to do today in the service of the Lord?

Servant Leadership

"For even the Son of man came not to be ministered unto, but to minister, and to give his life a ransom for many."

(Mark 10:45)

The preeminent model of leadership in the New Testament is **servant leadership**. Jesus modeled this type of leadership by reminding the disciples that He "... came not to be ministered to, but to minister (literally serve) and give His life a ransom for many" (Mark 10:45). Jesus' words in this text provide a paradigm from which those in spiritual leadership can function effectively and redemptively.

First, servant leaders are **sent**. Jesus was on a mission from the Master. His ministry was ordained by God the Father. Secondly, servant leaders are **sanctified**. Jesus was empowered and energized by the indwelling Holy Spirit which He received without measure. (See John 3:34). Finally, Jesus' leadership was **sacrificial**. He paid the ultimate sacrifice by offering up His perfect humanity as a sacrifice for sins. Those who serve in leadership for selfish or egotistical reasons are not only misplaced but misinformed.

The contemporary church is sorely in need of leadership today that aspires only to serve Christ and others. The Apostle Paul said it well: "For we preach not ourselves, but Christ Jesus the Lord; and ourselves your servants for Jesus' sake" (II Corinthians 4:5).

Totally In-Vested

**"And he called unto him his disciples, and saith unto them,
Verily I say unto you, That this poor widow hath cast more in,
than all they which have cast into the treasury:
For all they did cast in of their abundance;
but she of her want did cast in all that she had,
even all her living."**

(Mark 12:43-44)

Abraham was uniquely blessed of God to be a blessing to others. Abraham demonstrates that obedience always precedes abundance. Abraham trusted God who gave him property, prominence and posterity. The anonymous widow whose story is recorded in Mark 12:41-44 gave an offering to God that represented all her living or livelihood. Her offering signified that she was completely (totally) "in-vested" in the Master. She gave radically and was blessed by the approval and commendation of the Lord who observed how everyone gave to the Temple treasury. Our worship of God in general and our stewardship in particular should always be motivated by the desire to please God and to experience His approval.

David, the shepherd boy, singer, valiant warrior and king, was a man after God's own heart. With all his heart he desired to build a temple for the glory of God, a permanent residence for the Ark of the Covenant. This is the same David that danced before the ark when, after some years, it was returned to Israel after being in the possession of the Philistines. David's commitment and enthusiasm to this project was so contagious that "the people rejoiced, for that they offered willingly, because with perfect heart they offered willingly to the Lord" (I Chronicles 29:9b.) David's final prayer of thanksgiving is recorded in I Chronicles 29:10-19. This prayer reflects the intimate nature of David's relationship to God; a relationship that had evolved by faith to new depths of meaning over time and through many trying experiences.

If you and I hold on to something too tightly, we are sure to lose it. Read about the man that Jesus called a "fool" in Luke 12:13-21. This man had an unhealthy relationship to his possessions. After reading this striking passage we should reflect on the question, "What does God expect me to do with a blessing?"

Failing Forward

**"And the second time the cock crew.
And Peter called to mind the word that Jesus said unto him,
Before the cock crow twice, thou shalt deny me thrice.
And when he thought thereon, he wept."**

(Mark 14:72)

The Christian life spans both peaks and valleys. In the valley experiences of life our faith is tested. None of us pass these tests all the time! Often these straitened experiences leave us bewildered and disillusioned. This was certainly the case with the Apostle Peter who, when put to the test, denied that he even knew the Lord. Ironically, this was a new beginning for Peter. To use John Maxwell's popular phrase, "He failed forward." In failing forward, Peter's faith was bolstered and his calling as a preacher and an apostle validated. No longer was he dependent on the strength and tenacity of his own resolve, but on the matchless grace and mercy of the Lord Jesus Christ who picks us up when we are down.

According to C. S. Lewis in his classic Mere Christianity, "Faith is that which holds on to a belief which was formerly accepted by one's intellect or reason but is now either altogether doubted or suspect." This reminds me of what the French physicist Blaise Pascal said about faith. "Faith has its reasons that reason does not know." Pascal, who came to Christ well into his adult years, reminds us as does Lewis that Christianity compels us to trust God even when it does not make sense. When our lives wither, wilt and weaken because of our own disbelief or disobedience, or because of events or circumstances beyond our control, authentic faith stabilizes and reduces our vulnerability to either the facts or the feelings that we face.

Not only was Peter restored from his failure but, more importantly, his faith was restored. He learned a valuable lesson, as must we. Only the faith that attaches itself to God can take us through the valleys of life. Everything else will surely disappoint. The prophet Jeremiah spoke profoundly to this issue to another generation of believers when he said, "Thus saith the Lord, Cursed be the man that trusteth in man, and maketh flesh his arm, and whose heart departeth from the Lord. For he shall be like the heath in the desert, and shall not see when good cometh; but shall inhabit the parched places in the wilderness, in a salt land and not inhabited" (Jeremiah 17:5-6). Who or what are you trusting in today? As for me, I rejoice with the song writer who said, "I came to Him, weary worn and sad! I found in Him a resting place and that has made me glad!"

The Problem of Evil and Suffering

"And at the ninth hour Jesus cried with a loud voice, saying,
Eloi, Eloi, lama sabachthani? which is, being interpreted,
My God, my God, why hast thou forsaken me?"

(Mark 15:34)

The atheistic position is rationally untenable and inconsistent. The atheist absolutely denies the existence of the Absolute, making himself or herself God. A revision of the argument for the nonexistence of God addresses the evil, suffering and pain in the world. The argument proceeds like this: if there is a God, then God must be callous and cruel to allow suffering; or if God is loving, God must be powerless to destroy the evil, stop the suffering, and end the pain. In theology, this problem of evil and suffering is called <u>theodicy</u>.

What does the Word of God say about this problem? First, it is quite apparent from Scripture that in a universe where God permits the exercise of angelic and human free will, inevitably suffering will ensue as a result of decisions that are not consistent with the will of God. Yet, in the person of Jesus Christ, the only begotten of the Father, God's righteousness was not compromised, Jesus himself bearing our sins and suffering on the Cross. God's response to suffering is to suffer along with us and then to lead us beyond suffering to a condition of bliss and blessedness which eyes have not seen nor ears have heard. The Apostle Paul said it well: "For our light affliction, which is but for a moment, worketh for us a far more exceeding and eternal weight of glory" (II Corinthians 4:7).

A Resurrection Morning Prayer

**"And when the sabbath was past, Mary Magdalene, and Mary
the mother of James, and Salome, had bought sweet spices,
that they might come and anoint him.
And very early in the morning the first day of the week,
they came unto the sepulchre at the rising of the sun."**

(Mark 16:1-2)

God of all comfort and compassion, I thank you for your
faithfulness today as we experience your unfailing compassions;
for every morning new mercies we see. Your faithfulness is great
and glorious. It is like the spring season which blossoms and buds
radiant with perpetual possibility after the frigid chill of winter.
Your faithfulness is like the majestic march of the sun in its circuit
from east to west; it is like the harmonic and hypnotic roar of
ocean surf and tide.

Our Father, it is the resurrection of our Lord and Savior Jesus
Christ and Your Beloved Son that encourages our faith and our
hope in a world filled with sin and suffering. Because He lives we
can face tomorrow, because He lives all fear is gone. Those who
truly know, love and obey You live in the radiance of this hope
and are assured by Your Spirit that nothing can separate us from
the love of God in Christ Jesus.

And because the grave has been robbed of its victory and
death of its sting, we face our tomorrows with the certainty of the
poet who said, "So live that when thy summons come to join the
innumerable caravan which moves to that mysterious realm where
each shall take his chamber in the silent halls of death; that thou go
not down like the quarry slave at night, scourged to his dungeon
but, soothed and sustained by an unfaltering trust, approach thy
grave like one who wraps the mantle of his couch about him and
lies down to pleasant dreams" (William Cullen Bryant).

This we will surely do, Lord, through faith in the One who
is our righteousness, joy, peace and hope, and who died for our
sins, yet eternally lives. Amen.

And Peter ...

**"But go your way, tell his disciples and Peter
that he goeth before you into Galilee:
there shall ye see him, as he said unto you."**

(Mark 16:7)

While reading the Gospel of Mark devotionally this week, I was greatly moved by Mark 16:7. The angel said to Mary Magdalene, "But go your way, tell his disciples and Peter that he goeth before you into Galilee; there shall ye see him, as he said unto you." The words "and Peter" leaped off the pages of Scripture into my heart and mind. It made me think of what I call the power and priority of the personal in the Christian faith. Obviously, the angel's message to Mary and (by inference) the disciples, assured that the Apostle Peter, still reeling from the gravity and guilt of his denials, would know that the Lord retained a personal interest and concern for him, and still loved him despite his failure.

Christianity is first and foremost a relationship. It occurs in the personal domain and is what the Jewish theologian Martin Buber called an "I-Thou" relationship. This passage accentuates the glorious reality of this unique Christian distinctive. While God summons us collectively and corporately as "his disciples," He also knows each of us individually on a personal and intimate level. The Psalmist said it profoundly well: "Thou knowest my downsitting and mine uprising, thou understandeth my thought afar off" (Psalm 139:2). There are times when we must heed the call to discipleship as witnesses of His resurrection in rank and file unity with those with whom we share relationship in the body of Christ. Yet, how much sweeter the moments when the Creator and Lord of this universe and Redeemer of all mankind takes times to call a sheep by name. Jesus, the Good Shepherd "... calleth his own sheep by name and lead them out" (John 10:3). Later in this same Gospel, He summons Lazarus from the dead by calling his name. Had He simply said, "Lazarus," all the dead would have gotten up. (See John 11:43.)

Whatever you are going through today, be encouraged that our Lord has an intimate and personal knowledge of you and your circumstances. In a society that grows increasingly impersonal, how refreshing and encouraging this is. You and I are more than just a number or statistic; rather, we are persons made in His glorious image, of whom He has a personal interest so great that the very hairs of our heads are numbered. Like the Psalmist, I rejoice in breathless adoration at the thought of this. "How precious also are thy thoughts unto me, O God! how great is the sum of them!" (Psalm 139:17).

Making Waves

**"And they went forth, and preached every where,
the Lord working with them,
and confirming the word with signs following. Amen."**

(Mark 16:20)

God has determined that every believer and every local church have an outward and evangelistic focus. What begins in the innermost of our being moves to the uttermost of our world. This is the clear teaching of Acts 1:8. "But ye shall receive power, after the Holy Ghost is come upon you, and ye shall be witnesses unto me both in Jerusalem, in all Judea, and in Samaria, and unto the uttermost part of the earth." The abiding work of the Holy Spirit inside and upon each of us has world changing implications. We are called not only to be godly but global in our outlook and perspective.

The consistent inhale of the Word of God through the study of Bible doctrine and the filling of the Holy Spirit in the individual members of a local congregation creates spiritual density and a spiritual pivot that ripples from within to without and impacts the world for Jesus Christ. Rather than being weakened and wimpish waves tossed to and fro and carried about by every wind of doctrine, we become tidal waves, tempestuous torrents of truth that exalt the Savior, equip the saints and evangelize the lost. What begins with the message of the Gospel of the Lord Jesus Christ culminates in missions, evangelism and outreach that have local, regional, national and international impact. Enlistment and encouragement of members (those the Lord adds to the church), encouraging spiritual maturation through discipleship and equipping ministries, and the deployment of every member's spiritual gifts in meaningful ministry, are all significant aspects of this global venture.

The death of Jesus Christ, His resurrection, ascension and imminent return have significance for the whole world. In these latter days, we must prayerfully heed the summons to share the

Gospel with a broken world. Truly, "the world is hungry for the living grace. Lift the Savior up for the world to see. Trust him and do not doubt the words that He says, I'll draw all men unto me."

The Silent Partner

"And they went forth, and preached every where,
the Lord working with them,
and confirming the word with signs following. Amen."

(Mark 16:20)

The term "silent partner" is used often in the business world to communicate the capital investment and financial leverage of a party or parties active behind the scenes but whose identity is anonymous or unknown to others, except the primary owner or operator of the enterprise. There are many reasons why investors may want their involvement silent or hidden, but their participation in the business transaction is critical.

I thought of this business concept while contemplating recently the words recorded in Mark 16:20. "And they went forth, and preached everywhere, **the Lord working with them** [emphasis mine] and confirming the word with signs following. Amen." The very last verse of this remarkable Gospel that focuses on the servant ministry of our Lord and Savior Jesus Christ is a reminder that we are not alone and that God works with us to fulfill His purpose in our lives. Whatever the problem, we can be assured that God is not only <u>with</u> us and <u>in</u> us, but also <u>for</u> us. Indeed, the Apostle Paul reminded the believers at Rome that "if God be for us, who can be against us?" (Romans 8:31b).

So often while facing trial, crisis, or life's challenges, we sometimes forget this powerful truth. The Prophet Elijah, depressed and perhaps suicidal, thought that he was left all alone. He told God, "And I, even I only, am left; and they seek my life, to take it away" (I Kings 19:10b). To encourage His once valiant spokesman the Lord arranged a demonstration that included strong wind, earthquake and fire. The Lord did not manifest His presence in any of these. It was only in the "still small voice" (I Kings 19:12) that the discouraged prophet heard the voice of the Lord. The <u>Moffatt Translation</u> renders this phrase as *"the sound of a gentle whisper."*

We are not alone today! Whatever you or I are going through, the Lord is our sacred and often silent partner. Others who don't understand this truth look at us and ask, "What makes you so strong?" But we know the truth, because the Lord helps us to endure pressure through the powerful, pleasing, and ever-present sound of His gentle whisper.

Christmas Prayers

**"And his father Zacharias was filled with the Holy Ghost,
and prophesied, saying, Blessed be the Lord God of Israel;
for he hath visited and redeemed his people,
And hath raised up an horn of salvation for us
in the house of his servant David."**

(Luke 1:67-69)

After the birth of his son John the Baptist, Zacharias erupted in prayer and praise. The prayer of Zacharias recorded in Luke 1:67-80, has held a special place in the life of the church now for centuries. Some call it *The Benedictus*. For months he had been unable to speak, the consequence for his lack of faith. He doubted and expressed disbelief in the power of God when the angel of the Lord announced, "Thy prayer is heard and thy wife Elisabeth shall bear thee a son, and thou shalt call his name John" (Luke 1:13b). How difficult it must have been for him to endure the days, the weeks and months in silence as he watched the promise being fulfilled before his very eyes. Prior to the angelic announcement, his wife Elizabeth was barren and both she and Zacharias were advanced in age. Yet, she conceived and the child she carried in her womb would assume a special position as the forerunner of the Lord Jesus Christ. The angel promised Zacharias "joy and gladness" and "that many would rejoice at the birth of his son." (See Luke 1:14.)

When Elizabeth gave birth to their son and before he could speak again, Zacharias, when asked what name his son would be called, asked for pen and writing table and wrote the word "John." This was the name that the angel had assigned to the newborn child even before his birth. Zacharias acted in obedience to the special revelation he had received and it was at that moment that his speech miraculously returned. When he spoke, he was not just caught up in the moment or just expressing pent up emotions but, filled with the Holy Ghost and his faith now focused and fortified, he eloquently places the birth of his son in the context of God's special mission to Israel and the whole world.

Too often the contemporary church has been silenced by sin, deafened by disobedience, and muted by mangling or marginalizing the truth that has been supernaturally revealed in God's Word. This season provides every local church and every child of God the opportunity to break the silence and proclaim the Good News that "the Lord God of Israel hath visited and redeemed his people" (Luke 1:68). The barren places have now blossomed, springs have erupted in the desert, and deliverance rides triumphantly on the wings of the morning. Christ the Savior is born and we, like John the Baptist, are his announcers and forerunners called to "give light to them that sit in darkness and in the shadow of death, to guide our feet into the way of peace" (Luke 1:79).

As you and I count down the days leading to Christmas, let us be faithful and vigilant in seizing every opportunity that God the Holy Spirit gives us to break the silence and share with others that Christ the Savior is born! O come, let us adore Him!

Dear Lord,

A Christmas Prayer

During this season of remembrance, wonder and celebration, when we are so prone during the relentless rush of our lives to forget your choice blessings, we pause to offer you sincere praise and thanksgiving for all your precious gifts.

Thank you for the beauty and grandeur of your creations that give perpetual witness to your glorious name and essence. Thank you for blue skies, majestic sunsets, twinkling stars, the colors of autumn, the solemnity of winter, the roar of oceans and the trickle of streams.

Thank you Lord for the things we so often take for granted – food, shelter, clothing, jobs, and good health. Thank you for the countless expressions of your rich providence, for morning by morning new mercies we see. Thank you for the people we love – for family, friends and associates. Thank you for the people who, despite knowing our failures and faults and shortcomings, love us anyhow.

Thank you for the peace that passes all understanding that comforts us in despair, and the hope that refuses to be conquered by fear, intimidation or terror. Thank you for the faith that cannot be defeated or dismissed and that inspires us to hold on and hold out as we rise above the circumstances of our troubled times and envision a future pregnant with promise and possibility.

Most of all today, we thank you for your unfathomable love and your limitless grace, and for the glorious incarnation of Thine own self into the crucible of human experience. We thank you for the wonderful gift of your Son, the Lord Jesus Christ, who came to this world so that we might have life and have it more abundantly. For these and many other gifts, we give you unceasing thanksgiving and praise, now and forevermore. AMEN.

Heaven on Earth

"Glory to God in the highest,
and on earth peace, good will toward men."

(Luke 2:14)

The commemoration and celebration of the death, burial and resurrection of our Lord Jesus Christ this week has hopefully encouraged all of us to think critically about the implications of these events for our persons and our planet. As I have thought about who and what Jesus is, bursting into my own consciousnesses and riveting my thoughts and thinking has been the conceptual refrain "heaven on earth". It occurs to me that the melodic ministration of the angelic chorus at the birth of the humanity of Christ was profoundly significant when they sang, "Glory to God in the highest, and on earth peace, good will toward men" (Luke 1:27). The birth of Jesus linked heaven and earth together in a new and redeeming way. The "Peace" of heaven and peace on earth were now irreversibly intertwined and dually destined.

The thread and theme of this "heaven on earth" reaches its zenith in the life of Israel during the dedication of the Temple in the eleventh year of the reign of King Solomon. In II Chronicles 5:13b-14, it is recorded, "The house was filled with a cloud, even the house of the Lord; so that the priests could not stand to minister by reason of the cloud; for the glory of the Lord filled the house of God." This cloud and glory was none other than the SHEKINAH (or visible) presence of God that had led Israel in the wilderness as a cloud at day and a pillar of fire at night. As this glory indwelt the temple, "heaven on earth" was uniquely manifested in the reality and rituals of what I call "Temple #1". Tragically, according to Ezekiel 10:18, and because of the repeated and collected transgressions of the nation of Israel, this glory departed the house or temple and returned to heaven.

But God came to this earth in the person of Jesus Christ, and John wrote, "And the word was made flesh, and dwelt among us, (and we beheld his glory, the glory as of the only begotten of the

Father,) full of grace and truth" (John 1:14). Heaven on earth now is the presence of the Son whose temple (body) received the Spirit (glory) without measure (John 3:34). No wonder the Jews were stumped and stunned when Jesus, who I call "Temple #2", said, "Destroy this temple, and in three days I will raise it up" (John 2:19). He was not talking about the restored version of Solomon's temple, but His own humanity. Of course, Jesus (Temple #2) was crucified, buried, rose again and then ascended back to the Father. But this is not how the story ends.

Assembled in the Upper Room after His ascension on the Day of Pentecost were one hundred twenty disciples. They were in one accord and "suddenly there appeared a sound from heaven as of a rushing mighty wind, and it filled all the house where they were sitting ... and they were all filled with the Holy Ghost, and began to speak with other tongues as the Spirit gave them utterance" (Acts 2:3-4). Heaven on earth is now manifested in the life and witness of the individual disciples who are temples – where both the glory of God resides and reflects in the person of the Holy Spirit. This is undeniably Temple #3. What climaxed in the history of Israel as the most ornate, majestic and elaborate structure the world has known - which only pointed to the coming of the One who is the climax and apex of human history- is now resident in the life of the Church, particularly in the soul and spirit of the individual believer. Paul said it best in Colossians 1:27: "Christ in you, the hope of glory." This is why murder and violence in our society and world is so awful and ominous. Every human life is actually or potentially a temple, a depository and reflector of the glory of God, or "heaven on earth".

Preaching as "Trialogue."

"The Spirit of the Lord is upon me,
because he hath anointed me to preach the gospel to the poor;
he hath sent me to heal the brokenhearted,
to preach deliverance to the captives, and recovering of sight
to the blind, to set at liberty them that are bruised,
To preach the acceptable year of the Lord."

(Luke 4:18-19)

It is common in the African-American tradition to say that preaching is "not a monologue but a dialogue." But more is involved than a pulpit and an amen corner. In essence, preaching is a Trialogue. Preaching is uniquely triangulated and involves tri-lateral communication. It engages both the vertical (Theo centric) and horizontal (anthropocentric) dimensions. Preaching engages the ultra-personal relationship with God, the intrapersonal relationship with self and interpersonal relationships with others.

Ultimately, however, this private experience engages the Christian community. Gordon Fee in his book <u>Evangelical Spirituality</u> says, "In a balanced spiritual life private discipline must be related to the experience of the Christian community, which provides a source of nurture, an informal corrective and link to the continuing Christian tradition" (p. 5). This interface is possible and potent because the spirituality of the preacher permits an openness that reaches out and touches others.

The faith community, the church, is the point where the word of the Kingdom launches. Preaching loses intelligibility outside the context of the church. In every age of the church's demise, the prophetic vigilance of preaching has summoned the church back to her historic task. Such vigilance marked the ministry of Dr. Martin Luther King, Jr., a black Baptist Preacher, in whom was wedded the savvy of an international diplomat and the eloquence and transcendent vision of a prophet. He is to be honored not only for the contribution he made to the improvement of the plight of people of color all over the world, but for the genius he brought to the art and craft of biblical preaching.

Christian Character

"A good man out of the good treasure of his heart bringeth forth that which is good; and an evil man out of the evil treasure of his heart bringeth forth that which is evil: for of the abundance of the heart his mouth speaketh."

(Luke 6:45)

A popular quip says, "What we are speaks louder than what we say." Another one goes, "I'd rather see a sermon than hear one any day." One of my favorites is, "We teach what we know but we reproduce who we are." Jesus said that out of the abundance of the heart the mouth speaks (Luke 6:45). Even today in parts of Christendom, the church is reeling from an integrity crisis. Moral failure in Christian ministry has been and is our greatest enemy. The ever lurking reality of sin and temptation, the dynamics of the cosmic system under Satan's authority, seeking like a roaring lion to steal, kill and destroy, and the denigration of any vestige of spiritual authority in our secular, post modern age accentuate the essential urgency of consistent Christian character and morality.

In the devotional classic The Practice of the Presence of God, Brother Lawrence makes a relevant statement. When the occasion arose to practice some virtue he always said to God, "My God, I cannot do this unless You enable me to do so," and he was immediately given the strength needed, and even more. The Apostle Paul said, "I can do all things through Christ which strengtheneth me" (Philippians 4:13). Dr. Dallas Willard, my professor and mentor and the author of The Spirit of the Disciplines says, "Character is habituated willing." Character enables us to "walk the walk as we talk the talk." Character is the difference between trying and training. It is the quality and vitality of the inner life, indeed the reflected glory of God mirrored in our words and deeds. It is not just a public pose we strike at church, but rather the inner life turned inside out for all to see. The task of the church is empowering believers to discover, develop and deploy the awesome spiritual arsenal God has made available to us in our ongoing struggle of becoming.

Vocal Vitality

"And he said unto them, When ye pray, say,
Our Father which art in heaven,
Hallowed be thy name.
Thy kingdom come.
Thy will be done,
as in heaven, so in earth."

(Luke 11:2)

I find it extremely significant that, given the many needs and concerns they were facing, the disciples asked Jesus to teach them how to pray. (See Luke 11:2.) Jesus responded to their request by sharing with them what we now know as the Model Prayer. Their request is searching and significant because it reveals what is at the heart of personal spiritual vitality and piety as well as corporate spirituality. Prayer is undoubtedly the key that unlocks the treasures of heaven. The great practitioner of the Christian faith and the Lord's brother reminded his audience that "Ye have not because ye ask not" (James 4:2).

I am absolutely convinced that the church and Christian ministry grow and prosper in direct proportion to our commitment to prayer and the Word of God. "Except the Lord build the house, they labor in vain that build it; except the Lord keep the city, the watchmen waketh but in vain" (Psalm 127:1). God works with us and watches us through our prayers and praying. The late Dr. George Buttrick described prayers as "conversation with the ideal companion." How wonderful and gracious it is that God has given us the opportunity to come boldly to His throne of grace that we might find mercy and help in time of need!

Parties for Prodigals

"And the son said unto him, Father,
I have sinned against heaven, and in thy sight,
and am no more worthy to be called thy son.
But the father said to his servants,
Bring forth the best robe, and put it on him;
and put a ring on his hand,
and shoes on his feet:
And bring hither the fatted calf, and kill it;
and let us eat, and be merry:
For this my son was dead, and is alive again;
he was lost, and is found.
And they began to be merry."

(Luke 15:21-24)

The Gospel of Luke focuses on the humanity of Jesus Christ. He is not only a son of David and Abraham but also the son of Adam. Through His Son and our Savior, the Father reaches out to all of humanity with a suffering love that knows no boundaries and that is incomparable in its manifestation and its operation. In this gospel, Jesus "must be about His Father's business." For him, there is nothing more pressing and urgent then revealing the Father's essential character to those who are hurting, harassed and helpless. Compelled by a compassionate concern for those who were lost, Jesus gravitated toward those who were considered the outcasts in Jewish society. He incited the hostility of the religious leadership with what they considered to be His "unholy fraternization" with prostitutes, publicans and sinners. According to Chapter 15 of this gospel, Jesus responded to their narrow- mindedness with a trilogy of parables that provided poignant portrayal of His Father's deep and abiding love for those who were lost: the shepherd who had one hundred sheep but left the ninety-nine looking for the one that went astray; the woman who had ten pieces of silver but upon losing one, refused to cut her losses and swept the house clean looking for the valued coin.

But it is the third parable that Jesus shared in response to His critics that is undoubtedly the most endearing and enduring. God's love is like a man who had two sons. His very existence was consumed with an unrelenting concern for their well being. He made provisions for their every need and joyfully shared all his riches and wealth with them. One day, the younger of the two sons, weary of his father's fellowship, burdened by his father's expectations and disillusioned with his father's business, came to his father and asked for an early withdrawal on his estate account. I can hear him saying, "I want my freedom. There is something missing in my life. I want to taste life to the fullest and satisfy the deep desires ebbing inside me. Father, I want to live my own life and do my own thing. I can take care of myself. I don't need your help anymore!"

Bible students know how this story ends. The Parable of the Prodigal Son is one of the greatest love stories in all of the Bible. It is a powerful portrait of the unrivalled love and care of the Father of our Lord and Savior Jesus Christ. God still welcomes prodigals back home with celebration, not with condemnation; with joy, not with judgment. Far countries are cruel, cold and callous places. The truth of the matter is that you and I can travel to a far country without taking a step if we become careless, casual and cavalier in our commitment to God and God's business. And God's sole business is "soul business"; for He came to this planet in the person of the Lord Jesus Christ to save those which are lost. Where are you living today?

Fire the Rock!

"And he answered and said unto them,
I tell you that, if these should hold their peace,
the stones would immediately cry out."

(Luke 19:40)

Palm Sunday marks the triumphal entry of our Lord into Jerusalem during the week of His passion, which culminated in His trial, crucifixion, death and burial in a borrowed tomb. This week, Christians around the world will focus anew on the stupendous implications of these events for themselves and for the world in which we live. Jesus rode into Jerusalem not on a stallion but on a donkey, indeed a lowly ass, signally and signifying that His kingdom was of another world order. He did not arrive their as a conqueror but as a servant prepared to give His life a ransom for many.

He was met with a chorus of praise by the multitudes that gathered as He descended the applauding heights of Mt. Olive and entered the Holy City. Disciples rejoiced and praised God with a loud voice for all the mighty works they had seen. For the critics who bemoaned and criticized what they thought was an ostentatious and inappropriate display of acclaim and support, He said, "I tell you that, if these should hold their peace, the stones would immediately cry out" (Luke 19:40). I summoned every rocky imposter into my presence this morning and gave them their walking papers. I fired the rocks!

No genuine, true, sincere and passionate disciple would want a rock to serve as a proxy for his or her praise. Yet, this text is a reminder that if the church is silenced or remains silent, then even the natural order will rise up in homage and celebration of the King whose very presence on this planet ushered in a new world order. I don't know about you today, but I don't want a rock crying out for me! God has simply been too good. Like David as he gazed at the grandeur of the galaxy and was subdued by the majestic, luminous march of the stars through the Palestinian sky, I must declare, "O Lord, our Lord, how excellent is thy name in all the earth, Who hast set thy glory above the heavens. Out of the mouth of babes and sucklings hast thou ordained strength, because of thine enemies, that thou mightest still the enemy and the avenger" (Psalm 8:1-2).

According to Matthew's gospel, the response of the multitudes in Jerusalem was the fulfillment and actualization of this hope and inspiration in the hearts of the hordes who met Jesus as He entered the city. We dare do no less this week as we anticipate the celebration of events that took place in the life of our Lord that last eventful week; events that catapulted Him to an old rugged cross where He died for our sins as well as the sins of the whole world. (See I John 2:1-2.) Even more importantly, we are encouraged to look beyond the veil of His suffering and our own struggles to that radiant Resurrection morning when our Lord rose from the grave in incomparable power. In newness of a life eternal and a body incorruptible, He snatched the victory from the grave and extracted the sting from humanity's old enemy - death. Because of this reality, we can say with the Apostle Paul, "But thanks be to God, which giveth us the victory through our Lord Jesus Christ." His triumph is our own!

It's A Family Affair!

"But as many as received him,
to them gave he power to become the sons of God,
even to them that believe on his name:
Which were born, not of blood,
nor of the will of the flesh,
nor of the will of man,
but of God."

(John 1:12-13)

Recently, I found myself humming the melody and reflecting on the message of the very popular 1972 hit song by Sly and the Family Stone, "It's a Family Affair." I remember some of the lyrics,

One child grows up to be Somebody that just loves to learn And another child grows up to be Somebody you´d just love to burn Mom loves the both of them You see it´s in the blood Both kids are good to Mom ´Blood´s thicker than mud´

It's a family affair, it's a family affair It's a family affair, it's a family affair

These words contrast the constancy of a mother's love with the uncertainty associated with a child's growth and maturation. No parent really knows what a child will grow up to be. We certainly have and harbor our hopes and dreams and want the very best for our children. Yet in the final analysis, all we can do as parents is to raise our children in the nurture and admonition of the Lord. When their choices and behavior runs counter and contrary to our expectations, we must ask God for the strength to love them unconditionally. It is not always easy to do.

On a more profound level, the song points us to a deeper revelation. The lyrics say, "You see it is in the blood." While the artist did not intend or even anticipate this application, I welcome the implicit reminder that it is the blood of our Lord and Savior Jesus Christ that is the basis of true family. We are, potentially and actually, the children of God before we are the children of men. It is the blood that unites us into a family of faith and makes us heirs to unlimited possibility. The shedding of His blood on Calvary and His vicarious suffering is the compelling constant that unites us as the body of Christ. The Gospel writer John quiets and quells the excessive emphasis of the Jews on genealogy, lineage and bloodlines when he writes, "He came unto his own, and his own received him not. But as many as received him, to them gave he the power to become the sons (literally children) of God, even to them that believe on his name; which were born, not of blood, nor of the will of the flesh, nor of the will of man, but of God" (John 1:11-13).

From a spiritual perspective, what makes it a "family affair" is our relationship to the Son of God who is the quintessential revelation of grace and truth. Sly and the Family Stone were right when they said, "Blood's thicker than mud." While on one level we are nothing but dust, and these physical bodies of ours are prone to disease and death, as members of God's family we are also spiritual beings destined to transcend time for eternity. The great hymn by Charles Wesley says it best: "A charge to keep I have, a God to glorify, a never-dying soul to save, and fit it for the sky."

The Good Germ

**"But as many as received him,
to them gave he power to become the sons of God,
even to them that believe on his name."**

(John 1:12)

In the classic <u>Mere</u> <u>Christianity</u>, a moving and insightful treatise on the foundational truths of our faith, the late C. S. Lewis describes a saving relationship with the Lord Jesus Christ as a "good infection." Christianity is a "good germ"; a "virile virus" that one catches up close and personal in a dynamic relationship with another living Person who is and has always been the only begotten Son of God. This infection is permanent (incurable) and pervasive. It begins in the innermost of one's being and manifests itself ultimately in the uttermost of service and sacrifice for Christ, church and community. It attacks and destroys the corruption of the sinful nature, creating in the believer a "new" nature where old things are passed away and all things are continually becoming new. Our ancestors sang of this change and transformation when they said, "I went to the valley, I didn't go to stay; my soul got happy and I stayed all day; my hands looked new and my feet did too!"

This good infection transforms our perspectives, priorities, patterns and proclivities. It leverages our new birth experience, permeating the stream of the believer's being and leveraging a lifelong process that will culminate in nothing less than our being sons and daughters of God for eternity. This is what the Gospel writer John refers to when he says, "But as many as received him, to them gave he power to become the sons of God, even to them that believe on his name" (John 1:12).

The bad infection that started with Adam's transgression and the resultant death it caused is now subsumed by the good infection of the Son of God who "is made unto us wisdom, and righteousness, and sanctification and redemption" (I Corinthians 1:30). The Gospel represents God's compelling and consummate cure to the ills and ails of this planet. This good infection is first caught then taught. God was and is at work in Jesus Christ reconciling the world to Himself, and through the death, burial and resurrection of His Son has changed the course of human history. How infected and contagious are you today?

Celebrating Grace

**"For the law was given by Moses,
but grace and truth came by Jesus Christ."**

(John 1:17)

Phillip Yancey in the searching title of his bestselling book asks a very profound question: "What's So Amazing About Grace?" The Apostle John in the Prologue of his gospel says, "For the law was given by Moses, but grace and truth came by Jesus Christ" (John 1:17). The revelation of the humanity of Jesus Christ was at its essence a revelation of God's amazing grace. What the law was unable to do with its rituals and sacrifices, Jesus accomplished by grace.

The Bible affirms that grace is the ground of our salvation. "For by grace are ye saved through faith; and that not of yourselves, it is the gift of God" (Ephesians 2:8). Grace is God's gift to every member of the human race. Grace is God through Christ doing for us what we are unable to do for ourselves. Grace is God's gift of reconciliation at Christ's expense. While we can never celebrate our own righteousness, which is as filthy rags, we can celebrate the gift of God's grace.

When the Wine Runs Out

"And the third day there was a marriage in Cana of Galilee;
and the mother of Jesus was there:
And both Jesus was called, and his disciples, to the marriage.
And when they wanted wine,
the mother of Jesus saith unto him,
They have no wine."

(John 2:1-3)

The Gospel of John was written to encourage faith in the Son of God. The author expresses this intent very pointedly when he says, "These things were written that ye might believe in the name of the Son of God and believing, ye might have life in His name" (John 20:31). The very first miracle recorded in the Gospel is the turning of water into wine at a marriage feast in Cana of Galilee. When the wine ran out, Jesus performed a miracle of transformation and manifested His glory (John 2:11).

The presence of Jesus at the marriage feast is significant for three reasons. First, it was the reaffirmation of an unmerited provision. Marriage is a divine institution and, like salvation and the Word of God, is a grace gift that God has given to humanity based on God's integrity rather than our own worthiness. In Genesis 2:18-25, God implements the divine design of marriage because "it was not good for the man to be alone." While the presence of Jesus at the wedding feast was an afterthought on the part of the hosts, a crisis developed "when they wanted wine and there was none." How much this mirrors life; because, no matter what our level of preparation or anticipation, there are seasons in our lives when the "wine runs out". Relationships, marriages, families, careers, and finances are all vulnerable to this unavoidable problem and peril. Guests, some invited and others uninvited, enter and exit our lives and often consume more from us than they give to us. Like termites, these "guests" eat away at the very foundation of our marriage, families and society.

When (not if) the wine runs out, the presence of Jesus at the marriage feast reminds us of another truth and promise that should be the object of our faith and prayers during difficult seasons; and that is, Jesus can turn a crisis into a celebration because of the unrivalled possibilities that His presence creates in any trial or circumstance. In this miracle, He turned water (intended for the external washing involved in Jewish purification rituals) into the best wine the world has ever known. In the end, the governor of the feast could only say, "You have saved the best wine until last." Jesus is the very best that heaven and earth can offer, and we can through faith enjoy the vitality and joy of a relationship that has a beginning but will never end. Jesus is the "new wine" of life sent from heaven to a broken world and the very glory of God revealed in salvation and grace.

Authentic Worship

"But the hour cometh, and now is,
when the true worshippers shall
worship the Father in spirit and in truth:
for the Father seeketh such to worship him.
God is a Spirit:
and they that worship him
must worship him in spirit and in truth."

(John 4:23-24)

The Christian apologist Ravi Zacharias describes worship as "the sense and service of God." Worship necessitates the totality of the believer's response. True worship is essentially "total praise". According to Bishop William Temple, "Worship is the quickening of conscience by His holiness, the nourishment of the mind by His truth, the purification of the imagination by His beauty, and the opening of the heart to His will." Jesus said, "But the hour cometh, and now is, when the true worshippers shall worship the Father in spirit and in truth: for the Father seeketh such to worship him. God is a Spirit: and they that worship him must worship him in spirit and in truth" (John 4:23-24).

Therefore, true worship involves both objective reality (truth) and subjective reality (Spirit). Authentic worship is a powerful and pleasing pendulum that pulsates within the tension between these two polarities. When we worship authentically with the totality of being, there is both structure and spontaneity. There is order and opportunity when worship is informed by the Word of God and inspired by the Spirit of God. In this context, it is essential that the worship celebration is planned prayerfully and intentionally. This is a primary consequence of the creative and corroborative synergy between the Pastor of the local congregation and the Minister of Music. Discord, disharmony and diffusion in this primary and pivotal relationship will be disruptive and detrimental to the creation of a liturgical environment that is conducive to compelling worship in the corporate domain.

Authentic worship, like a pulsating pendulum, moves between the polarities of praise and thanksgiving. We praise God for who God is and we thank God for what God has done! Consequently, there should never be a time when the true believer is not worshipping God either in praise or thanksgiving. Yet, the devil aims to stifle, stagnate and stymie authentic worship by causing the believer to move off the true and solid foundation of praise and thanksgiving.

Our knowledge of God empowers and encourages genuine praise; for truly the more we know, the more we glow. The recognition of God's faithfulness and grace – saving grace (the removal of sins at the Cross), logistical grace (God keeps us alive in the devil's world) and super-grace blessings (God brings about spiritual impact and production) in our lives should ignite an attitude of gratitude in the heart of the child of God. This attitude is at the heart of the Psalmist's pledge: "I will bless the LORD at all times: his praise shall continually be in my mouth" (Psalm 34:1).

Authority and Freedom

**"And ye shall know the truth,
and the truth shall make you free."**

(John 8:32)

Authority, structure, and accountability have become unpopular words in a culture where self-expression, self-centeredness and self-absorption are prized, paraded and promoted. Our culture more and more mirrors the times recorded in the Book of Judges. "In those days there was no king in Israel. Every man did that which was right in his own eyes" (Judges 21:25). A wise person said once that "freedom without authority is anarchy and authority without freedom is tyranny." The point is obvious! Authority and freedom are but different sides of the same coin.

God created Adam and Eve and placed them in a perfect environment called Eden. However, their freedom and happiness were conditioned on proper authority orientation toward God, who prohibited them from eating of the Tree of the Knowledge of Good and Evil. (See Genesis 2:17.) The penalty for disobedience was death. The sad record of human history is that their disobedience propelled themselves and all of us into the downward and deadly spiral of sin. Only the obedience of the unique Son of God, who perfectly obeyed the Law and submitted unconditionally to the will of the Father, could reverse the consequences of Adam's sin.

And it is the Son, the Lord Jesus Christ, who gives us the principle that leads to perfect happiness and freedom. He says, "And ye shall know the truth, and the truth shall make you free" (John 8:32). The truth that Jesus speaks of is Himself. Truth is much more than propositions, principles and platitudes, but is ultimately experienced in a relationship with the Savior who can make us "free indeed". On the day in which we celebrate our country's commitment to human freedom and our "inalienable rights", let us never forget that the price of our spiritual freedom was the death of the Son of God who came that we might have life and have it more abundantly.

Both Body and Bride

"My sheep hear my voice,
and I know them, and they follow me:
And I give unto them eternal life;
and they shall never perish,
neither shall any man pluck them out of my hand.
My Father, which gave them me, is greater than all;
and no man is able to pluck them out of my Father's hand."

(John 10:27-29)

In the letter to the Church of Ephesus recorded in Revelation 2:1-7, Jesus is described as "he that holdeth the seven stars in his right hand, who walketh in the midst of the seven golden candlesticks" (vs. 1b). This description of the risen and ascended Lord is striking; for it affirms two realities that should be the basis of great confidence and comfort for those who are members of His church. First, the "seven stars in his right hand" refers to the seven churches that are the subjects of Revelation Chapters 1-3. Those churches (and ours) are not only in His hand, but the hand of reference is the "right hand". This communicates both significance and security. During his earthly ministry Jesus made the following promise: "My sheep hear my voice and I know them, and they follow me. And I give unto them eternal life; and they shall never perish, neither shall any man pluck them out of my hand. My father, which gave them me, is greater than all; and no man is able to pluck them out of my father's hand" (John 10:27-29).

For those who bemoan the present condition of the contemporary church, it is refreshing to know that the security and significance of the church has nothing to do with the plans or machinations of men and women, but the faithfulness and promises of God. The right hand in the Bible relates to special favor, prominence, access and preeminence. The church of which Jesus is the Head and every believer is a member in particular (Colossians 1:1 and Ephesians: 5:13) is the object of special favor and blessing from the Lord. On the earth, the church is the body of Christ; but in glory, the church is destined to be the bride of Christ. The Apostle Paul mirrored the passion of our Lord as he wrote to the Corinthians, "For I am jealous over you with a godly jealousy, for I have espoused you to one husband, that I may present you as a chaste virgin of Christ" (II Corinthians 11:2). We offer continual praise to God for His powerful presence in the church and His persistent preoccupation with the lives of those who He has called from darkness into His marvelous light!

Insufficient Conclusions and False Realities

"Therefore his sisters sent unto him, saying, Lord, behold, he whom thou lovest is sick. When Jesus heard that, he said, This sickness is not unto death, but for the glory of God, that the Son of God might be glorified thereby."

(John 11:3-4)

Interestingly, the Latin word from which we derive our English word "illusion" means "mocking" or "to mock". One of the subtle and seductive ploys of Satan is to encourage us to look at life and our circumstances in a way that is inconsistent with the truth. One way this is done is by creating a false world or alternative reality that only gives the appearance of reality, but in essence is fleeting and fictitious. Satan seeks to blind our eyes to the truth as it is ultimately revealed in the Lord Jesus Christ, offering us rather the illusion of happiness – pleasure without God, worship without God and success without God.

There is an interesting story of a man who was driving his car rather fast on an isolated rural road. While passing an oncoming car, he heard the driver yell, "Cow!" Thinking that an insult had been hurled his way, he yelled back, "Pig!" and even accelerated as he approached a curve in the road. After entering the curve he came suddenly upon a cow in the middle of the road and was just barely able to avoid a collision. This story brings in bold and urgent relief the necessity to critically evaluate our circumstances before drawing conclusions or making judgments. When the disciples overheard the message delivered to Jesus from Mary and Martha that their brother Lazarus was grievously ill and that Jesus should come see about him right away, they immediately assumed the worst. Jesus reminded them, however, "This sickness is not unto death, but for the glory of God!" (John 11:4).

Someone once said that "life is the art of drawing sufficient conclusions from insufficient premises." The truth of the matter is that often our conclusions about the reality before us are insufficient as well. This is true because, like Mary and Martha and the disciples, we are guilty of underestimating the awesome power of God, disregarding the timeless plan of God and misinterpreting what it really means to be related to the person of God. When circumstances encourage us to accept a false reality or make misinformed decisions, remember God always has the last word and can add a compelling conjunction to every period of our lives no matter how bad things look on the surface.

Paradox

**"Therefore his sisters sent unto him, saying,
Lord, behold, he whom thou lovest is sick."**

(John 11:3)

The dictionary defines paradox as statement or situation that is contradictory or absurd. Mary and Martha's urgent message to the Lord on behalf of their sick brother Lazarus is cloaked in the language of paradox. "He whom thou lovest is sick" (John 11:3). Consecrated ministry to the Lord necessitates that we worship, witness, and work through our paradoxes. As believers live "in time, for eternity", we experience the tension of the "now" and the "not yet." Our faith is stretched and strained when we face our "fiery furnaces" and must affirm both that "God is able" and"if not." (See Daniel 3:13-18.)

As our spirituality evolves and progresses into a greater likeness of Christ, we often live frustrated between, "the good I would do, I do not and the evil I would not do, that I do." In the body of Christ we recognize that wheat and tares grow together, and we painfully discover that those who claim domicile in the household of faith often inflict the deepest wounds.

What are we to do in these conflicted and constricted corridors where we must live out our faith? Like Isaac of old, we must dig again the wells of our fathers until we find the spiritual waters of Rehoboth. (See Genesis 26:22.) Rehoboth means "more room." When facing life's paradoxes, we just need more room; room to believe, room to hope and room to love!

Divine Delays

**"Now Jesus loved Martha, and her sister, and Lazarus.
When he had heard therefore that he was sick,
he abode two days still in the same place where he was."**
(John 11:5-6)

Jesus Christ is the supreme revelation of God; so much so that in the Gospel of John, Jesus says to Philip, one of the twelve, "He that hath seen me hath seen the Father" (John 14:9b). I don't think it is coincidental that in this same Gospel we have one of the most profound verses of the Bible, "Jesus wept" (John 11:35). These words, while brief, pierce the darkness of our understanding like a flash of lightning in a turbulent storm. Jesus, the supreme and perfect image of God, not only wearies with us in our suffering (John 4:6) but weeps with us in our sorrow as well.

Is this not a significant clue to the meaning of Hebrews 4:15? "For we have not a high priest which cannot be touched with the feeling of our infirmities; but was in all points tempted like as we are, yet without sin." What we must conclude is that not only are we made in God's image but God made Himself in our image in the person, passion and perfect humanity of Jesus Christ. Jesus, the only begotten Son of God, is not only the perfect representation of who God is but what God intends for each of us to be in Him. One theologian called him the "human face of God." Jesus is the model of the ideal destiny that God planned for humanity and the ultimate consummation of redemption and reconciliation. In the epistle that bears his name, John says, "Beloved, now are we the sons of God, and it doth not yet appear what we shall be: but we know that, when he shall appear, **we shall be like him** [emphasis mine] for we shall see him as he is" (I John 3:2).

Therefore, Jesus weeping at the tomb of Lazarus is not a token of timidity, a litany of limitation or an insignia of ineptness, but rather the revelation of the God who loves us so much that He enters with us into the veil of incomprehensible suffering. After all, Lazarus had died even though Jesus knew of his illness. The sisters had sent word to the Lord, but He purposely postponed

His arrival in Bethany until Lazarus had been entombed for four days and it appeared all hope was lost. Some of us are dealing with the difficulty and painful contradiction of a Divine delay right now! We have prayed and prayed and prayed, and yet God seems silent. Our pain and problem remains and at times seems to have worsened. Be encouraged today that the Lord has not forgotten about you or me. For God not only wearies and weeps with us <u>but</u> <u>He</u> <u>waits</u> with those who are His beloved. As the Apostle Paul learned, it is through the fellowship of our sufferings that we experience the fellowship of His sufficiency. (See Philippians 3:10.) Ultimately, it is not God's plan or purpose to make us comfortable but to conform us to the image of His Son who "Though he were a Son, yet learned he obedience through the things which he suffered; and being made perfect, be became the author of eternal salvation unto all that obey Him" (Hebrews 5:8-9).

Life Together

"A new commandment I give unto you,
That ye love one another; as I have loved you,
that ye also love one another.
By this shall all men know that ye are my disciples,
if ye have love one to another."
(John 13:34-35)

Christianity is both spiritual and social. At the point of salvation, every believer is baptized by the Holy Spirit into the body of Christ. We are many members but one body. The unity and diversity in the body of Christ (the church on earth) reflects the essence of the triune God. Therefore, it is significant that God calls us not only into relationship with God's Self but with one another. Christianity has both vertical and horizontal dimensions.

Through Christian fellowship, the church grows warmer. Whenever and wherever we see God working in the Bible, whether creating or redeeming, one undeniable aspect of God's activity is the formation of genuine community. In the Genesis narrative, God creates all that is "out of nothing" by simply saying, "Let there be." However, when human beings are created, God says, "Let us make man in our own image … "(Genesis 1:26a). With these words, God in His triune essence was signaling that there is something unique about human beings that necessitates not only a relationship with God, but interrelationship with others. Viewing man in isolation in the Garden for the first time, God said, "It is not good that man should be alone" (Genesis 2:18a). We are made for fellowship; while this is a fundamental affirmation of our creation in God's likeness, it is also an essential part of God's intent in redemption.

In the Upper Room as Jesus anticipated His impending arrest, trial and crucifixion, He encouraged the disciples to "love one another." Their love would be the primary and preeminent insignia of their relationship to Him. Ultimately that love expressed and experienced in Christian community is self-giving and sacrificial. It cannot be coerced or orchestrated, but is inspired unconditionally by the integrity content of the lover for the beloved. This is at the heart of John 3:16. "God so loved the world that He gave His only begotten Son ... "God is so intent upon assuring relationship and fellowship with those who bear His image that He gave His very best.

The German theologian Dietrich Bonheoffer wrote a classic book on Christian fellowship that he called <u>Life</u> <u>Together</u>. Our fellowship in the Sprit is fundamental to the external witness or evangel of the church. Shortly before His arrest and crucifixion, Jesus exhorted His disciples, "A new commandment I give unto you, that ye love one another; as I have loved you, that ye also love one another. By this shall all men know that ye are my disciples, if ye have love one to another" (John 13:34-35). Our experience of fulfilling fellowship today is an essential part of the center and the circumference of the Christian message.

Religion or Relationship?

**"Jesus saith unto him, I am the way, the truth, and the life:
no man cometh unto the Father, but by me**

(John 14:6)

Christianity is not a religion but a relationship. The Bible does not reveal a God who is an impersonal absolute, but rather One who is absolutely personal. God's definitive disclosure is a relationship and is in relationship. Christianity is a relationship and not a rule book. Jesus said, "Come unto me all ye that labor and are heaven laden and I will give you rest." While the relationship cannot ever be exhausted, it is perpetually exhilarating. In the faith tradition of the Black church we say, "Every day with Jesus is sweeter than the day before." In relationship, we encounter the truth, the prerequisite to our spiritual freedom and the basis of our liberation from the trials and victory over the circumstances that beset us. Jesus said to the Jews who had believed on Him, "If ye continue in my word, then are ye my disciples indeed; And ye shall know the truth, and the truth shall make you free" (John 8:31-32). Ultimate truth is experienced in relationship with Jesus Christ. Pontius Pilate's question was tragically misguided. Rather than asking, "What is truth?", he should have asked, "Who is truth" (John 8:38).

God's ultimate revelation in Jesus Christ is consistent and continuous as well, with the essence of God as a trinity of three Persons. While Jesus the Christ makes known the Father, the Holy Spirit glorifies the Son. The essence of Trinitarian community is the model and the motivation for our interpersonal relationships in the body of Christ. God, who is community, is calling us into community as well. This is the focus of John the Apostle when he says, "That which we have seen and heard declare we unto you, that ye also may have fellowship with us: and truly our fellowship is with the Father, and with his Son Jesus Christ. And these things write we unto you, that your joy may be full" (I John 1:3). The experience of life-changing relationship with God in a vertical dimension is the impetus for healthy and wholistic relationships in the horizontal dimension of the family of faith that is the church. These two realities are interdependent and inseparable. One wise writer said it well: "We are all strings in the concert of His joy." The God who delights in the intimacy of His own community of Father, Son and Holy Spirit desires the same for those who have been made in His image and likeness.

Grapes of Grace

"I am the vine, ye are the branches:
He that abideth in me, and I in him,
the same bringeth forth much fruit:
for without me ye can do nothing."

(John 15:5)

As I reflected upon the transformation of grapes on the vine, some compelling realities emerged in my mind. First of all, ripened grapes only reach that stage when connected securely to the vine, having received fully the nutrients required for full maturation. The grapes cannot exist or ripen apart from their connection to the vine or the source of sustenance. Grapes that are severed fall to the ground and rapidly decay and deteriorate. On the other hand, the ripening of grapes (or any other edible fruit for that matter) requires not only the penetrating heat of the sun, but the refreshing showers of rain that water the ground as both sun and rain collaborate as companions in the process of maturation.

The source [the vine], sun and rain, are the ingredients that eventuate in the ripening of fruit. The vine originates, the sun radiates and the rain permeates the ground. Each ingredient is vital. In much the same way, God encourages the maturity of the believer. What begins in a personal and intimate relationship with the Lord Jesus Christ, the ground of our being culminates in the production of spiritual fruit in our lives to the glory of God. Along the way, our lives are watered and refreshed with His blessings, and our growth encouraged and stimulated by the sometimes scorching and discomfiting rays of tribulation and distress brought about due to the presence of sin and suffering in and around us. Through it all, we are encouraged that God will hold us up and hold on to us with His hands until we reach our fullest potential in Him. This is the clear teaching of John 15:1ff. Jesus said, "I am the true vine, and my Father is the husbandman.

Every branch in me that beareth not fruit he taketh away; and every branch that beareth fruit, he purgeth it, that it may bring forth more fruit" (John 15:1-2).

Christian maturity is not a destination but a journey, a process that God guides and which connects us to the Constant Center of our true being and the source of our joy, but exposes us as well to the torrents of a contingent existence. Yet, we are encouraged because our Source and Savior reminds us that, while in the world we shall have tribulation, we can be of good cheer because He has overcome the world. (See John 16:32-33.)

The Comforter

**"But when the Comforter is come,
whom I will send unto you from the Father,
even the Spirit of truth,
which proceedeth from the Father,
he shall testify of me."**

(John 15:26)

The Upper Room Discourse is recorded in the Gospel of John Chapters 13-16. This section of the Gospel records the interaction between Jesus and his disciples prior to His arrest in the Garden of Gethsemane. These words are a kind of last will and testament to the disciples and to us. Much occurs in these verses. Most importantly, Jesus assures the disciples that He must go away so that another Comforter (of the same kind that He is) will come. Just as He was with the disciples, so would the Holy Spirit be with them (and us) as well.

The ministry of the Holy Spirit begins at salvation and is the basis for our growth in the likeness of our Lord and Savior Jesus Christ. The Holy Spirit is the down payment the Father and Son make on the promised redemption of body, soul and spirit that is to come. The Holy Spirit reveals the truth about Christ to the believer and allows the believer to reflect the glory of Christ to a broken world. When led by the Spirit, the believer abides in Christ, who abides in the believer and brings forth fruit unto everlasting life.

Christ, Creation and Community

"And now I am no more in the world,
but these are in the world, and I come to thee.
Holy Father, keep through thine own name
those whom thou hast given me,
that they may be one, as we are."

(John 17:11)

Jesus, the second Adam and true Israel, perfectly fulfills the covenant that embraces redemption and creation. Jesus builds the church with those who have the law written in their hearts as a new community whose centrifugal mission (Matthew 28:18-20) is, according to Michael Williams in his book Far As The Curse Is Found, the "redemptive historical fulfillment of what Israel was called to do." The local church is called to proclaim God's kingdom rule in a world where His sovereignty is contested. The glorious ascent of Jesus Christ to heaven makes us more children of heaven than of earth. The church waits with hope (and with a commitment to holiness) for His imminent return and promised restoration of this planet to its glorious ideal. The bodily incarnation and resurrection of Jesus are the prototypes of our own glorious destiny and, through the empowerment of the Holy Spirit, is the earnest of our inheritance until the glorious redemption.

One remarkable implication of the Lord's commitment to restore creature and creation to the pristine patterns and paradigms experienced before the Fall recorded in Genesis 3 is the expression and experience of oneness with God, self and others. This goal is a primary focus in the high priestly prayer of our Lord recorded in John 17. Three times in this chapter (verses 11, 21 and 22) He prays that "they may be one" as He and His Father are one. Jesus is the melody that integrates the discordant keys of human experience. The most damnable and dismal expression of that discord is the division, disunity and separation that abounds all around us, even in the Church, the body of Christ here on earth. Today's first annual Dr. Martin Luther King, Jr. Unity

Celebration sponsored by our Global Reach Unity Corporation is an attempt to narrow the gulf and impasse that separates us in this community. It is my prayer that walls will become windows and barriers bridges as we seek to transform our personal and collective weaknesses into strengths. God would have it so!

God is at work with us in this endeavor. What a wonderful story this is! We are destined not only for greatness but for oneness. And like all good stories, it has a happy ending. The phrase Williams uses for the title of his book is a refrain in the great Isaac Watts hymn, "Joy to the World". It is preceded by the words, "No more let sins and sorrows grow, nor thorns infest the ground; he comes to make his blessings flow." Because of God's covenant commitment to a sin cursed world, the weeping that erupted in a night of sin, suffering and death has been removed by the joy that arrived in the radiant morning of the glorious resurrection of our Lord and Savior Jesus Christ, who took the sting out of death and snatched the victory from the grave.

Celebrating Unity and Diversity

**"And the glory which thou gavest me I have given them;
that they may be one, even as we are one:"**

(John 17:22)

The revelation in Scripture of the triune God encompasses both unity and diversity. God is one in essence but three Persons in revelatory particularity. The reconciliation of unity and diversity in the creation, and by implication, the redemption and reconciliation of human life, must be inevitably extrapolated from our certitude that there is unity and diversity in the Creator. It is most revealing, then, that Jesus prays in His high priestly prayer, "And the glory which thou gavest me I have given them; that they may be one, even as we are one." (See John 17:22.)

The impetus for ministry and missions to the society in which we live begins with the recognition of the social dynamic in the Godhead. Therefore, our dependence on God and our interdependence on others is an inherent concomitant of the *imago deus* (Latin for our spiritual and relational likeness to God). Dr. Martin Luther King, Jr. made a profound statement when he said, "We are bound in an inescapable network of mutuality, tied in a garment of destiny."

Therefore, the observance of the Lord's Supper is not only a sublime recognition of our faith in God and participation in the death of God's Son on the cross, but also a compelling reminder of our own interrelationships in the body of Christ. We remember the Lord by not only eating the bread and drinking the cup, but by remembering as well that we are one body but many members.

A Mother's Love

"When Jesus therefore saw his mother,
and the disciple standing by, whom he loved,
he saith unto his mother, Woman, behold thy son!
Then saith he to the disciple, Behold thy mother!
And from that hour that disciple took her unto his own home."
(John 19:26-27)

One of the words used in the Greek language to express love is *storge*. Unlike the word agape, which communicates the unconditional love of God, storge expresses the reality of parental love; the love of a mother and father for their children. On this very special day as we celebrate the wonderful gift of "motherhood", we are reminded that every good and perfect gift comes from God. All true love, no matter the channel, has as its ultimate source the love of God ultimately revealed in the life, death and resurrection of our Lord and Savior Jesus Christ.

We all thank God today for the godly women past and present that have nurtured and encouraged us, impacting our lives in inestimable ways. The true essence of motherhood transcends a mere biological/reproductive relationship and includes as well the psychological, emotional and mental support that we experience when another person comes alongside us in a truly personal, redemptive and transformational way.

A mother's love and commitment is foundational to the well-being of the family. The tragedy in our society today is the destruction and dysfunction that is eating away like an incurable virus at the very heart of the family because the biblical model and spiritual principles related to parenting and family have been forfeited. We need more "Proverbs 31 Women" who with meticulous and matchless care give themselves unconditionally and wholeheartedly to God and then to their families with the very heart of Christ. It is said of this type of woman that, "She looketh well to the ways of her household, and eateth not the bread of idleness. Her children arise up, and call her blessed; her husband also, and he praiseth her" (Proverbs 31:27-28).

Any of us who have experienced the loving touch and compassionate care of a true and spiritual "Mother" must be moved to praise and thanksgiving to God today for giving such a gift to us. Reflecting on the constancy of a mother's love, one poet wrote, "Youth fades; love droops; the leaves of friendship fall; but a mother's secret love outlives them all."

Feed My Sheep

**"So when they had dined, Jesus saith to Simon Peter,
Simon, son of Jonas, lovest thou me more than these?
He saith unto him, Yea, Lord; thou knowest that I love thee.
He saith unto him, Feed my lambs."**

(John 21:15)

The Word of God is a supernatural reality. It is inspired by God and reflects God's perfect nature. During the temptation in the wilderness, Jesus said to Satan, "Man cannot live by bread alone but by every word that proceedeth out of the mouth of God" (Matthew 4:1).

Jesus understood the critical importance of the Word of God for the spiritual life of the believer. Just as the body requires balanced diet and nutrition, the soul and spirit must be nourished by the consistent and daily intake of the Word of God. Every believer must make Bible study a priority if we are to resist the devil and persist in the plan of God for our lives.

The primary function of the gift of pastor-teacher is feeding the people (flock) of God with the Word of God. (See John 21:15-16.) When this is done faithfully and consistently, the saints will be perfected (literally fitted for combat) for the work of the ministry and the body of Christ will be built up. The church is built up one believer at a time. Have you made Sunday School and Bible Study a priority in your life?

The Blessing Beyond the Brokenness

**"So when they had dined, Jesus saith to Simon Peter,
Simon, son of Jonas, lovest thou me more than these?
He saith unto him, Yea, Lord; thou knowest that I love thee.
He saith unto him, Feed my lambs."**

(John 21:15)

"The Blessing Beyond the Brokenness" is the title of our new sermon series. It has been both challenging and refreshing to take a close look at one of the most endearing passages in all of Scripture - Peter's restoration to ministry as recorded in John 21:15-19. This passage accentuates the truth inherent in the title of a popular leadership book by John Maxwell, <u>Failing</u> <u>Forward</u>. Because of God's amazing and sufficient grace, we have learned that "failure" is not the last word. God reserves the right to place a footnote at the end of our failures. This is exactly what the Lord did for the Apostle Peter. After his denials, the Lord lovingly and intentionally met Peter and moved him from brokenness to blessedness by doing three things: (1) redeeming his past, (2) reigniting his passion and (3) reshaping his purpose.

It is significant to me that Peter's restoration occurred in the context of a meal that the Lord shared with His disciples. As this faith family celebrates the Lord's Supper today, I believe a proper orientation and perspective of this ordinance will encourage our work, witness and worship as well. The implications of the Supper span and embrace past, present and future. It is a perpetual reminder that we have been saved from the penalty of sin in the past, the power of sin in the present, and the presence of sin in a glorious future. The Apostle Paul provided timeless teaching to the Corinthian church regarding the Supper. He said, "For as often as ye eat this bread, and drink this cup, ye do shew the Lord's death till he come" (I Corinthians 11:26). In this remarkable statement, Paul gives a panoramic assessment of the symbolic implications of the Lord's Supper for past, present and future.

In the privacy of our priesthood today as we share the bread and drink the cup, each of us can be assured that God has already met us at our place of brokenness and, through His vicarious death on the cross, covered our sins with His blood. After his restoration, the Apostle Peter wrote to the church, "Forasmuch as ye know that ye were not redeemed with corruptible things … But with the precious blood of Christ as of a lamb without blemish and without spot" (I Peter 1:18-19).

The Promise and Provision of Power

"But ye shall receive power,
after that the Holy Ghost is come upon you:
and ye shall be witnesses unto me both in Jerusalem,
and in all Judaea, and in Samaria,
and unto the uttermost part of the earth."

(Acts 1:8)

There are two power systems in the Christian life. First, the filling of the Holy Spirit. Every believer is indwelt by the Spirit of God at the point of salvation (Phase 1 of the Plan of Salvation). (See I Corinthians 6:19.) However, while there is one and only one indwelling, there are many fillings. We are filled by the Holy Spirit (Ephesians :18) as we yield our wills to the leadership of the Spirit in all things. The filling of the Holy Spirit is prerequisite to any lasting spiritual production in the believer's life. At any point in time, the believer is either producing the works of the flesh or the fruit of the Holy Spirit. (See Galatians 5:19- 25.) The primary purpose of the Holy Spirit is to glorify the Lord Jesus Christ.

The second power system in Phase 2 of the Plan of Salvation (the believer in time; Phase 1 is salvation and Phase 3 is the believer in eternity) is the metabolizing or inhale and exhale of Bible doctrine. This requires consistent inhale and exhale of the Word of God through systematic Bible study. The teaching of the Word of God is the primary responsibility of the Pastor-Teacher and is essential for individual and corporate growth in the body of Christ. Experience of the second power option results in strengthening of the inner person, characterized by occupation with Christ, a relaxed mental attitude, and enhanced spiritual comprehension and discernment. (See Ephesians 3:16-19.)

Lack of faithful, systematic study of the word of God is a primary reason for the powerlessness that haunts and hobbles many Christians today. Remember, Jesus said when tempted by Satan, "It is written, Man shall not live by bread alone, but by every word that proceedeth out of the mouth of God" (Matthew 4:3).

Back to Basics

**"And they continued stedfastly in the apostles' doctrine
and fellowship, and in breaking of bread, and in prayers."**

(Acts 2:42)

Acts 2:37-47 is a primary passage for understanding the dynamics of church growth and corporate spiritual production. The early church was founded on and grounded in the Word of God. On the Day of Pentecost, the Gospel was preached with compelling clarity by a compassionate courier (the Apostle Peter) with unprecedented Christological ("about Christ") content. Those who listened and heard were pricked in their hearts and asked, "What shall we do?" (See Acts 2:37.) The apostles directed them to repent (change their minds) and be baptized for the remission of sins and receive the Holy Spirit.

This passage also provides a snapshot of the priorities and precedents that characterized the life of the early Christian community. They engaged in four primary or basic spiritual activities according to Acts 2:42: the <u>apostles</u> <u>teaching</u> (Bible Study), <u>breaking</u> <u>of</u> <u>bread</u> (worship/observing the ordinance of the Lord's Supper), <u>fellowship</u> (they were connected to the community) and <u>prayer</u>. Because of their persistence and sheer tenacity in putting first things first, the Lord continued to add to the church those that were being saved. This passage is pivotal for the contemporary church. We experience blessing and success as we go back to the basics and are faithful in following God's blueprint.

Prison Proclamations

"And when they had laid many stripes upon them,
they cast them into prison,
charging the jailor to keep them safely:
Who, having received such a charge,
thrust them into the inner prison,
and made their feet fast in the stocks.
And at midnight Paul and Silas prayed,
and sang praises unto God:
and the prisoners heard them."

(Acts 16:23-25)

What do the books The Long Journey Home by Nelson Mandela, Why We Can't Wait by Martin Luther King, Jr., and The Pilgrim's Progress by John Bunyan have in common? I'm glad you asked. They were all written from prison. Though imprisoned for their beliefs, these men were able to pen thoughts that moved and motivated millions. Dr. Martin Luther King, Jr. wrote his treatise from a Birmingham jail, effectively and eloquently challenging and admonishing the white clergy who questioned his concern about the disenfranchised and disinherited of that city. John Bunyan wrote from a prison cell in London one of the most beautiful allegories of the Christian life and the spiritual journey the world has ever known. In December 2004, I visited the cell on Robben Island in South Africa where Nelson Mandela contemplated thoughts and transcribed words that would fuel the fires of liberation in his country and focus the world's attention on the injustices and atrocities of apartheid.

These men are remarkable examples of the resiliency and resolve of the human soul. We can literally be locked in but never locked out because of the mind's capacity to soar beyond its captivity and its captors. God has made us in His image. And God is a spirit; they that worship Him must worship Him in Spirit and truth. (See John 4:24.) Just as God cannot be contained or confined behind bars, bricks, or barriers, neither can we. Jesus told His disciples, "And ye shall know the truth, and the truth shall make you free... If the Son therefore make you free, ye shall be free indeed" (John 8:32, 36).

This is an important spiritual principle to remember. All prisons are not made of bricks, concrete, steel, or mortar. There are situational prisons, relational prisons, financial prisons and even conceptual prisons. Whatever enslaves us, snares, and stymies us is a prison. Whatever keeps us from fulfilling our God-given potential and purpose is a prison. For the Jewish leaders addressed in the Gospel of John, the prison was their conceptual and ritual attachment to the Law and their unwillingness to embrace the dawning of abundant grace and matchless mercy incarnated in the life, mission, and message of Jesus Christ.

From a prison Paul wrote, "I can do all things through Christ which strengthens me" (Philippians 4:13). This is Paul's **Declaration of Dependence** and ours! Only through Christ can we soar beyond our limits and constraints. Otherwise, "dreams die and life becomes a broken-winged bird that cannot fly" (Langston Hughes). As I write to you, I am contemplating words that I can share with a family whose hearts are broken by the unexpected loss of a loved one. They find themselves suddenly in a prison of bereavement wondering what tomorrow will bring. A husband, father, grandfather and friend is dead. What are we going to do? I can find no better words of hope, help and healing than these: "But my God shall supply all your need according to his riches in glory in Christ Jesus" (Philippians 4:19). This is the truth that will set us free!

The "Right-Side-Up Church."

**"And when they found them not, they drew Jason
and certain brethren unto the rulers of the city, crying,
These that have turned the world upside down
are come hither also."**

(Acts 17:6)

The new sermon series on the Book of Acts is based on the accusation that unbelieving Jews made against the Apostle Paul in Thessalonica during his second missionary journey. They claimed that the Christians were guilty of turning the word upside down. Upon reflection, this statement provides a point of analysis for the entire Book of Acts when the question is asked, "What kind of church turns the world upside down?" At the least, such a church must be a *"right-side-up" church*.

Jesus commissions the church in Acts 1:8 to take the Gospel to the uttermost parts of the world. Any local church that takes this commission seriously will be the salt of the earth and a light that sits on a hill that cannot be hidden. In other words, such a church will impact its community and region for Jesus Christ. That church, that is, that "right-side-up" church will not only be Christ-centered but Spirit-filled.

The Holy Spirit is the third person of the Trinity. We are in fact living in the dispensation of the Spirit. Just as the Father is the author of the Plan of Salvation, the Son is the executor, and the Holy Spirit reveals the plan to men and women. No serious consideration of the Christian life is possible apart from significant reference to the pre-salvation and post-salvation ministries of the Holy Spirit. On the Day of Pentecost, the one hundred twenty disciples in the Upper Room were filled with the Holy Spirit. The Gospel was preached with power and three thousand souls were added to the church. Not only was the church characterized with power without, but with fellowship and compassionate sharing within. How true the words of Oswald Smith's inspiring hymn, "Lord, possess me now, I pray, Make me wholly Thine today; gladly do I own Thy sway, with Thy Spirit fill me!"

Jesus the Son of God

**"Paul, a servant of Jesus Christ, called to be an apostle,
separated unto the gospel of God,
(Which he had promised afore
by his prophets in the holy scriptures,)
Concerning his Son Jesus Christ our Lord,
which was made of the seed of David according to the flesh."**

(Romans 1:1-3)

The Apostle Paul began his Roman epistle with a sweeping statement about the nature and significance of the Lord Jesus Christ. This passage is significant for a number of reasons. First, Jesus is the Son of God, although a descendent of David the King according to the flesh. The Lord Jesus Christ is one person with two natures - divine and human, whose uniqueness and sinlessness the very power and holiness of God validate.

Secondly, the resurrection of Jesus from the grave is the basis of the church's proclamation of the Gospel to the whole world. It was the resurrected Lord that summoned Paul to the ministry of an apostle. It is the reality of the resurrected Lord in our lives today that is the incentive for worship, witnessing and work within the context of the ministry of the church. We are the "called out" of Jesus Christ. Those who believe in the crucified yet risen Savior have been called from darkness into His marvelous light.

Finally, a cursory reading of the aforementioned text will reveal that the Apostle Paul writes with such urgency and unction to his readers, hardly able to capture the grandeur of the truth he communicates. In this same chapter he says, "I am not ashamed of the gospel of Christ; for it is the power of God unto salvation to everyone that believeth" (Romans 1:16). The empty tomb should create in all of us an urgency to tell others that, indeed, Christ is risen today and, because He lives, I can face tomorrow!

The Sinless and the Endless Life

"Concerning his Son Jesus Christ our Lord,
which was made of the seed of David according to the flesh;
And declared to be the Son of God with power,
according to the spirit of holiness,
by the resurrection from the dead:
By whom we have received grace and apostleship,
for obedience to the faith among all nations, for his name."

(Romans 1:3-5)

The popular movie *The Passion of the Christ* has heightened awareness among believers regarding the tremendous cost that Jesus paid to secure our salvation. The graphic and riveting depiction of the arrest, trial, scourging and crucifixion of our Lord awakened in me and many others who have seen the movie a deep and abiding appreciation for depths of the Savior's love for all persons.

However, we must not forget that apart from the resurrection, the sufferings of Christ would have been in vain. In this important passage, Paul clearly emphasizes the critical role the resurrection plays in the declaration of Jesus as the Son of God who triumphed over death and the grave with power, securing the hope of salvation for all humanity, not only with a sinless life but an *endless* life! This sets Jesus and Christianity apart from all other religions, for the Author and Finisher of our faith yet lives and has become the first fruits of them that sleep. It is not the Suffering Servant of Isaiah 53 that is the ultimate object of our faith and hope, but it is the Risen Savior of I Corinthians 15: "And Christ be not risen, then is our preaching vain, and your faith is also vain" (I Corinthians 15:14).

The resurrection of Jesus Christ is the foundation of the Christian Gospel. As the Apostle Paul said, "And if Christ be not risen, then is our preaching vain, and your faith also vain" (I Corinthians 15:14). The physical, bodily resurrection of Jesus is the supreme apology or defense of our faith. The empty tomb validates the message, ministry and mission of the One who was crucified for our sins and was raised from the dead for our justification.

If the Gospel is true (and it is) in its primary assertion, then it must be true as well in every other regard. While the wages of sin is death, the gift of God is eternal life. This life was secured for us through the death, burial and glorious resurrection of the Son who is the first fruits of them that sleep. On the Cross, Jesus secured for all humanity a strategic victory of such proportions that the kingdom of darkness has been put to flight and history changed forever. We celebrate today not only a sinless life but an endless life! Yes, because He lives, I can face tomorrow!

The King Has One More Move!

"Therefore being justified by faith,
we have peace with God through our Lord Jesus Christ:
By whom also we have access by faith
into this grace wherein we stand,
and rejoice in hope of the glory of God."
(Romans 5:1-2)

The greatest war of all is fought on the battleground of the hearts of men and women. This war began in angelic history when Lucifer, the anointed cherub, attempted to usurp the power and authority of God. The war entered time when Adam and Eve sinned in response to the sinister insinuation of the Serpent who said they could be "as gods" if they ate of the Tree of the Knowledge of Good and Evil. (See Genesis 3:1-7.)

Sin entered the human race and death by sin. Sin has made us a fallen race on a fallen planet. (See Romans 5:12). Yet God, like a master chess player, always has the last move. Where sin abounded, grace did much more abound. God prepared a sacrifice to atone for sins and to reverse the deadly consequences of angelic and human rebellion. That sacrifice was Himself – the perfect humanity of the Son. Jesus' death on the cross was a strategic victory on the historic battleground of sin and suffering. (See I John 2:1-2.) For this reason, the Apostle Paul signaled ultimate triumph for the believer in our struggles with sin and suffering. He said, "Therefore being justified by faith, we have peace with God through our Lord Jesus Christ: By whom also we have access by faith into this grace wherein we stand, and rejoice in hope of the glory of God" (Romans 5:1-2). It is hope and glory that is in our purview today because, when sin has done its worst, Jesus Christ still has the last move. Where sin abounds, grace much more abounds!

In a museum hung a famous painting called *Checkmate* depicting two characters, Faust and Mephistopheles, jostling for supremacy over a chess board. One represents Satan and the other the human race. They are playing chess and the pieces are arranged on the board to apparently look like a checkmate in favor of our old enemy the devil. But one day, a renowned chess master visited the museum and stood looking at the painting. He walked back and forth immersed in deep thought and reflection. Something about the position and placement of the pieces on the board troubled him. As he paced, examining the painting from different angles, he exclaimed, "Wait! The king has another move."

Palm Sunday marks the Lord's triumphant entry into the City of Jerusalem as the Messiah and the beginning of Passion Week. It is a perpetual reminder to the Church that the King has one more move! Whatever else we do this week, we must take time to reflect upon the completed work of Christ on the Cross for the sins of all people. Deliverance from sin has been secured by the victory of the Lamb. To God be the Glory!

The Symbolism of Baptism and the Lord's Supper

**"Therefore we are buried with him by baptism into death:
that like as Christ was raised up from the dead
by the glory of the Father,
even so we also should walk in newness of life."**

(Romans 6:4)

The two ordinances of the New Testament Church are Baptism and the Lord's Supper. While these symbolic rituals portray significant aspects of the message, mission, and ministry of Jesus Christ to a broken and sinful world, they cannot save or sanctify. However, they beautifully concretize the great truths that are at the very heart of the salvation relationship.

Water baptism by immersion symbolizes the believer's identification with Christ in His death, burial and resurrection. The Apostle Paul writes, "Therefore we are buried with him by baptism unto death: that like as Christ was raised from the dead by the glory of the Father, even so we also should walk in the newness of life" (Romans 6:4). The late Baptist theologian Dr. W. T. Conner said, "Our baptism, then, in symbolizing our spiritual death and resurrection commemorates the Death and Resurrection of Jesus as the fundamental facts of the gospel. Outside Christ's death for our sins and His resurrection from the dead, there is no gospel" (p. 279, <u>Christian</u> <u>Doctrine</u>).

The Lord's Supper symbolizes Jesus' unique deaths on the cross for our sins. While the bread symbolizes his physical death, the cup emphasizes His spiritual death. On the cross, Jesus became sin for us that we might become the righteousness of God, which is in Him. (See II Corinthians 5:21.) It was the spiritual death of our Lord on Calvary that paid the penalty for our sins and the sins of the whole world. (See I John 2:1-2.) The observance of the Lord's Supper provides a wholesome context for personal self-evaluation and spiritual assessment in the privacy of one's own priesthood. Prior to eating the bread and drinking the cup, all known sin should be confessed as a basis of unhindered fellowship with the Lord through the Spirit.

According to the Scriptures, Baptism precedes the Lord's Supper. Participants in these ordinances are believers only. As we faithfully observe these ordinances, the essence of the Gospel message is kept alive in our hearts as we express symbolically our utter dependence on the death, burial and resurrection of Jesus Christ as the only sure ground of our salvation.

The Shadow and the Substance

"For we know that the law is spiritual:
but I am carnal, sold under sin.
For that which I do I allow not:
for what I would, that do I not;
but what I hate, that do I."

(Romans 7:14-15)

The New Testament believer resides in what Richard Niebuhr calls the "meanwhile". We live not only in the shadow of the Cross, but bask by grace in the glorious radiance of the Resurrection as well. This is not only a theological reality but one that is borne out by experience. Shakespeare has an excellent line that says,

"The web of life is a mingled yarn, filled with good and ill. Our virtues would be proud if they were not whipped by our faults and our crimes would despair if they were not cherished by our virtues."

These words of the English playwright communicate quite eloquently the paradox that we find ourselves in as we try to live out our lives to the praise and glory of God. The Apostle Paul conveys the same tension in his epistle to the Romans when he says, "For we know that the law is spiritual: but I am carnal, sold under sin. For that which I do I allow not: for what I would, that do I not; but what I hate, that do I" (Romans 7:14-15). Both the cross and the empty tomb are enduring realities and truths of the Christian faith. They are interdependent, different sides of the same spiritual coin. We could not long endure the tragedy and trauma of all that is embodied in the cross apart from the hope of the resurrection. Nor can we truly appreciate the treasured triumph of the resurrection apart from the deliverance and hope from the agony of sin, suffering and death the Empty Tomb gives.

It is indeed the radiant reflection of sunlight upon an object that causes it to cast a shadow. Because Christ lives, not only can each of us face tomorrow, but we can also face the shadows in life whose varied and vicious forms haunt, hobble, harass and even sometimes hinder us as we move by grace into the radiance of God's glory. Be encouraged today that the shadow of our own faults, flaws and frailties can never be greater than the substance of the new life that is assured to those who are in Christ. No wonder Paul catapulted from the despair prompted by the contradictions in his own life experience to a joyous anthem of praise by acknowledging, "There is therefore now no condemnation to them which are in Christ Jesus, who walk not after the flesh, but after the Spirit. For the law of the Spirit of life in Christ Jesus hath made me free from the law of sin and death" (Romans 8:1-2). Let us all remember today that difficulties are only opportunities to plunge deeper into our faith and find our faith stretched and strengthened through the struggle.

The War Within

**"For I delight in the law of God after the inward man:
But I see another law in my members,
warring against the law of my mind,
and bringing me into captivity
to the law of sin which is in my members.
O wretched man that I am!
who shall deliver me from the body of this death?"**

(Romans 7:22-24)

Holiness is not a pose one strikes or the designation for a particular religious denomination, but rather the supreme expectation and ideal for the Christian life. God who is Holy calls every believer to be holy in relationship to Him. In the Sermon on the Mount, Jesus says, "Be ye therefore perfect, even as your Father in heaven is perfect" (Matthew 5:48). Is this standard beyond our capacity to reach or achieve? Indeed, it is not in our own strength and power, but only through the grace of God and the indwelling ministry of the Holy Spirit that perfection of holiness can be experienced in our lives. This occurs each and every time we yield to the Holy Spirit and allow Him to control our emotions, mind and will. This is the essence of the Apostle Paul's teaching in Galatians 6:16. "This I say then, Walk in the Spirit, and ye shall not fulfill the lust of the flesh. For the flesh lusteth against the Spirit and the Spirit against the flesh; and these are contrary the one to the other; so that ye cannot do the things that ye would."

Is there among us anyone who does not know or empathize with this incessant struggle; this civil war that is raging within us? In our efforts to walk right and talk right, "evil is present on every hand." In fact, we have "resident evil' inside us because of the existence of the old sin nature in each of us. Only as we resolve to yield ourselves to the Holy Spirit can we experience holiness in word and deed. A very important function of Christian ministry is to strengthen our resolve and spiritual production through the systematic inhale/exhale of the Word of God.

In his book Learning to Walk by Grace in the chapter he titled, *"Portrait of a Struggling Christian"*, Chuck Swindoll writes, "When we try to fight sin in the flesh we lose. We cannot have victory in our struggle if we draw only from ourselves. Furthermore, when we focus on the flesh, we quit. If we try to overcome sin on our own, then we will eventually become disillusioned and give up the fight" (p. 13). What then is the solution to living a holy life? Swindoll continues by saying, "God does not hate failure. After all, He loved failures so much that He sent His only Son to die for them. The Lord simply asks that we learn from our mistakes and use them to move closer to Him" (p. 14). Are you and I moving closer to the standard of holiness that is the ideal for every child of God? While defeats and disappointments will surely come, remember God's promise: "There is therefore now no condemnation to them which are in Christ Jesus, who walk not after the flesh, but after the Spirit" (Romans 8:1).

Someone Is On the Line

"Likewise the Spirit also helpeth our infirmities:
for we know not what we should pray for as we ought:
but the Spirit itself maketh intercession for us
with groanings which cannot be uttered."

(Romans 8:26)

As I reflect on the centrality of prayer in the believer's life and in the experience we call "church", somehow my mind wanders down a seldom visited corridor associated with my childhood. I remember one of my sisters getting a play telephone for Christmas. As a little boy, when I had my go at this new and amusing gadget, I discovered something quite startling. While the phone was bright red, rang loud and the dial worked, when I put the receiver to my ear and talked, no one answered back. There was only stark silence on the other end. The only conversation I could muster was talking to myself. Only a child's naiveté would have expected otherwise.

When you and I talk to God, God speaks to us in the very innermost part of our beings, reminding us that there is someone on the other end. I remember now an old hymn that I heard in the church of my childhood and youth called "A Royal Telephone." God has placed in the bosom of every believer a royal telephone whose service can never be suspended or interrupted. Our problem so often is inconsistent or inappropriate use of this spiritual resource.

Eugene Peterson says that when we pray we are paying attention to God and God is paying attention to us. Naturalistic skeptics would say that prayer is only autosuggestion or the projection, indeed the reflection of our desires and insecurities on the mirror of our own self-consciousness. In essence, what they are saying is that there is no one on the other end. However, I know that your and my experience of prayer is quite different. When you and I call, God does indeed answer. There is no "call waiting" or "voice mail"; the Spirit welcomes our requests and ushers them into the very presence of the Holy. God's Holy Spirit prays in us, with us, and for us. This is certainly what the Apostle Paul was alluding to in Romans 8:26. Praise God on this Pentecost Sunday for the privilege and power of prayer. It is truly more than a play thing!

Responsible and Responsive

"I beseech you therefore, brethren, by the mercies of God,
that ye present your bodies a living sacrifice,
holy, acceptable unto God, which is your reasonable service.
And be not conformed to this world:
but be ye transformed by the renewing of your mind,
that ye may prove what is that good, and acceptable,
and perfect, will of God."

(Romans 12:1-2)

The basic call initiated by God in grace to every believer presumes responsibility and responsiveness in those whose humanity, while fractured, flawed, finite and frail, maintain within the realm of time and space a bodily existence. Christian maturity is the process where the believer willfully receives the fullness of God in the body, soul and spirit as connection points between the Kingdom of God and this fleeting world. In particular, the human body is the domicile of human personality, but more importantly, it is the temple where the Holy Spirit takes up residence in every believer at the point of salvation and becomes the surpassing stimulus for authentic growth, maturity and spiritual production.

Through holy obedience and submission to the leading of the indwelling Spirit, the believer glorifies God in body, soul and spirit, which is the outward manifestation of an inward transformation. Therefore, in the Christian life, God does not just want to do something through and with us, but God wants to do something in us. The Christian life is a life of perpetual surrender to God's Spirit. This daily surrender and submission in the life of the individual believer is the foundation of the church's ministry — which is nothing less than our desire to reach out and up to God and through him to other people.

A Sure and Steady Foundation

**"According to the grace of God which is given unto me,
as a wise masterbuilder, I have laid the foundation,
and another buildeth thereon.
But let every man take heed how he buildeth thereupon.
For other foundation can no man lay than that is laid,
which is Jesus Christ."
(I Corinthians 3:10-11)**

A few weeks ago, while visiting a small rural church that had recently completed a new addition, I experienced a surprising insight. The new annex at this church, consisting of a fellowship hall, additional classroom and bathrooms, was attached to the original structure. The deacon who was giving me the tour also served as chairman of the building committee. His excitement and joy over the expansion of their facility left no doubt that it was a major accomplishment for their small, yet historic, congregation. When we came to the place where the two buildings were joined, I noticed that a significant part of the wall of the older structure had to be moved to accommodate the new construction. I asked my guide and host, "Was this a load bearing wall?" He responded by saying that it was. While I make no boast of being accomplished or adept in the science of building construction, Basic Construction 101 teaches that any disturbance or disruption of a load bearing wall in a construction project must be done with care and caution.

According to Matthew 16:18, The Lord Jesus Christ has built His church on a sure and steady foundation. This foundation is none other than the crucified and risen Lord Himself and is unshakeable and unmovable. The superstructure of the church consists of the apostles and others who served after them, who came to believe on the Lord through their word. You and I are included in this vast chorus spanning the generations of the church, because Jesus said, "And for their sakes I sanctify myself, that they also might be sanctified through the truth. Neither pray I for these alone, but for them also which shall believe on me through their word" (John 17:19-20). It is apparent that the teaching of the apostles or the "apostles' doctrine" was primary to the growth of the early church. The Bible records that after the Day of Pentecost, "They continued steadfastly in the apostles' doctrine and fellowship and in breaking of bread, and in prayers" (Acts 2:42). Every component of this compelling agenda constituted a spiritual "load bearing wall" in the life of the early church. Fellowship, doctrinal integrity, worship, prayer and praying were essential to the church's growth, then and now.

As the church faces the growing challenge of confronting new realities in our contemporary culture and world, we must be careful that we do not destroy, distort or diminish the "load bearing walls" that bear the weight, worth and wealth of our worship, witness and work as a community of faith. Compromise and complicity with the forces at work in our culture that would undermine the church's historic commitment to the biblical model of marriage and family is an example of the challenges we face today. How sobering then the ancient yet timeless warning and witness of the psalmist who asked, "If the foundations be destroyed, what can the righteous do?" (Psalm 11:3). The Bible answers the very question it raises! What are we to do? The Apostle Paul said it best: "Therefore, my beloved brethren, be ye stedfast, unmoveable, always abounding in the work of the Lord, forasmuch as ye know that your labour is not in vain in the Lord" (I Corinthians 15:58).

In the Shadow of the Cross

"What? know ye not that your body
is the temple of the Holy Ghost which is in you,
which ye have of God, and ye are not your own?
For ye are bought with a price:
therefore glorify God in your body,
and in your spirit, which are God's."
(I Corinthians 6:19-20)

The Apostle Paul begins his epic and magnificent letter to the Romans with a salutation that was designed to establish his apostolic credentials and credibility. (See Romans 1:1-6.) Paul identified himself as a servant, called to be an apostle and separated unto the gospel of God. The term "servant" translates the word in the New Testament for *bond slave*. Such a person was absolutely committed to his or her master during their lifetime. The word *called* expresses the apostle's understanding that he was selected to his sacred office because of the sovereign activity of God and not for any merit of his own. "Separated" translates a word that means literally *off the horizon*. Paul was moved from one sphere of service (a servant to sin) to another sphere or horizon (a servant of God).

These verses are applicable to those who serve in the church today. We too must establish a credible and contagious apologetic to those who are outside the veil of Christ. (See I Peter 3:15.) This is accomplished by consistent Christian living, prayer, the study of the Word of God, development of an intimate personal relationship with God, and the sacrifice and commitment that is such an essential part of Christian ministry. It is no wonder, the bridge that separates the great doctrinal sections of the letter to the Romans and the practical and life application sections begins with these words: "I beseech you therefore, brethren, by the mercies of God, that ye present your bodies a living sacrifice, holy, acceptable unto God, which is your reasonable service" (Romans 12:1).

During the observance of the Lord's Supper, it is appropriate, indeed essential that we examine ourselves in the shadow of the Cross. We must view sin as the ominous and awful thing it is; in order to be expiated, it necessitated nothing less than the death of the perfect Son of God on an ignominious cross. Our salvation, sanctification and glorification have been secured at a great cost. The shadow of that cross should encourage reflective humility.

Christian Preaching

"For though I preach the gospel,
I have nothing to glory of:
for necessity is laid upon me;
yea, woe is unto me, if I preach not the gospel!"
(I Corinthians 9:16)

What is preaching? Who is the preacher? What is the place and purpose of preaching in the history of the church and the development of community and nation? According to Albert Mohler, Jr., President of Southern Baptist Theological Seminary, preaching begins and ends with God. Hence, preaching is a divine transaction and theocentric in origin, history and destiny. Preaching is not optional for the church of Jesus Christ but obligatory. Preaching is the communication of the great imperative indicatives of our faith.

The reality of the Christ event is so resilient and redemptive that failure to communicate it is tantamount to sin. Preaching is an audacious proclamation that springs from the authoritative pronouncements of a sovereign, all-powerful God to a broken world. Furthermore, this God, eternally bent on communicating with a fallen race, has spoken definitively and with finality in and through His Son, who is the brightest star in the constellation of revelation. (See John 14:6; Acts 4:12.)

In Christian preaching, Jesus is posited and proclaimed with exclusivity. He is the preeminent and paramount symbol who redemptively embraces human sin and suffering in order to reveal God's incomparable glory in the midst of brokenness and bewilderment. What makes preaching unique is that it is distinctively and exclusively Christological. God perpetuates this awesome message by commandeering fractured, finite and frail humans, illuminating our hearts and heads by His Spirit so that we might hear and herald the Gospel. God is both the ground and glory of preaching. Preaching is sacred business faithfully ascribing glory to the Father who speaks, the Son who saves, and the Spirit who sanctifies. No wonder the Apostle Paul said, "For the preaching of the cross is to them that perish foolishness; but unto us which are saved it is the power of God" (I Corinthians 1:18).

The Undeniable Echo

"For though I preach the gospel,
I have nothing to glory of:
for necessity is laid upon me;
yea, woe is unto me, if I preach not the gospel!
For if I do this thing willingly, I have a reward:
but if against my will,
a dispensation of the gospel is committed unto me."

(I Corinthians 9:16-17)

Christian ministry is not a vocational decision made merely in the context of one's own desires and abilities, but is a supernatural call that interrupts and invades one's experience that is both compelling and irresistible. Whatever we do for Jesus Christ and the advance of His Kingdom must be bolstered by an unshakable sense that God has spoken to us in the deep places of the heart, creating the very desire that only He can satisfy. The Apostle Paul said, "For it is God which worketh in you both to will and to do of his good pleasure" (Philippians 2:13).

Therefore, we do not minister to be seen or heard, or to receive the approval of others, but rather because God has placed within us the undeniable echo of His own essence. How challenging the words of the great hymn, "A charge to keep I have, a God to glorify, Who gave his Son my soul to save, and fit it for the sky. To serve the present age, my calling to fulfill, Oh may it all my powers engage to do my Master's will."

A Marathon Mindset

**"Know ye not that they which run in a race run all,
but one receiveth the prize? So run, that ye may obtain."**

(I Corinthians 9:24)

Recently I've encountered more than one person who has indicated that they are training for or participating in marathons. The thought of running for twenty-six miles non-stop makes me want to repent in sackcloth and ashes and spend forty days in prayer and fasting. Seriously though, influenced and infiltrated of late by this "marathon mentality", I recently shared with another pastor in Houston, Texas during the marriage of my daughter's best friend that marriage is at best a "monogamous marathon". There are hills to climb, valleys to go through, fertile fields, flowered gardens and even stretches of parched earth and rugged terrain through which we must travel and traverse until "death do us part". Surprisingly, he told me that he would never forget that description.

However, upon reflection, it occurs to me that all of God's children are marathoners. Of course, our churches have their fair share of "dashers" who on any given Sunday make their weekly worship dash (some even before the service is over). They are not seen again until the following Sunday when the ritual is repeated. In essence though, the Christian life requires persistence and perseverance. Truly, the race is not given to the swift or the strong, but to the one who endures unto the end. Eugene Peterson, the author of <u>The Message</u>, a refreshing paraphrase of the Word of God, also has an excellent commentary on the Psalms. He gave it the searching title, <u>A Long Obedience in the Same Direction - Discipleship in An Instant Society</u>. The title of this book is an excellent description of Phase 2 (the believer in time) of the Christian life. It is this same mentality that drives the Apostle Paul and encourages him to write, "Brethren, I count not myself to have apprehended; but this one thing I do, forgetting those things which are behind, and reaching forth unto those things which are before, I press toward the mark of the high prize of the calling of God in Christ Jesus" (Philippians 3:13-14).

Isn't it interesting that one of the more popular salt substitutes is called "Mrs. Dash"? This is insightful to me in light of the fact that the church and every believer are called to be the salt of the earth. In the Sermon on the Mount, Jesus said, "Ye are the salt of the earth; but if the salt have lost his savour … it is thenceforth good for nothing, but to be cast out, and to be trodden under the foot of men" (Matthew 5:13). We season our surroundings through consistent demonstration of the truth with our lips and our lives. Salt substitutes simply won't do in this present age. Don't be a Mr. or Mrs. Dash, but run with patience the race that is set before you, looking unto Jesus, the Author and Finisher of our faith.

History is His-Story

"Now all these things happened unto them for ensamples: and they are written for our admonition, upon whom the ends of the world are come."

(I Corinthians 10:11)

The Swedish theologian Gustav Aulen described history as "the workshop of God". This insight sparked a collage of reflections in my heart and head regarding the significance of history from a Christian and spiritual viewpoint. First of all, I believe history fulfills a <u>descriptive function</u>. The retrospection and reflection that reported and recorded history encourages provides a framework for understanding and assessing past trends and events. Indeed, those who do not comprehend the past are destined to repeat it for good or for ill. The Wisdom writer said it best and with remarkable redundancy: "there is nothing new under the sun" (Ecclesiastes 1:19). For this reason, Moses reminded a new generation of Israelites (and us) of the danger of forgetting where the Lord had brought them from. (See Deuteronomy 6:10 -15.) He encouraged them to maintain tangible reminders of their pilgrimage and to share their faith stories and testimonies with their children.

History also has a <u>prescriptive function</u>. This is what the Apostle Paul had in mind when he wrote to the Corinthians, "Now all these things happened unto them for examples: and they are written for our admonition, upon whom the ends of the world are come" (I Corinthians 10:11). The great theologian Karl Barth would often say that serous preachers prepared their sermons with the Bible in one hand and the newspaper in the other. His point was that good preaching touches people where they are, and that past and current events are powerful incentives for the preacher truly committed to sharing a Word in "due season". In the Twenty-Third Psalm, David says, "He leadeth me in the path of righteousness for His name's sake" (vs. 3b). The phrase "paths of righteousness" is a beautiful word picture that describes one wagon traveling in tracks made by another that preceded it. Whose tracks are you following today? Is grace and mercy close behind?

Finally, I believe history has a <u>predictive function</u>. History points toward something, indeed SOMEONE who is greater than the sum of its collected parts and plots. History is God at work in time and space making history HIS-STORY. The late C.S. Lewis said, "History is the story written by the finger of God." History is nothing less than our communion and community with the Ideal Companion, in whom and by whom we live, move and have our very being. Jesus Christ controls history and is indeed the melody that transcends the discordant notes of our temporal existence. Jesus gives life meaning and assures us that while "now we see through a glass darkly, but THEN *(emphasis mine),* face to face" (I Cor. 13:12a).

Body Chemistry

**"For as the body is one, and hath many members,
and all the members of that one body,
being many, are one body: so also is Christ."**

(I Corinthians 12:12)

I have been helpfully haunted during the past few days while reflecting on the dynamics, indeed the imperative of Christian growth and maturity. This is the clear command of II Peter 3:18: "But grow in grace and in the knowledge of our Lord and Savior Jesus Christ, to him be glory both now and forever. Amen." How appropriate that these inspired words and this exhortation to grow emerge from the experience of one who was so uniquely challenged in this area. One cannot read the Gospels and not witness the struggles of the Apostle Peter to be more like Jesus. There were times when he succeeded and, at other times, he failed miserably. Isn't this reflective of our own experience as well?

While contemplating this critical issue in the Christian life, there is a sight and scene that continually recurs in my mind and imagination which I believe has relevance to our growth in the Lord and His likeness. Perhaps recounting the many blood samples that were taken during my recent hospitalization, in my mind's eye I see some microbiologist or laboratory technician peering through a powerful microscope and observing how healthy cells from a blood sample are both separating and coagulating in order to ensure the wellness and healthy growth of the subject. It occurs to me that even on the level of our essential biological functions as creatures made in the image of God, that cell separations are as important to our physical growth and well being as when cells come together or cohere.

In the Christian life, while God wants us to come together (coagulate) as a body of Christ in faith, hope and love, God also encourages our growth through separation. There are seasons in our life when the Lord takes us apart literally to Himself in order to deepen our dependence on Him and to encourage our appreciation of spiritual realities. God indeed breaks us (as a cut from a sharp instrument breaks the skin) so that He might bless us. During these unexpected separations, our faith is strengthened as we learn anew that God works all things according to the counsel of His will. You may be aware right now in a special way of God's presence experienced not so much in the unity and fellowship of the body of Christ, but rather in the trial and trauma of individual pain and suffering. Be encouraged that even in our separations God is at work in us to will and do of His good pleasure.

Biblical Hope

**"And now abideth faith, hope, charity, these three;
but the greatest of these is charity."**

(I Corinthians 13:13)

One of the prominent and persistent themes of the Old and New Testament is "hope." Hope is included in Paul's triumvirate of Christian virtues recorded in I Corinthians 13:13. At the heart of the Christian message is the belief that God is at work in this universe and in our lives with a determined resolved to redeem both creature and creation to Himself. Biblical hope presupposes a linear view of history. Life does have meaning. We are not going in circles but moving toward the consummation of God's purpose and plan. And because God is sovereign, no power or force in the universe can thwart or derail what God has prepared for those who love Him.

Biblical hope, however, is not passive resignation to some predetermined and distant end, but rather an active expectation that God is at work in the lives of His people right here and now. And while God is the ultimate arbiter of our destinies, our decisions do matter. The late Amy Carmichael said it well. She likens our walk with the Lord as an ascent toward a mountain summit. She said,

"Make us thy mountaineers We would not linger on the lower slope, Fill us afresh with hope, O God of hope."

Hope compels our ascent toward God. But the very hope that satisfies our deepest needs is itself a gift from God who creates in us the awareness that our tomorrows can be better than our yesterdays and our todays. There is no need to linger on the "lower slopes" of life in despair, disappointment or despondency.

"I." Witnesses

"And last of all he was seen of me also,
as of one born out of due time.
For I am the least of the apostles,
that am not meet to be called an apostle,
because I persecuted the church of God."
(I Corinthians 15:8-9)

The Word of God is clear that Jesus was seen by many witnesses after His glorious resurrection from the dead. According to I Corinthians 15:5-11, the Lord was seen by Peter and the apostles, five hundred disciples at once, and then by Saul, the persecutor of the church who became the Apostle Paul. These "eyewitnesses" gave historical validity and credibility to the miraculous and stupendous claims associated with the empty tomb on that first Easter morning. "He is not here," the angel said, "He is arisen!" Undoubtedly, something had happened to them that was so marvelous and momentous that the apostles were transformed from timidly cowering in corners from the Jewish authorities to openly and boldly declaring the Gospel to anyone who would hear. Luke informs us in the opening words of the Book of Acts that "he (Jesus) shewed himself alive after his passion by many infallible proofs, being seen of them forty days, and speaking of the things pertaining to the kingdom of God" (Acts 1:3).

I am intrigued by the critical role of eyewitnesses in these accounts of our Lord's resurrection. I am reminded of how precious and how pivotal our testimonies are regarding our experiences with and relationship to the Lord and Savior Jesus Christ. Our ancestors sang, "I am a witness for my Lord, I am a witness for my Lord ... my soul is a witness for my Lord!" God is still in need of witnesses today; witnesses who can declare without reservation that, "Yes, God is real!" Such witnesses are not so much "eyewitnesses" as they are "I - witnesses." An "I — witness" is one who has a personal testimony and who is ready, willing and able to share it with others. An "I—witness" boldly declares, "This is my story and this is my song!" The Apostle

Peter, who tragically flunked his first "I—witness" test by denying the Lord three times, got it right and wrote these words: "But sanctify the Lord God in your hearts and be ready always to give an answer to every man that asketh you a reason of the hope that is in you with meekness and fear" (I Peter 3:15).

What a wonderful opportunity we have today to share the wonderful truths of the Gospel that "Jesus died, was buried and rose again the third day according to the Scriptures" (I Corinthians 15:1ff) with others who are experiencing difficulty, doubt and disappointment. I challenge each of you today to commit this week to sharing with at least one person an "I— witness" testimony of the goodness and the grace of God. You can do this not only with your lips but, more importantly, with your life as you demonstrate the truth of the words of the ancient hymn, "I serve a risen Savior, He's in the world today, I know that He is living, whatever men may say. I see His hand of mercy, I hear His voice of cheer, and just the time I need Him, He's always near. He lives, He lives, Christ Jesus lives today!"

Beyond the Grave

"And if Christ be not risen, then is our preaching vain,
and your faith is also vain.
Yea, and we are found false witnesses of God;
because we have testified of God that he raised up Christ:
whom he raised not up, if so be that the dead rise not."
(I Corinthians 15:14-15)

A few month ago while shopping at a discount book store I purchased a book, the title of which immediately caught my attention. While I didn't know the author (Dave Breese), the title was provocative - Seven Men Who Rule the World From the Grave. This book narrates the intellectual contributions of seven men whose ideas have changed the way we think about ourselves, others and the world around us. Charles Darwin, Karl Marx, Sigmund Freud and Julius Wellhausen are among those chronicled in this book. For many today, Charles Darwin's theory of evolution still challenges and critiques the biblical view of creation. Karl Marx's social and political theories are the philosophical foundations for communism. Sigmund Freud gave us the *id, ego,* and *super-ego* as a paradigm for looking within and understanding the human psyche. Julius Wellhausen's literary critique of the Old Testament, particularly the Pentateuch (Genesis, Exodus, Leviticus, Numbers and Deuteronomy), transformed the science of biblical interpretation, or hermeneutics, almost overnight.

While the information in this book was intriguing and it remains one of the favorites in my library, what really grasped and gripped me and encouraged my initial purchase was that the title agitated my thoughts in a helpful way in another direction as it relates to Christianity. While all the men whose contributions were annotated in the book are buried and dead, there remains One who is the hope of humanity and the supreme and superlative object of Christian faith who still rules the world from beyond the grave. The celebration of Resurrection Sunday accentuates the affirmation of the Apostle Paul who said, "And if

Christ be not risen, then is our preaching vain, and your faith is also vain ... if in this life only we have hope in Christ, we are of all men most miserable" (I Corinthians 15:17, 19).

Jesus got up from the grave because no power on earth could hold him down. He rules and super-rules this creation and is one day returning in glory to establish His kingdom on this planet. He has risen from the grave and He alone is Lord. While we can acknowledge with measured and critical respect the contributions of great men and women over the course of human history, none could ever compare to Jesus who is still making history "His-story". I pray that this is true of each of you on a personal basis; for only Jesus as our Savior and Lord is capable of meeting us and redeeming us beyond this veil of death and tears.

Bridging the Gap—
The Bible and the Newspaper

"Ye are our epistle written in our hearts,
known and read of all men:
"Forasmuch as ye are manifestly declared to be
the epistle of Christ ministered by us, written not with ink,
but with the Spirit of the living God; not in tables of stone,
but in fleshy tables of the heart."
(II Corinthians 3:2-3)

Karl Barth, the eminent German theologian, was fond of saying that every preacher should read and reflect with the Bible in one hand and the newspaper in the other. By doing so biblical principles would merge, meld, and marry practical applications and concerns in the lives of people. The result of course and implications for preaching is that the message shared would be both spiritually revealing and socially relevant.

In these trying and troubling days when so much effort is being expended in both the private and public sector to choose and charter paths and polices that will encourage economic stability in our nation and to formulate programs that are socially relevant and politically expedient, the church has an unprecedented opportunity to focus our nation's concerns on the moral imperatives that undergird every society. It is still true that "righteousness exalts a nation but sin is a reproach to any people" (Proverbs 14:34). However, to maximize and seize this moment, we must read the signs of the time with eyes wide open. In so many instances today, false securities have been stripped and ripped away from the lives of so many who based their ultimate confidence in position, privilege, prosperity and power. We have learned the truth of the words of the song that says, "'Today can be as bright as the noon day sun, but you can look up tomorrow and everything you have is gone!'

The daily newspaper when laid alongside the Bible encourages the recognition that there is "nothing new under the sun". The Bible is always contemporary because it speaks to needs and concerns that are timeless. For example, the drought that gripped Israel in an iron claw of recession and depression during the reign of Ahab is not much unlike the tenor of our own times. Ahab and Queen Jezebel had encouraged and officially sanctioned the worship of Baal in the northern Kingdom. God was displeased and, through the ministry of the prophet Elijah, providentially placed the heavens on atmospheric lock down. No rain had fallen for forty-two months. Yet, the prophet, sensitive to the spiritual drought in the hearts of the people, asked God for a demonstration of power, and fire fell down from heaven. (See I Kings 17–18.)

So many people are desperate today, searching for answers and in urgent need of a demonstration of power from on high. They should be able to look at the lives of those of us who claim to know the Lord and trust His Word and find help and hope in a time of need. We are, as the Apostle Paul said, "epistles [letters] … known and read of all men" (II Corinthians 3:2b). What do those around us see when they read the text of our lives? Can they see a real, sincere and consistent connection between what we say and what we do? We are God's newspapers; each of us a spiritual daily and diary that others may read and see in the light that shines from within, a living demonstration of a living Word. There is something more to life than money, sex and power. "Extra, extra, extra; read all about it!"

Leadership Is Influence

"Forasmuch as ye are manifestly declared to be
the epistle of Christ ministered by us, written not with ink,
but with the Spirit of the living God; not in tables of stone,
but in fleshy tables of the heart."

(II Corinthians 3:3)

Leadership is influence – nothing more and nothing less. There is a real sense in which every Christian is involved in leadership, for we have been called by God to be the salt of the earth and a light that is set upon a hill. Undoubtedly, we influence those who are in our periphery. The real question is whether our influence is positive or negative; whether others can see Christ living in us.

Those who aspire to be persons of influence must first be influenced themselves by the Spirit of God and the Indwelling Christ. The Apostle Paul understood that our lives must be a perpetual expression of the intimate relationship we share with the Lord Jesus Christ. He said, "I am crucified with Christ; nevertheless I live; yet not I, but Christ liveth in me; and the life which I now live in the flesh I live by the faith of the Son of God, who loved me, and gave himself for me" (Galatians 2:20).

Two of the greatest leaders of the Old Testament were Joshua and Caleb. Joshua and Caleb were selected by Moses to search out the land of Canaan along with ten others. Only these two brought back a good report. While the others discouraged the people greatly, they said, "If the Lord delight in us, then he will bring us into this land, and give it us; a land flowing with milk and honey (Numbers 14:8). A careful review of the lives of these two great leaders will reveal two things. Joshua was a leader that *never gave in* and Caleb was a leader that *never gave up*. (See Joshua 14:6-14; 24:14-16.)

What type of influence do you have in your home, the neighborhood, on your job and in the church? Does your presence inspire and encourage others? Positions do not make leaders and true leaders make straight paths to the Lord for themselves and others.

Fixing Our Affections

"Now the Lord is that Spirit:
and where the Spirit of the Lord is, there is liberty.
But we all, with open face beholding
as in a glass the glory of the Lord,
are changed into the same image from glory to glory,
even as by the Spirit of the Lord."

(II Corinthians 3:17-18)

My new sermon series is titled **The Seven Compelling C's of Christian Ministry** and is based on II Corinthians 3:17-4:12. In the first sermon we determined that the first "C" of Christian ministry, *Character*, is rooted in the progressive transformation of the believer by the Holy Spirit. This is primarily the result of intimacy with God in the vertical plane. It is what the late A. W. Tozer called in his devotional classic The Pursuit of God, "the gaze of the soul." Eugene Peterson in his book Working the Angles – The Shape of Pastoral Integrity describes it as "paying attention to God." While drawing a significant parallel between the experience of Moses on Mount Sinai and our own, the Apostle Paul said,"Now the Lord is that Spirit: and where the Spirit of the Lord is, there is liberty. But we all, with open face beholding as in a glass the glory of the Lord, are changed into the same image from glory to glory, even as by the Spirit of the Lord" (II Corinthians 3:17-18).

Needless to say, it is the ongoing challenge of the Christian life to fix our affections and sustain our attention on the Lord; humbly submitting to the inner working of God the Holy Spirit, whose aim is to transform us into the very likeness of our Lord and Savior. We are bombarded with distractions that disrupt and distort our view. The world, the flesh and the Devil constantly transmit images to, in and around us that are designed to literally jam our "sense and service of God", which is the nature of true worship. These fleeting and seductive images offer us the illusions of success without God, pleasure without God, and worship without God.

Only as we determine to look at Jesus and look to Jesus can we begin to experience the resolve and engage the resources that are fundamental to Christian ministry and the basis of blessing in the Christian life. The writer of the Book of Hebrews said it better than I ever could: "Wherefore seeing we also are compassed about with so great a cloud of witnesses, let us lay aside every weight, and the sin which doth so easily beset us, and let us run with patience the race that is set before us, **Looking unto Jesus** *[emphasis mine]* the author and finisher of our faith; who for the joy that was set before him endured the cross, despising the shame, and is set down at the right hand of the throne of God. For consider him that endured such contradiction of sinners against himself, lest ye be wearied and faint in your minds" (Hebrews 12:1-3). It is my fervent prayer that during the coming week of consecration that each of us will renew our gaze on the Lord and be changed, be renewed and be set free to worship, witness and work more authentically by His Spirit of truth.

The Unique God-Man

**"But if our gospel be hid, it is hid to them that are lost:
In whom the god of this world hath blinded the minds of
them which believe not, lest the light of the glorious gospel of
Christ, who is the image of God, should shine unto them."**

(II Corinthians 4:3-4)

Jesus Christ is the unique God-Man of human history. While His humanity was born in a stable in Bethlehem, from everlasting to everlasting He has always been the Son. With compelling specificity and clarity the prophets of old foretold the coming of the One who, being God Himself, would take away the sins of the world. During the Christmas season, amidst the maze and malaise of commercialism, it is easy to lose sight of the real reason we celebrate the season. When Jesus entered the world, the religious leadership of Israel failed to grasp His true essence. The Bible says, "He was in the world, and the world was made by him, and the world knew him not. He came unto his own, and his own received him not" (John 1:10-11). Israel's leadership was blinded by a zealous but misguided commitment to legalism and tradition.

The Apostle Paul reveals the fundamental and sinister reason for spiritual blindness as it relates to the thing of God. "But if our gospel be hid, it is hid to them that are lost; in whom the god of this world hath blinded the minds of them which believe not, lest the light of the glorious gospel of Christ who is the image of God, should shine unto them" (II Corinthians 4:3-4). No wonder Jesus would say to Nicodemus, "And this is the condemnation, that light is come into the world, and men loved darkness rather than light, because their deeds were evil" (John 3:19).

We must be vigilant in confessing and acknowledging any sin that keeps us from seeing the light of the glorious Gospel. Then we must ask God the Holy Spirit to illuminate within us the vision and view of the Son who is Wonderful, Counselor, the Mighty God, the Everlasting Father, and the Prince of Peace. (See Isaiah 9:6.)

A Becoming Proposal

"Therefore if any man be in Christ,
he is a new creature:
old things are passed away;
behold, all things are become new."
(II Corinthians 5:17)

The new sermon series on 2 Corinthians 5:17-21 is titled **"A Becoming Proposal."**. In Part 1 of the message we clarified terms, accentuated relevance, and addressed three areas in the text that make the Gospel a "becoming proposal". First, the Gospel is a becoming possibility. This is true because of the unprecedented inclusiveness packed in the phrase "if any man [literally, anyone] be in Christ" in verse 17 of the text. This is one of many texts in the Word of God that affirms and validates the open-endedness of the salvation afforded in a personal relationship with Jesus Christ. Secondly, the Gospel involves a becoming position. The Apostle Paul uses the phrase "in Christ" at least one hundred seventy times in the New Testament. What anointing and abiding is to the Apostle John, immersion in the person of Christ is to Paul. This constitutes a perpetual reminder in the Pauline writings that there is no essential or authentic being (existence) apart from Christ. The source of all true joy, hope, life and peace is "in Christ".

Finally, the Gospel represents a becoming progression. Old things are passed away and all things become new. The believer in Christ experiences new vistas and horizons of spiritual opportunity and growth. Indeed, he or she is a new species, for The Divine Assurance Adjuster has totaled the old you and me because the flesh is beyond repair or rehabilitation. Every good and perfect gift comes from God. We cannot please God in the flesh. The spiritual progress that begins in Christ and in time extends into eternity. God's ultimate goal is to make you and me a little Christ. This progressive process is at times painful, for some people change when they see the light while others of us change only when we feel the heat.

New Things

"Therefore if any man be in Christ,
he is a new creature:
old things are passed away;
behold, all things are become new."
(II Corinthians 5:17)

The original language of the New Testament is <u>Koine</u> <u>Greek</u>. It was the common vernacular of the people living at that time. I am sure one reason this language was chosen for the inspired writings of New Testament scriptures is its ability to express with compelling clarity the nuances and shades of meaning of biblical concepts and principles. One example is the word translated <u>new</u> in our Bibles. In II Corinthians 5:17, the Apostle Paul writes, "Therefore if any man be in Christ, he is a **new** creature: old things are passed away; all things become **new**." The word **new** occurs twice in this passage. However, Paul has something distinct and unique in mind for his readers. The word does not mean "new in time" (Greek *meos*) but rather "new in kind" (Greek *kainos*). Paul reminds the Corinthians that a relationship with Christ is not just something that happens in time, but rather an experience that brings about a different quality of life altogether.

I pray that your experience of this <u>New</u> Year is not just the passive observation of the procession of hours, days, weeks and months ahead, but something altogether new in quality and significance as you go further out and deeper down in the secret things of God. Isaiah encouraged Israel of old with this promise, "Behold, I will do a new thing, now it shall spring forth; shall you not know it? I will even make a road in the wilderness and rivers in the desert" (Isaiah 43:19). This is my prayer for each of you and this faith family in the coming year.

White Out

"For he hath made him to be sin for us, who knew no sin; that we might be made the righteousness of God in him."

(II Corinthians 5:21)

The first book of the Bible and the fourth Gospel have something in common. Both start with the word "beginning." The Hebrew of Genesis 1:1 and the Greek of John 1:1 is similar in that the word "beginning" literally means "a beginning that was not a beginning." These words stretch and strain to communicate a particular point in time and space when the eternal timelessness of God punctuated our existence in a unique and compelling way.

The God who transcends time and who created all that is by the power of His word, and the Word (or Logos) who in the person of Jesus Christ is face to face with God from eternity to eternity, is one and the same. Jesus Christ is the ultimate and quintessential revelation of God's grace and truth. He became flesh and dwelt among us and, through his life, offers to each of us the possibility of a fresh start and new beginning.

Even with the endless avalanche of word processing and publisher programs and software, I still find myself going old school and using a typewriter and white out. While ancient and antiquated to some, the white out or liquid paper allows me to cover my errors and, when it is dried, to replace it with the correct text. I keep an ample supply in my desk drawer. I use it often. I also use correction tape. A clear strip of tape (shiny side facing out) is placed over the incorrect letter or word and the appropriate key or keys are struck. The impact of the tape on the text already imprinted on the paper removes it from the document and allows the typist to replace it with the proper letter or word. Interestingly, upon observation, one can see the removed letter or word on the correction tape which now bears the error.

I celebrate with each of you the possibility of a fresh start and new beginning. Allow God to use His redemptive white out and the liquid paper of His grace and mercy on the unsightly blotches and unholy blemishes of our lives. As the light of God shines in our hearts (the shiny side is out today), recognize that our Lord and Savior Jesus Christ has absorbed the impact and received the penalty of our sins, "becoming sin for us that we might be made the righteousness of God in Him" (II Corinthians 5:21). He is the propitiation (mercy seat) of our sins; and not ours only, but the sins of the whole world. (See I John 2:1.) And every new beginning and every fresh start is already bound up in the never-ending existence of the One who is the same yesterday, today and forevermore.

Sticking the Landing — Truth and Traction

"(For the weapons of our warfare are not carnal,
but mighty through God
to the pulling down of strong holds;)
Casting down imaginations,
and every high thing that exalteth itself
against the knowledge of God,
and bringing into captivity every thought
to the obedience of Christ."

(II Corinthians 10:4-5)

In Proverbs 29:18, King Solomon offered timeless wisdom: "Where there is no vision, the people perish: but he that keepeth the law, happy is he." The late Dr. Stephen Olford called this principle "spiritual acuity". Acuity has to do with awareness, alertness or the ability to maintain a proper perspective regarding the things around us. The dearth or distortion of this quality in a leader will doom and diminish the strivings of any institution or, for that matter, any relationship. For almost three decades now as a pastor-teacher, I have embraced and encouraged the consistent inculcation (intake) of divine viewpoint or Bible doctrine through the study of the Word of God as the primary means and mode of encouraging spiritual acuity or alertness. The Word of God sharpens our vision and heightens our awareness of the things of God. And the Word of God shades, shields and shelters us from the persistent and pernicious assaults of our culture, the human viewpoint that "exalts itself against the knowledge of God" (II Corinthians 10:5a).

Recently, I was reflecting on the findings of a Cambridge University funded study that surprisingly revealed how bumble bees are very selective and intentional about the flower petals on which they choose to land. While some flower petals are smooth and slippery, others are comprised of cone-shaped cells that give the petals a kind of Velcro-like traction that allows bees searching for nectar and honey to stick their landing. Bees instinctively choose to land on the latter. The advantage for the bees is the ability (because of a more efficient landing) to access the honey in the flower more quickly. The advantage for the flower is that pollination by the bees (carrying flower seeds to other areas) is significantly enhanced. This article somehow reminded me anew that the local church has an urgent responsibility to provide a learning environment conducive to the creation of spiritual traction (or acuity) so that we can "stick our landings" in life and access the honey of God's Word. When this becomes a reality, the possibility of pollination is significantly enhanced, not only in the heart and mind of the child of God, but in marriage, the home, our communities and ultimately in our world. Spiritual traction keeps us from "being conformed to the world but rather transformed by the renewing of our minds" (Romans 12:1-3). Remember when the apostles in the early church made the preaching and teaching of the Word of God a priority, the Bible reports that "The word of God increased; and the number of disciples multiplied in Jerusalem greatly; and a great company of the priests were obedient to the faith" (Acts 6:7)

In his commentary on Proverbs 29:18, Stephen Olford argues that vision inspires venture. I believe that without vision, we only have vacuum (emptiness) and vanity (self-absorption). However, when there is vision, there will not only be venture (faith perception), but vigilance (attention to and mastery of the details of life), victory (conquest), value (significance) and validation (purpose in life). These are the attributes that determine whether we are casualties (constantly missing our landings in life) or conquerors (experiencing the traction that allows us to access the truth, or "honey", of God's Word) in victorious Christian living, effective and expanding Christian witness in this world that is so in need of the Gospel of grace.

Undertow

"For the flesh lusteth against the Spirit,
and the Spirit against the flesh:
and these are contrary the one to the other:
so that ye cannot do the things that ye would."

(Galatians 5:17)

Phase Two of the Christian life (the believer in time) involves primarily the transformation of the believer into the image of Christ by the renewing of the mind. While progressive in nature, we have the hope that this process will be completed when we see Jesus face to face. This is the essence of John's reference in I John 3:1-2. "Behold, what manner of love the Father hath bestowed upon us, that we should be called the sons of God: therefore the world knoweth us not, because it knew him not. Beloved, now are we the sons of God, and it doth not yet appear what we shall be: but we know that, when he shall appear, we shall be like him; for we shall see him as he is." However, just as Satan and the legions of evil opposed Jesus as He in Phase One (redemption) secured our salvation through His vicarious suffering and death on the Cross, we too face cosmic contention and demonic assault as we seek to be made in His likeness.

As I think of this sobering reality, I'm reminded of my work years ago as a high school student during a summer internship with the U. S. Coast Guard. I remember even now the trauma and tragedy of looking for the bodies of drowning victims in the Kentucky River basin. Many of those who drowned were excellent swimmers but were carried under the waters by what the Guardsmen called an "undertow." I learned that an undertow is a swift current under the surface of the waters that runs in the opposite direction with as great a force as the current on the surface. Some areas of the river were posted "off limits" so swimmers would be aware of the danger. In the spiritual life there is an undertow as well. Could this be what the Apostle Paul was thinking about when he wrote, "For I know that in me (that is, in my flesh,) dwelleth no good thing: for to will is present with me; but how to perform that which is good I find not. For the good that I would I do not: but the evil which I would not, that I do" (Romans 7:17-19). (Compare Galatians 5:17.)

The old sin nature (OSN) does not cooperate with us as we seek to be more like Jesus; rather, it is a subtle, seductive and sinister current that runs in the other direction. Coupled with the "pull of the world" and Satan himself, every believer experiences this undertow. However, the good news is, if you have been saved, washed in the blood of Christ, and indwelt by God's Holy Spirit, nothing can separate you from the love of God in Christ. You nor I will be a victim of drowning, for God has placed within us His Spirit which is not only the earnest of His inheritance until the day of redemption, but a spiritual flotation device that prevents us from being pulled under by the currents of sin and evil. While we may feel as if we are drowning sometimes in our trials, temptations and tribulations, the truth of the matter is that God is in control and will never allow us to be pulled under by life's swift and uncertain currents.

The Church — Visible and Invisible

"For this cause I Paul,
the prisoner of Jesus Christ for you Gentiles,
If ye have heard of the dispensation of the grace of God
which is given me to you-ward:
How that by revelation he made known unto me the mystery;
(as I wrote afore in few words)"
(Ephesians 3:1-3)

The church exists in this dispensation in both invisible and visible manifestations. The invisible church will be unveiled at the Rapture. The visible church includes both born again and unsaved elements; for in this age both wheat and tares grow together, and everyone that says "Lord, Lord" shall not enter into the Kingdom of Heaven. The invisible church is a perfect organism. The visible church is an imperfect organism. There are no perfect churches on this side of glory. You become a member of the invisible church by Spirit baptism. (See I Corinthians 12:13.) This occurs the moment a person accepts Jesus Christ as their personal Savior. One way to become a member of the visible church is water baptism. Water baptism is a ritual that symbolizes the reality of an inward change.

Jesus Christ is the unrivaled head of the invisible church. He was declared to be so with power after His resurrection from the dead. (See Romans 1:3-4.) Pastors after God's own heart are called to give spiritual leadership and nurture to the visible church. The invisible church is one true church that transcends culture, ethnicity, race, social and economic status and gender. The visible church is multicultural, multiethnic, multiracial and irrespective of gender. The church of the Lord Jesus Christ was a hidden mystery in the Old Testament. The prophets of old saw the suffering of Christ and His return to the earth in glory, but not revealed truth about the Age of the Church. (See I Peter 1:10-11; Ephesians 3:1ff.) Mystery in the Bible has to do with the truth that cannot be apprehended by unassisted natural intellect, but is disclosed only by divine revelation.

The church is the Body of Christ on Earth and will be the Bride of Christ in glory. I'm excited to be a part of the ministry and historic faith legacy of this church. But I have even greater joy and confidence in knowing that I am a member of the one true church of which Jesus is the Head. This church is being adorned even now to meet Jesus in the air. Oh what a day of rejoicing that will be! Are you going to be in that number when all the saints of the ages make it home?

Walking

**"I therefore, the prisoner of the Lord,
beseech you that ye walk worthy of the vocation
wherewith ye are called"**

(Ephesians 4:1)

One of the Apostle Paul's favorite metaphors for the Christian life is walking. This is certainly true in the Book of Ephesians where the word "walk' or its derivatives is used seven times. (See Ephesians 2:2, 10; 4:1, 17; 5:2, 8, 17.) The parallels are thought provoking. The physical act of walking requires balance, coordination, maturity, and strength. It also involves progressive advance (unless you are walking in place, of course). Pace varies with the person involved and must be adjusted to the terrain one traverses. All these concepts have relevance for the life of the believer in Phase 2 of the Christian life, which is the "believer in time."

Perhaps one of the most suggestive applications of the metaphor is that walking is often experienced in the context of companionship. Enoch walked with God and their paths became so intimately intertwined that one day God just took him. (See Genesis 5:24.) The prophet Amos exhorted his audience with these challenging words: "Can two walk together, except they be agreed?" (Amos 3:3). David encouraged himself in the Lord by assenting that, "Yea, though I walk through the valley of the shadow of death, I will fear no evil: for thou art with me; thy rod and thy staff they comfort me" (Psalm 23:4).

One of the most memorable sermons in the history of the Christian church was preached by Timothy Dwight [1752-1817]. He was the grandson of the great revivalist preacher Jonathan Edwards and one of the first presidents of Yale University. The title of the message was *"Each Man's Life a Plan of God."* The biblical text was John 21:18-23. While encountering this riveting message anew I thought of Shakespeare's immortal words, "There is a divinity that shapes our end, rough hew them how we will!" This is exactly the resonating theme in Psalm 37:23-25: "The steps of a good man are ordered by the LORD: and he delighteth in his way. Though he fall, he shall not be utterly cast down: for the LORD upholdeth him with his hand. I have been young, and now am old; yet have I not seen the righteous forsaken, nor his seed begging bread."

Be encouraged today that God is leading us, and as we walk toward the glorious light of His presence, He will not suffer our foot to be moved and will watch our going out and coming in not only today but forevermore. (See Psalm 121.) Our ancestors said it best when they sang, "Walk with me Lord, walk with me ... all along my pilgrim journey, I want Jesus to walk with me!"

Communication Gifts

"And he gave some, apostles; and some, prophets;
and some, evangelists; and some, pastors and teachers;
For the perfecting of the saints, for the work of the ministry,
for the edifying of the body of Christ."

(Ephesians 4:11-12)

The church, the body of called-out believers during this dispensation, exists in a unique relationship to the Lord. While described as the body of Christ on earth, the church will be the bride of Christ when the Lord returns. The church consists of all Spirit baptized believers saved from the Day of Pentecost until the Rapture. Those who are members of the church are not only saved but are being progressively transformed into the image and likeness of Christ. Fundamental to this process is the sanctifying ministry of the Holy Spirit and the spiritual vitality and nourishment provided by the Word of God.

During the period the church waits for the Lord's return, communication gifts have been provided to the church for the "perfecting of the saints, for the work of the ministry for the edifying of the body of Christ." These gifts are apostle, prophet, evangelist, and pastor-teacher. Since the completion of the New Testament canon, the primary active gifts are evangelist and pastor-teacher. The evangelist helps the church grow larger through preaching of the Gospel. The pastor-teacher helps the church grow deeper through the teaching and assimilation of Bible doctrine.

Spiritual Drift

**"That we henceforth be no more children, tossed to and fro,
and carried about with every wind of doctrine,
by the sleight of men, and cunning craftiness,
whereby they lie in wait to deceive."**

(Ephesians 4:14)

Ships that are rudderless, not properly anchored in the harbor, lacking an accurate compass or missing a skilled navigator at the helm, risk drift and collision. In much the same way, spiritual drift is also a danger to the believer. On the sea of life, we can drift, losing both purpose and perspective if our minds and hearts are not properly fixed on Jesus, occupied with the Word of God, and guided by the Holy Spirit. There are many distractions in life that can cause us to lose our focus and drift into the tempestuous and treacherous waters of disillusionment, moral failure, disappointment, frustration, bitterness and hopelessness. In such waters, we risk the shipwreck of our faith and can easily run aground in the shallow waters of spiritual collapse.

Spiritual drift can be avoided by the continued application of some powerful and proven principles. First, we must have **a renewed commitment to worship God** with praise and thanksgiving. When we worship God, we are fulfilling our highest destiny. "Thou art worthy, O Lord, to receive glory and honour and power; for thou hast created all things, for thy pleasure they are and were created" (Revelation 4:11).

Secondly, we must **renew our concentration and contemplation of the Word of God**. As we do this, we are "transformed by the renewing of our mind that we might prove the good, acceptable and perfect will of God." (See Romans 12:1-2.) As we focus on God's Word, we develop a greater capacity to align our wills with His will.

Finally, spiritual drift can be avoided when we **relinquish control of our lives to the Holy Spirit**. Jesus said, "Howbeit when he, the Spirit of truth is come, he will guide you into all truth: for he shall not speak of himself; but whatsoever he shall hear, that shall he speak and he will shew you things to come" (John 16:13). The Holy Spirit is the internal compass that every believer receives at the point of salvation.

If you feel that your life (ship) has moved off course and is drifting, return to Jesus, the Captain and Anchor of our souls, and let Him take complete control of your vessel.

Mastering the Details

"But ye have not so learned Christ;
If so be that ye have heard him,
and have been taught by him, as the truth is in Jesus:
That ye put off concerning the former conversation the old man,
which is corrupt according to the deceitful lusts;
And be renewed in the spirit of your mind;
And that ye put on the new man,
which after God is created
in righteousness and true holiness."

(Ephesians 4:20-24) .

The experience and enjoyment of financial prosperity and blessing is directly related to our ability to orient to and master the details of life. This requires the accumulation of residual Bible doctrine in the soul of the believer in order that the capacity to make decisions (volitional responsibility) can be strengthened. (See Ephesians 4:20-24.) Failure is not a *destination* but rather a *journey*, the result of many choices made from a position of weakness.

Either we master the details of life — relationship, jobs, and necessity issues — or they master us. Gaining and retaining Bible doctrine in our souls allows us to view our circumstances from God's viewpoint. The great Apostle Paul reminded the Corinthians that they had the very *mind of Christ*. (See I Corinthians 2:16.) As we deploy the mind of Christ (the very Word of God) in our situations, we experience the Life Principle (Zoe) that Jesus, the Good Shepherd promises in John 10:10. "The thief cometh not, but for to steal, and kill and to destroy; I am come that they might have life and that they might have it more abundantly."

Failure to orient to the Plan of God and Bible Doctrine results in a frantic search for happiness in all the wrong places. Adversity in life is converted to stress in the soul as a result of the failure to apply the Word of God to the details of life. (See Matthew 4:4; Hebrews 4:1-2.)

A Father's Instruction

"Children, obey your parents in the Lord: for this is right.
Honour thy father and mother;
which is the first commandment with promise;
That it may be well with thee,
and thou mayest live long on the earth.
And, ye fathers, provoke not your children to wrath:
but bring them up in the nurture and admonition of the Lord."

(Ephesians 6:1-4)

A man who was the president of a very large construction company was asked the question, "When you are thinking of hiring an employee - - especially a man - - what do you look for?" His answer was "I look primarily at the relationship between the man and his father. If he felt loved by his dad and respected his authority, he's likely to be a good employee." Then he said, "I won't hire a young man who has been in rebellion against his dad. He will have difficulty with me too."

This response and a myriad of other possible references point to the critical importance of the father's role in the family. Solomon emphasized the importance of the father's role when he wrote:

Hear, ye children, the instruction of a father, and attend to know understanding. For I give you good doctrine, forsake ye not my law. For I was my father's son, tender and only beloved in the sight of my mother. He taught me also, and said unto me, Let thine heart retain my words: keep my commandments, and live. (Proverbs 4:1-4)

The alarming breakdown of the family and the emotional and spiritual fragmentation that contributes to the troubling tide of violence, drug abuse, early sexual activity and other forms of rebellious behavior in so many of our youth can be traced to the fundamental tragedy of fathers who have either abandoned their children or forfeited their role as priest and spiritual leader in the marriage and home. Every Christian father should with a sense of urgency seize every opportunity to relate to our children and to teach them about our faith. We should never become so distracted by career or other concerns that we become virtual strangers in the home. The memories we sow in the hearts of our children today will be the harvest that impacts their lives for years to come.

Under Attack

"Put on the whole armour of God,
that ye may be able to stand against the wiles of the devil.
For we wrestle not against flesh and blood,
but against principalities, against powers,
against the rulers of the darkness of this world,
against spiritual wickedness in high places."

(Ephesians 6:11-12)

Many believers live from day to day totally unaware of the spiritual conflict that wages around them. I find it quite remarkable that the Apostle Paul launches a discussion in this arena in the Book of Ephesians after an extended treatment of marriage, parent-child relationships and servant-master (employee-employer) dynamics. (See Ephesians 5:18-6:9.) Upon reflection, however, the connection is apparent. The enemy always attacks us at our points of vulnerability. He focuses his assaults on those aspects of our lives where we invest the most time, concern and passion. If he can create confusion and chaos in these areas, then he will preempt our ability to access the spiritual resources and reserves that God has already laid up for us in heavenly places.

The devil is no fool! He relentlessly assails us at those points where failure and frustration can impact our spiritual walk, negate the filling of the Holy Spirit, and disrupt our fellowship with Christ and the Church. His volleys are deviously and diabolically designed to cloud our prayers, compromise our praise and cripple our proclamation of the Truth as it has been revealed in Jesus Christ. Therefore, it is imperative and urgent that we heed Paul's instructions: "Be strong in the Lord, and in the power of his might. Put on the whole armor of God, that ye may be able to stand against the wiles of the devil."

God's Blueprint for the Church

"Paul and Timotheus, the servants of Jesus Christ,
to all the saints in Christ Jesus which are at Philippi,
with the bishops and deacons: Grace be unto you, and peace,
from God our Father, and from the Lord Jesus Christ."

(Philippians 1:1-2)

Philippians 1:1 is a remarkable biblical passage and a uniquely revealing description of the structure and leadership of the local church. This passage reminds us that the church has design, order and structure. To disregard or disrespect this is to the detriment of any local congregation.

The church consists first of all of saints. Sainthood is not a status granted after death, but it is the result of the glorious union of believer's life with the life of the Lord Jesus Christ. (See II Corinthians 5:17.) While our position in Christ is secure, because of the presence of the old sin nature, we still have "sinner's problems". The word "saints" in this text validates the called-out, set-apart nature of membership in the New Testament church. (See I Peter 2:9-10.)

The church also consists of "overseers'. This is one of the words used in the New Testament to describe the office and function of the pastor-teacher. The pastor gives spiritual oversight to the local congregation. (See Hebrews 13:7, 17.) This authority is God-given and is the essential basis for teaching, preaching and leading the congregation, and "for the perfecting of the saints, for the work of the ministry for the edifying of the body of Christ" (Ephesians 4:12). (See also Acts 20:28.) The apostle greets the church by identifying himself and Timothy as "servants of Christ Jesus." The word translated "servants" means (literally) bond slave and describes one who gives himself up to another's will and who is devoted to another to the disregard of one's own interests. While the gift of pastor-teacher functions in the local church, it is a gift to the whole church of which Jesus Christ is the head.

Finally, the passage reminds us that even during the infancy of the church, deacons functioned as servants in the church to assist and encourage pastors in accordance with Acts 6:1-8. The word translated deacon is the Greek *diakanos* and means "to run on errands"; it identifies one who executes the commands of another, especially of a master. The apostle reminds faithful deacons in I Timothy 3: 13, "For they that have used the office of a deacon well purchase to themselves a good degree, and great boldness in the faith which is in Christ Jesus.

The Greatest Soldier of All!

And being found in fashion as a man, he humbled himself,
and became obedient unto death, even the death of the cross.
Wherefore God also hath highly exalted him,
and given him a name which is above every name:
That at the name of Jesus every knee should bow,
of things in heaven, and things in earth,
and things under the earth;
And that every tongue should confess
that Jesus Christ is Lord,
to the glory of God the Father."

(Philippians 2:8-11)

Memorial Day was originally known as Decoration Day because it was a time set aside to honor the nation's Civil War dead by decorating their graves. It was first widely observed on May 30, 1868, to commemorate the sacrifices of Civil War soldiers. An order was issued stating, "The 30th of May, 1868, is designated for the purpose of strewing with flowers, or otherwise decorating the graves of comrades who died in defense of their country during the late rebellion, and whose bodies now lie in almost every city, village, and hamlet churchyard in the land. In this observance no form of ceremony is prescribed, but posts and comrades will in their own way arrange such fitting services and testimonials of respect as circumstances may permit."

When Memorial Day is observed, a special ceremony is held at Arlington National Cemetery in our nation's capitol during which a small American flag is placed on each grave. Also, it is customary for the President or Vice-president to give a speech honoring the contributions of the dead and lay a wreath at the Tomb of the Unknown Soldier. It is estimated that about 5,000 people attend the ceremony annually. A few years ago while visiting Washington, D.C., my wife and I had the opportunity to witness the meticulous and methodical changing of the guard at this tomb. The sacredness and solemnity of the moment did not escape either of us or others who stood in silent tribute and veneration. However, I was moved then and now to think about the experience of the Apostle Paul who, while ministering in Athens, passed by and beheld an altar with the inscription, **"TO THE UNKNOWN GOD."** This observation prompted and propelled one of the most memorable sermons in the Apostle's stellar apostolic career. He said to the skeptical and cynical philosophers that made up the audience on that day, "Whom therefore ye ignorantly worship, Him declare I unto you... For in Him we live, and move, and have our being" (Acts 17:23-28).

In a culture increasingly permeated with doubt, the Church and every Christian has an unprecedented opportunity to declare Him, the Savior of all mankind who will one day judge this world of ours, from every rooftop. The greatest soldier of all is not UNKNOWN, nor are His remains encased in an unmarked tomb; but He came to this planet over two thousand years ago, bled and died on an old rugged cross and was resurrected on the third day in majesty and glory with all power in His hands! He is the Unrivalled and Supreme Commander of the forces of good, and has been highly exalted, decorated and given a name which is above every name. And "at the name of Jesus every knee shall bow and every tongue shall confess that He is Lord, to the glory of God our Father" (Philippians 2:9-11). During this weekend, as we remember the sacrifices of loved ones and a multitude of others who paid the ultimate sacrifice to defend our freedom and insure our liberty at home and abroad, let's not ever forget the most compelling Combatant of all who defeated death and the grave and even now is making His (and our) enemies His footstool!

Spiritual "Pick-Me-Up."

**"I know both how to be abased, and I know how to abound:
every where and in all things I am instructed
both to be full and to be hungry,
both to abound and to suffer need.
I can do all things through Christ which strengtheneth me."**

(Philippians 4:12-13)

A few weeks ago, an installment of the cartoon **"Hagar the Horrible."** caught my attention. It shows Hagar, the boisterous Viking, retreating to the cellar of his house in response to the relentless chastening of his wife Helga who is complaining that he "get in here and pick up all the clothes you threw on the floor." In the next frame of the cartoon, Hagar is in the cellar filling a mug from a tap in a whiskey keg stored there. He says, **"I always say if you have to "pick up." it's important to have a little "pick-me-up." beforehand."**

While I found this humorous, it was also quite revealing as it made me ponder the challenges and responsibilities we face as believers. Difficulties abound in the Christian life; some we experience as a result of the actions or attitudes of others, and some because of our own sin and disobedience. Others are beyond our control. We incur and endure them because of the pains and perils that are part and parcel of life. Sometimes it's difficult to pick up the pieces lying tattered and shattered around us. We too need a "little pick-me-up" to get us through the day or the situation.

I have found (and perhaps you too) my spiritual help, yes my "pick-me-up", in various places. There are times that it emerges as a starburst of insight from prayerful reflection on a biblical text during a period of private and personal devotion. Sometimes it is encapsulated in the kind and encouraging words of a dear friend. There are also times during worship, while hearing a song or listening to a testimony, that something uplifting and strengthening resonates and rings deep down in the chords of my soul and spirit. As a pastor, there are times I've experienced a "pick-me- up" during a moment of profound insight while ministering to others in need. How encouraging it is to witness firsthand the merciful and miraculous mystery of the Divine at work in the trenches and tracks of human pain and suffering, proving beyond all doubt that God is able.

Unfortunately, so often in life, people and even those who call themselves Christians are looking for help and support in the wrong places; shallow kegs like material possessions, superficial friendships, popularity, fleeting carnal pleasure or short-lived worldly success and fame. These things have only limited value and will not help us go the distance. Only in a growing, vibrant and vital relationship with the Lord Jesus Christ can one find strength for the journey.

The All-Knowing God

**"But my God shall supply all your need
according to his riches in glory by Christ Jesus."
(Philippians 4:19)**

God is omniscient, or "all knowing". There is nothing in this universe (spatial reality) or in past, present or future (temporal reality) that God does not know. God's knowledge is perfect, complete and comprehensive. On the basis of God's foreknowledge, believers enter the predestined plan of God. That plan has three dimensions—salvation, the believer in time and the believer in eternity. Because of God's perfect knowledge, all of our needs are supplied according to His riches in Christ Jesus. (Philippians 4:19) In other words, because of the believer's position in Christ, which was foreordained even before the foundation of the world, God provides grace for living and dying that exceeds all that we ask or think.

It should encourage those of us who are tempted to be anxious about the unknown that God already knows what things we have need of and has placed those things in a wonderful portfolio of blessings designed to advance us in the Plan of God. (See Mathew 6:32; Ephesians 1:3.) So no matter what you are going through, remember God is in charge. While I don't know about tomorrow, I know who holds tomorrow in His hands.

Eternally Specific

"Giving thanks unto the Father,
which hath made us meet to be
partakers of the inheritance of the saints in light:
Who hath delivered us from the power of darkness,
and hath translated us into the kingdom of his dear Son:
In whom we have redemption through his blood,
even the forgiveness of sins:
Who is the image of the invisible God,
the firstborn of every creature:
For by him were all things created, that are in heaven,
and that are in earth, visible and invisible,
whether they be thrones, or dominions,
or principalities, or powers:
all things were created by him, and for him:
And he is before all things, and by him all things consist."

(Colossians 1:12-17)

In the New Testament, the eternality of Jesus Christ is attested by His involvement in creation. Ultimately though, it is the incarnation of God in the historical person of Jesus Christ that represents the decisive moment in the revelatory constellation. (See Hebrews 11:1 -3.) It is the incarnation interface, this unprecedented point of particularity, where all that is God-ness and goodness engages human frailty and finiteness. It is this sphere of specificity, God's sacrificial concern and redemptive identification with humanity in our sufferings, that is anticipated in His unique covenant relationship with the nation of Israel. Anticipating that covenant relationship, it is significant that in a prelude on Mount Sinai, God meets Moses in a bush that burned but did not consume.

At the point of Moses' commissioning as the Liberator of Israel, God reveals His essential Self as "I am that I am." The declaration of God's true essence was prior and preparatory to any experiential engagement of the plight of the oppressed Israelites. The tumultuous struggle that ensued in Egypt and began with Moses' initial confrontation of an oppressive Pharaoh provides timeless insight here. It was prefaced with these words, "The LORD God of the Hebrews hath sent me unto thee, saying, Let my people go, that they may serve me in the wilderness: and, behold, hitherto thou wouldest not hear. Thus saith the LORD, In this thou shalt know that I am the LORD: behold, I will smite with the rod that is in mine hand upon the waters which are in the river; and they shall be turned to blood" (Exodus 7:16-17).

The implications are clear that it is in the context of missions and our identification with those with whom God identities that unbelievers come to know that the God of Israel, the Father of our Lord Jesus Christ, is the One True God. The holistic nature of God's redemption of Israel can only be understood in light of God's timeless intent to vindicate and validate God's true essence in the context of human suffering. This irrepressible passion reached its zenith in the life, death, burial and resurrection of the Lord Jesus Christ who is the propitiation (mercy seat) for our sins as well as the sins of the whole world.

Made By God and For God

**"For by him were all things created, that are in heaven,
and that are in earth, visible and invisible,
whether they be thrones, or dominions,
or principalities, or powers:
all things were created by him, and for him."**

(Colossians 1:16)

In the Gospels, Jesus commended the poor widow for giving out of her need and not her abundance. She gave everything she had. Jesus said, "For all they did cast in of their abundance; but she of her want did cast in all that she had, even all her living" Mark 12:44. This woman's actions are consistent with the clear teaching of Romans 12:1-2. God does not desire our half-hearted commitment but rather a total sacrifice. When our hearts are totally committed to God and our lives reflect the lordship of Jesus Christ, it will impact our giving significantly.

Giving from a biblical viewpoint is the acknowledgment that "every good gift and every perfect gift is from above." (See James 1:17a.) In fact, when we give, we represent in a tangible way that not only has God made us but He has created us for Himself! (See Colossians 1:16.) When we give from the overflow of a full heart, we feel the pleasure of God who has made us for Himself.

The Bible specifies the tithe (10% of our gross income) and offerings as the means of supporting the work of the ministry and advancing the arena of God's Kingdom. (See Malachi 3: 6-8.) God blesses our obedience at this point, opening up the windows (not doors) of heaven and pouring out to us a blessing. I believe the tithe establishes a biblical principle: "equal giving and equal sacrifice." But tithing is not the limit of our giving. Through sacrificial offerings we who know the Lord in the covenant of grace are compelled to do more than what the Law requires. As we sow bountifully, we will also reap bountifully, for the Lord loves a cheerful giver.

Melody from Heaven

"Let the word of Christ dwell in you richly in all wisdom;
teaching and admonishing one another
in psalms and hymns and spiritual songs,
singing with grace in your hearts to the Lord."

(Colossians 3:16)

Genesis 4:21 is a significant biblical passage that records that Jubal (a descendant of Lamech, a descendent of Cain) was "the father of all such as handle the harp and organ." From the dawn of time and the beginning of creation, it is apparent that music has played a very important part in the lives of men and women and the worship of God. This musical chord was not severed by the ravages of original or imputed sin resulting from the Fall that occurred in Genesis 3. The 150th psalm is a clarion call to all of creation to praise God. The forms of this include praising Him through trumpet, psaltery, harp, dance, stringed instruments and organs. It is evident that God has invested humanity with a musicality that is a very integral part of worship.

In the New Testament, the Apostle Paul exhorts the believers at Colossae to "Let the word of Christ dwell in you richly with all wisdom; teaching and admonishing one another in psalms and hymns and spiritual songs, singing with grace in your hearts to God" (Colossians 3:16). Spiritual songs and singing are sacred and substantive because they represent a heart response controlled by the Holy Spirit. Therefore, music plays a significant role in our worship, work and witness as believers. Music is not a performance but a profession that is rooted in the heart (mentality of the soul) of the believer-priest and is energized by the filling of the Holy Spirit. As God's Spirit brings to our remembrance all that God has done for us, our hearts erupt in joyful praise.

Did you worship with a melody and song in your heart? I believe the Lord has given us a song that even angels cannot sing, because we have been washed in the blood of the Crucified One and we are Redeemed. God is the One who provides the melody to the discordant strands of our experiences. "Let everything that hath breath praise the Lord. Praise Ye the Lord."

The Feminine Voice

"In like manner also,
that women adorn themselves in modest apparel,
with shamefacedness and sobriety;
not with braided hair, or gold, or pearls, or costly array;
But (which becometh women professing godliness)
with good works."
(1Timothy 2:9-10)

I thank God for the precious gift of motherhood! Who among us has not been touched in a special and lasting way by the caring, compassionate and compelling presence and person of a mother? God is awesome! Every good and perfect gift comes from Him. No gift in the timeless tapestry of His creativity, other than that of Himself in the person of the Lord Jesus Christ, is as precious and priceless as mothers.

While we could consider the limitless list of things that mothers do to make us feel special, loved and cared for, one thing in particular is very important to our development physically, spiritually and emotionally. Mothers are the primary source of the feminine voice in our lives. It is the feminine essence that God literally manufactured (from a rib taken from the man's side) in the Garden, a beautiful woman and soon-to-be mother named Eve who completed Adam and satisfied His longing for companionship. (See Genesis 2:18-25.) I had a seminary professor who was fond of saying that God is a "fatherly mother and a motherly father." Over the years, I have paused at many points to contemplate the implications of that statement. The Bible says, "So God created man in his own image, in the image of God created he him; male and female created he them" (Genesis 1:27). This text affirms that whatever else it means to be made as human beings in the image of God, it necessarily involves and embraces both masculine and feminine dimensions. Apart, either the man or the woman are incomplete, but together in union with each other and with God, they constitute and comprise a synergy that is nothing less than supernatural!

Our mothers and those who have been motherly to us are the primary conduits and channels that God uses to inform and infect us from infancy forward with the awareness of the feminine voice in creation and in our lives. This voice originates in the Divine. It is the voice glimpses of it at many places in the Bible. Failure to recognize this reality is the primary problem of the feminist theologies so in vogue today. In an effort to level the playing field between men and women, these errant perspectives run the risk of diminishing and dismissing altogether the unique patterns and possibilities that women, deeply conscious of and committed to their own femininity, give to the marriage, family, the church, the interpretation of the Scriptures and to ministry. Our mothers are part and parcel of this beautiful mosaic that God painted at the beginning of time and perpetuates even now. How bland and bleak our lives would be without their loving and caring voices.

Legacy Matters

"When I call to remembrance
the unfeigned faith that is in thee,
which dwelt first in thy grandmother Lois,
and thy mother Eunice;
and I am persuaded that in thee also."

(II Timothy 1:5)

Recently, I was asked to prepare a ten to fifteen minute video taped meditation for a member who wanted to encourage spiritual growth, worship and maturation at their upcoming family reunion celebration. I was both humbled and daunted by the request. I was humbled that my feeble thoughts and reflections on the subject would be so esteemed and valued, but daunted because of the challenge of saying something significant and substantive in such a limited context of time.

My heart and mind rushed down many compelling and competing corridors. Emerging in the mentality of my soul was the thought **"legacy matters."**. The dictionary defines legacy as "anything handed down from an ancestor". Having recently celebrated a memorable reunion with my own family – the descendants of my maternal grandparents in Nashville, Tennessee, a wonderful time of blessing and bonding - I was reminded anew that legacy matters. It mattered to Abram (later called Abraham), an unknown Bedouin tribesman and the beneficiary of bountiful blessing from God. God promised him life, lineage, land and LEGACY in Genesis 12:1 -3.

The more I contemplated legacy matters, the more my thoughts converged around the question of what matters about legacy? To resolve this theological and conceptual challenge, I was led of the Spirit to a wonderful passage in II Timothy 1:1-7; 11-12. Here we have, literally, Paul's last will and testament to Timothy, his son in the ministry. This classic text represents the magnificent musings of a mature minister, the wonderful witness of a wise warrior, the solemn sentiments of a seasoned saint, the audacious affirmations of an aged apostle, and the daring declarations of a dedicated disciple. This text reveals what matters about legacy. Legacy is the **evidence of a providential purpose**. The will of God is the focus and fulcrum of Paul's opening salvo to Timothy. Legacy is also the **experience of a personal privilege**. Timothy was Paul's legitimate son in the ministry. Bereft of a stable and satisfying relationship with his natural father, God had provided Timothy a spiritual father in Paul who was model and mentor.

Legacy is also the **encouragement of persistent prayerfulness**. Paul's affection for Timothy was expressed and articulated in his constant praying for Timothy's good. The most important thing parents can do for their children is pray for them. This text reminds us also that the matter of legacy is the **evidence of a parental priority**. Timothy contracted an infectious (unfeigned) faith from his mother and

grandmother. Truly, more is "caught than taught". Finally, legacy matters and is important to you and me because of the **enablement of a proven power**. Paul encouraged Timothy's faith in God as an antidote to fear. He says to him, "God hath not given us the spirit of fear but of power, and of love and of a sound mind" (I Timothy 1:7). I also learned these things from my family of origin and extended family, many of whom are present in our worship celebration today. I learned that God can be trusted and that God is able to keep that which is committed unto His hands. I thank God for my spiritual legacy. What are you and I doing to leave a legacy for others?

Trained or Trapped

**"Study to shew thyself approved unto God,
a workman that needeth not to be ashamed,
rightly dividing the word of truth."**

(II Timothy 2:15)

The article in the newspaper caught my attention. The caption read, **"Bank employee suffocates being trapped inside huge vault."** It was the tragic account of a Brooklyn, New York woman who worked for a securities holding company. The story reported that the woman suffocated inside a huge Manhattan bank vault after she triggered an alarm system that released carbon dioxide, eliminating most of the oxygen in the vault. The woman mistakenly activated the system which was designed for quashing fires by depleting the oxygen supply. Apparently working alone during the late shift, her whereabouts were not determined by firefighters who responded to the alarm until it was much too late.

The church has been entrusted with the Gospel of the Lord and Savior Jesus Christ. It is a treasure of incomparable value. As we work the spiritual "late shift" in a world that is growing increasingly hostile toward the Word of God, it is important that we not work alone, but exhort and encourage one another. Also, we must be properly trained and equipped to handle any emergency that arises. Otherwise, that which has been provided to give us security and strength can be used by the evil one to kill, steal and destroy.

Cleared for Departure

"For I am now ready to be offered,
and the time of my departure is at hand."
(II Timothy 4:6)

During the past few months, I have found myself at a number of points and places viewing the arrival and departure screens in concourses and terminals in various airports in the continental United States and abroad. These checks were important and critical during my travels to assure proper gate identification and secure accurate flight connection information. While preaching in Chantilly, Virginia and a guest at a hotel near Washington Dulles International Airport, I was reminded anew of the transitory nature of life. As plane after plane rocked and roared in thunderous and almost rhythmic ascent and descent over the hotel going to or coming from the airport, I remembered the words of the Psalmist who said, "The Lord shall preserve thy going out and thy coming in from this time forth and even for evermore" (Psalm 121:8). Our lives are lived out in the brief dash between our arrival and our departure; the time of our birth and the time of our death.

Two short verses in the Pauline epistles speak profoundly to this reality. "And last of all he was seen of me, also as one born out of due time" (I Corinthians 15:8); and "For I am now ready and the time of my departure is at hand" (II Timothy 4:6). These powerful passages are bookends marking pivotal points and periods in the life of the Apostle Paul. They are reminders that the apostle was steeped in the awareness that His life was encapsulated in a transcendent timetable, a divine diary and an intergalactic itinerary. In both passages, he speaks of "time". Paul reflects upon the two significant moments and movements of his life: the time of his spiritual birth and the time of his death. While he experienced a late arrival to the family of faith, his departure from this veil of sin, suffering, and sorrow was on time. In both passages, he is reflective and contemplative. He writes to the church at Corinth and he is looking back over the tracks and trails of his storied ministry. He writes the last letter of his stellar apostolic career (from a Roman prison) to Timothy, his son in the ministry, while awaiting certain execution and martyrdom, and he is looking forward to the inviting horizons of a never-ending future. He tells Timothy, "I have fought a good fight, I have finished my course, and I have kept the faith" (II Timothy 4:7).

How we start out in life pales in significance and comparison to how we end up. Paul, the persecutor turned preacher, the adversary and now apostle, knew this. Time is one of the greatest gifts and resources God gives us in the epic battle of life, and time is running out for us all. How are you and I doing with the dash? Are we maximizing every moment and seizing every situation to and for the praise and glory of God? Are we faithful, focused and fitted for the fight? As we taxi through life, are we ready to respond by faith to our Supreme Pilot—who will one day pierce and propel the soul and spirit of every child of God—when He announces, "You have been cleared for departure"? Like Paul, the Apostle James understood this profound truth. He wrote, ""Whereas ye know not what shall be on the morrow, For what is your life? It is even a vapor that appeareth for a little time, and then vanisheth away" (James 4:14).

The Ministry of Encouragement

"Do thy diligence to come shortly unto me:
For Demas hath forsaken me,
having loved this present world,
and is departed unto Thessalonica;
Crescens to Galatia, Titus unto Dalmatia.
Only Luke is with me.
Take Mark, and bring him with thee:
for he is profitable to me for the ministry."

(II Timothy 4:9-11)

I thank God for the ministry of encouragement. Encouragement comes in many forms in the Christian life. First, there is the encouragement that comes from God. The Holy Spirit encourages the worship, work and witness of every true believer. For this reason, the Gospel of John calls Him the Comforter. This word is derived from a Greek word that means to "come alongside". Jesus said, "And I will pray the Father, and he shall give you another Comforter, that he may abide with you forever" (John 14:16). It is for this reason that we can be assured that God will never leave us or forsake us.

We also receive encouragement from the Word of God. The Psalmist declared, "Thy testimonies also are my delight and my counselors" (Psalm 119:24). In the same Psalm he said, "I rejoice at thy word, as one that findeth great spoil" (Psalm 119:162). The supernatural and inspired word of God is living and dynamic. It refreshes the spirit and waters the parched ground of our being. No wonder Paul, when facing martyrdom in a Roman prison, asked Timothy to bring with him "... the books but especially the parchments" (II Timothy 4:13b). Even to his dying hour the great Apostle found strength and encouragement in the Word.

God also places in our lives those who have the gift of encouragement and exhortation. A smile, an encouraging comment, a phone call or card can go a long way toward lifting the dark clouds that sometimes descend upon us. Thank God for the true friends and special encouragers that He gives us who understand that "A man hath joy by the answer of his mouth: and a word spoken in due season, how good is it!" (Proverbs 15:23). They minister to us with sincere compassion, and an unconditional love that has as its primary object our well-being. If you are blessed by this rare gift today, thank God for such a wonderful expression of His grace. Be thankful today that God encourages us by His indwelling Holy Spirit, through His Word, and by calling alongside us those who bless us with the ministry of presence and encouragement.

Not Alone

"At my first answer no man stood with me,
but all men forsook me:
I pray God that it may not be laid to their charge.
Notwithstanding the Lord stood with me,
and strengthened me;
that by me the preaching might be fully known,
and that all the Gentiles might hear:
and I was delivered out of the mouth of the lion."
(II Timothy 4:16-17)

II Timothy is considered by most expositors and commentators to be the Apos- tle Paul's last will and testament; dying words to Timothy (his son in the ministry), the book that was written from prison and cast in the shadows of his imminent martyr- dom. I am always intrigued and amazed when reading II Timothy 4:16. Paul says, "At my first answer no man stood with me, but all men forsook me; I pray God that it may not be laid to their charge." How could this be? How could the great church planter and apostle be left alone in the hour when he most needed companionship? Where were those whose lives he had touched? Why weren't there representatives from the congregations he had served at his first defense before Caesar?

In his hour of great need and privation, Paul felt the haunting, hobbling sting of isolation and loneliness. No one stood with him! We, too, experience loneliness as we seek to be good ministers of the Lord Jesus Christ. In one sense, this loneliness is occu- pational. There are times when our commitments and convictions necessitate that we walk alone. We cannot serve the Lord faithfully if we are merely moved and motivat- ed by the crowd. Because of this reality, there are times one can be in a room full of people and feel the chill of loneliness. In our Christian experience, loneliness occurs when God wants to have us completely to God's Self. Like the loving Shepherd that God is, He parts and separates us from the flock, calls us by name and has His own way with us as He shapes and conforms us into the image of His Glorious Son!

Paul Tillich, the great theologian, said, "Language has created the word loneli- ness to express the pain of being alone, and the word solitude to express the glory of being alone." The Apostle Paul was lonely and forsaken but not alone; for in the soli- tude he experienced the grace and glory of God. He says to Timothy, "Notwithstanding, the Lord stood with me, and strengthened me; that by me the preaching might be fully known, and that all the Gentiles might hear: and I was deliv- ered out of the mouth of the lion" (II Timothy 4:17). I am thankful for the blessed as- surance believers have that God will never leave us alone. Even as Jesus shouted from the cross the words of God-forsaken-ness (Mark 15:34), He was experiencing unfath- omable and unbroken intimacy with the Father and Holy Spirit. Be encouraged that when you feel lonely, isolated, forgotten and forsaken, YOU ARE NOT ALONE.

The Great Communicator

God, who at sundry times and in divers manners spake
in time past unto the fathers by the prophets,
Hath in these last days spoken unto us by his Son,
whom he hath appointed heir of all things,
by whom also he made the worlds;
Who being the brightness of his glory,
and the express image of his person,
and upholding all things by the word of his power,
when he had by himself purged our sins,
sat down on the right hand of the Majesty on high."
(Hebrews 1:1-3)

The Bible affirms unapologetically that God has spoken. God is the Great Communicator, doggedly intent on bridging the chasm between the Creator and the creature. God is the Divine Suitor who is determined to redeem the brokenness of creature and creation and make history "His-story", bringing many sons and daughters to glory. God is the great I Am who simultaneously inhabits past, present and future, always addressing the human predicament with commanding clarity and compelling compassion, transforming the dry ground of our existential deserts into holy ground. Beginning in Genesis 1:3, God speaks authoritatively to the primeval chaos which, although formless and void, erupts with life and vitality at God's command. In a similar fashion, the Gospel of John opens with a thunderous assent to the primacy of the Eternal Word, or Logos. (See John 1:1 -14.)

The Fall, as recorded in Genesis 3, is precipitated by an inappropriate response to the satanic and mister suggestion that God had not spoken; or if God has spoken at all, God had done so without integrity, comprehensiveness or authentic concern for man and woman. The serpent said to the woman, "Did God really say that?" This is the position of what Dr. D. A. Carson calls "philosophical pluralism". If God has spoken at all, then God's speech is muffled, muddled, and mangled in a multiplicity of manifestations, claiming only a subjective and relativistic authority to hearers who themselves are the architects of God' declarations and the captains of their own souls and destinies. Philosophical pluralism flagrantly denies, deconstructs and diminishes God's authoritative and spoken word, spawning what has been called a "culture of disbelief". Skepticism and disbelief, twins birthed by an arrogant pride, are at the heart of Adam's sin and ours.

The magnificent prologue of the Book of Hebrews reminds us that not only has God spoken, but God has spoken and acted in history with infinite creativity, unparalleled diversity, and determined and definitive finality. God's Word is not only spoken, but it happens as God intervenes and invests recurrently and redemptively into the life of the covenant community. (See Hebrews 1:1-3.)

The Morphology of Salvation

"Since the children have flesh and blood,
he too shared in their humanity
so that by his death he might destroy him
who holds the power of death--that is, the devil--
and free those who all their lives
were held in slavery by their fear of death."
(Hebrews 2:14-15 NIV)

Hardly a day passes without some mention of the very legitimate and serious concerns regarding the expectation that this year's flu season will be one of the most brutal and challenging for health agencies and, especially, public schools. These concerns are fueled primarily by the growing number of cases of a new strand of the virus called the swine flu in the continental United States and in many foreign countries, particularly Mexico. Vaccines have been developed for this new flu virus but will not be available until later this year.

I reflected upon the morphology or toxicology of vaccines (*our resident health professionals can help me here*) when I read recently the profound statement of the writer of the Book of Hebrews regarding the humanity of the Lord Jesus Christ. He wrote, "Forasmuch then as the children are partakers of flesh and blood, he also himself likewise took part of the same; that through death he might destroy him that had the power of death, that is, the devil; And deliver them who through fear of death were all their lifetime subject to bondage" (Hebrews 2:14-15). My basic understanding of the nature and composition of an effective vaccine is that it is developed from the virus itself and particularly from subjects who were infected and then survived the attack and onslaught of the disease. How interesting that C. S. Lewis in his classic <u>Mere Christianity</u> refers to Jesus Christ as a "good infection" in the human race whose presence as the sinless Son of God has changed, indeed transformed everything radically and dramatically. Because He lived, died and lives again, nothing can or will ever be the same. The "good infection" has changed the course and trajectory of human history.

The pre-incarnate Son of God who is the second member of the Trinity has always borne the image of the heavenly. The Apostle Paul in Philippians 2:6 said of Him, "Who, being in the form of God, thought it not robbery to be equal with God." Jesus praying to the Father made mention of this in His high priestly prayer when He said, "And now, O Father, glorify thou me with thine own self with the glory which I had with thee before the world was" (John 17:5). Yet, Jesus became a flesh and blood man primarily because it was the only way He could truly be the sin bearer of the human race, receiving into His own perfect humanity the virus of sin and death. According to the teaching of II Corinthians 5:21, "For he hath made him to be sin for us who knew no sin; that we might be made the righteousness of God in him." Jesus survived the infection of sin and death, the evidence of which is His glorious resurrection from the dead! He is now the vital and vicarious vaccine, the inviting inoculation, the compelling cure, and redemptive remedy for our sins.

The season of sin, suffering and death has been trumped and triumphed by the morphology of the Savior, who according to the prophet Isaiah, "Was pierced for our transgressions, he was crushed for our iniquities; the punishment that brought us peace was upon him, and by his wounds we are healed." I anticipate, as many of you do, once again fortressing my immune system by taking the flu shot when it is available. However, I am more confident and sure in the reality that my faith and life are secure now and forever in the knowledge and experience of He that is "able to keep you from falling, and to present you faultless before the presence of his glory with exceeding joy. To the only wise God our Savior, be glory and majesty, dominion and power, both now and ever. Amen" (Jude 1:24-25).

The Rest that Jesus Gives

"There remaineth therefore a rest to the people of God.
For he that is entered into his rest,
he also hath ceased from his own works,
as God did from his."
(Hebrews 4:9 -10)

Jesus Christ invited those who heard Him to enter into the place with Him where "ye shall find rest for your souls" (Matthew 11:29). This relational rest is experienced by those who acknowledge Jesus as Savior and Lord. It requires submission of the soul to the authority of the Holy Spirit and the consistent inhale and exhale of the Word of God. (See Matthew 4:4). No wonder this rest is associated with faith and the Word of God in Hebrews Chapter 4.

This rest is the "peace of God that passeth all understanding" (Philippians 4:6- 7). A believer anchored in the Word of God enjoys spiritual density and will not be tossed to and fro or carried about as a wave at sea. As we experience the rest that Jesus gives, we are able to boldly face the inevitable adversities of life without fragmenting.

Accessorizing Our Faith

**"But, beloved, we are persuaded better things of you,
and things that accompany salvation, though we thus speak."**

(Hebrews 6:9)

There is an interesting phrase in the Book of Hebrews that relates profoundly to the integrity and consistency of the Christian life during Phase Two of salvation (the believer in time). After encouraging his audience to advance beyond the principles of the faith – baptism, the laying on of hands, the doctrine of the resurrection, and eternal judgment - the author says, "But, beloved, we are persuaded better things of you, and things that accompany salvation" (Hebrews 6:9). Every time I read this passage, I think of this as a challenge to "accessorize our faith".

Fashion conscious men and women know how just the right piece of jewelry, or the right color blouse, shirt or necktie can bring out the salient features and patterns of a suit or dress. These accessories can make an otherwise plain or bland garment look much better. A few years ago, a book with the appealing title <u>Dress for Success</u> caught my attention. This book provided practical guidance in choosing, purchasing and accessorizing clothes so that one's appearance would make the maximum impact.

While we can do nothing to earn or merit salvation, there are accessories that we should diligently seek to adorn as those who through faith and well doing inherit the promises of God. The Apostle Peter enumerated these accessories in his second epistle. He said, "And beside this, giving all diligence, add to your faith virtue; and to virtue knowledge; and to knowledge temperance; and to temperance patience; and to patience godliness; and to godliness brotherly kindness; and to brotherly kindness charity. For if these things be in you, and abound, they make you that ye shall neither be barren nor unfruitful in the knowledge of our Lord Jesus Christ" (II Peter 1:5-8).

The failure to accessorize our faith cheapens the priceless garment of salvation, causing it to look plain and unattractive to a world that is in desperate need of a demonstration of true faith, hope and love at work in the lives and hearts of those who profess they are Christians.

The Perfect Sacrifice

"But Christ being come an high priest of good things to come, by a greater and more perfect tabernacle, not made with hands, that is to say, not of this building; Neither by the blood of goats and calves, but by his own blood he entered in once into the holy place, having obtained eternal redemption for us."
(Hebrews 9:11-12)

The Book of Leviticus regulates the worship and social life of ancient Israel. In great detail God communicates through Moses to the people regarding their relationship to Him and to those in the covenant community. In addition, the priestly service was regulated, and only Aaron the high priest was allowed to go beyond the veil in the Tabernacle into the Holy of Holies. He did this on the Day of Atonement, offering a blood sacrifice for his own sins and the sins of the people.

Each passing day, week, month and year animals were sacrificed and offerings made. There was a seemingly endless parade of innocent animals brought to the Tabernacle and sacrificed as each priest served in his course. Through the sacrificial system, Israel was reminded over and over again that without the shedding of blood there was no remission of sin.

The Old Testament sacrificial system pointed toward the coming of Christ, the perfect Lamb of God who would fulfill the requirements of the Law once and for all by His death on the Cross. "But Christ being come an high priest of good things to come, by a greater and more perfect tabernacle, not made with hands, that is to say, not of this building; neither by the blood of goats and calves, but by his own blood he entered in once into the holy place, having obtained eternal redemption for us" (Hebrews 9:11-12). This profound passage in the Book of Hebrews is a reminder of the completeness of our salvation. The death of Jesus Christ for the sins of the world made obsolete the Levitical priesthood and the intricate rituals of sacrifice associated with it. Each of us can now go beyond the veil into the person and presence of Christ, our High Priest and the Author and Finisher of our faith.

Faith Perception

**"Now faith is the substance of things hoped for,
the evidence of things not seen."
(Hebrews 11:1)**

There are three primary means of perception in the human race. First, one can perceive through the exercise of the rational mind. This type of knowing is called <u>rationalism</u>. The world around us can also be perceived by the use of the senses – touch, sight, smell and hearing. This type of knowing is called <u>empiricism</u> and is the basis of the scientific method. Both rationalism and empiricism are based on merit. The use of the mind and intellect can be enhanced by education and training. And obviously, a person with perfect sight could enjoy the radiance of a sunset more than a person who could not see at all.

The third means of perception or knowing is called <u>faith.</u> The Bible describes faith in this manner. "Now faith is the substance of things hoped for and the evidence of things not seen" (Hebrews 11:1). Furthermore, the Bible tells us that God has designated faith as the primary means of perceiving spiritual truth and reality. "But without faith it is impossible to please him; for he that cometh to God must believe that he is, and that he is a rewarder of them that diligently seek him" (Hebrews 11:6).

Chapter Eleven of the Book of Hebrews is the great faith chapter of the Bible. It chronicles the exploits of many of the great characters of biblical history who pleased God and experienced blessing and prosperity by faith. Over and over again, we hear the refrain "by faith" in this chapter. It is apparent that God wants us to be men and women of faith who do not depend ultimately on what we know or what we can see or sense, but rather persons who stand on the promises of God.

This is not only the legacy of our Christian faith, but this is also the rich heritage of Black people. While moving from slavery to freedom, former slaves appropriated the truths of the Christian faith in their own experience of oppression and bondage and discovered they could still sing the Lord's song in a strange land.

Faith and Reason

"But without faith it is impossible to please him: for he that cometh to God must believe that he is, and that he is a rewarder of them that diligently seek him."

(Hebrews 11:6)

The primary means of perception in the spiritual realm is <u>faith</u>. We cannot ultimately know and experience God from the vantage point of reason or our senses. Therefore, the writer of Hebrews declares emphatically that without faith, it is impossible to please God. (See Hebrews 11:6). Unlike reason and sensory perception (the scientific method or empiricism), faith is non-meritorious. Faith focuses on the object and not the subject. For those persons who say they have no faith, all human beings exercise faith on a daily basis. In fact, it is unreasonable to think that we could live normal lives apart from faith. Every doctor's visit, drink from the water fountain, meal at a restaurant, or drive to work is predicated on faith.

Blasé Pascal, the French scientist and philosopher, became a Christian during an extreme crisis in his life, largely because of the witness of his sister. He once said, "Faith has its reasons that reason does not know." A sophisticated intellect or a scientific approach to life will not ultimately sustain you or me during seasons of difficulty, challenge and turmoil. Something deep and wrenching inside cries and clamors for us to move beyond the limits of the mind and senses, to walk by faith and not by sight. This faith, while often viewed as inconsequential by the world, when directed to God can enable us to face and move our mountains. (See Matthew 17:20.)

Compelled by Joy

"Looking unto Jesus the author and finisher of our faith; who
for the joy that was set before him
endured the cross, despising the shame,
and is set down at the right hand of the throne of God."
(Hebrews 12:2)

On Palm Sunday, the Gospels record that Jesus ride into Jerusalem on a donkey. Roman generals often returned from battles in parade dress, riding on white stallions. Jesus entered the city on a servile beast amidst the jubilant hosannas of the masses who acclaimed Him as the Messiah of Jewish prophetic expectation. This event has often been referred to as His triumphant entry into the city. Five days later, our Lord was crucified like a common thief outside the city gates on a hill called Golgotha, or Calvary. When asked to choose between Jesus and Barabbas, the crowd chose a murderer over Jesus. Are these two scenes only tragic contradictions that witness to the fickleness and foolishness of people? Or is there some greater purpose and will to be determined in the solemn events?

This last visit of the Lord to the holy city of Jerusalem was indeed the beginning of a strategic victory for all humanity. It initiated a chain of events that culminated in His fulfilling a divine destiny and becoming once and for all the sin bearer for the whole human race. (See I John 2:1-2.) It was a victory that was secured not with sword or shield, cannon or catapult, arrows or lances but with the precious blood of the spotless Lamb of God. The writer of Hebrews said that He was compelled by the joy set before Him and therefore endured the cross and despised the shame and is now set down at the right hand of the throne of the Majesty on high. (See Hebrews 12:2.)

During this season we must be reminded that the power of God unto salvation was manifested ultimately and decisively in the death of the Lord Jesus Christ on the cross. While He could have called twelve legions of angels to His side, He laid His life down for your sins and mine. While those who condemned Him then and now must be responsible for their actions, it is reassuring to know that the power of God transcends the machinations of those who seek to thwart His program and purposes.

The Sacredness and Sanctity of Marriage

"Marriage is honourable in all, and the bed undefiled: but whoremongers and adulterers God will judge."

(Hebrews 13:4)

Recently while attending a national conference on biblical counseling, upon exiting a very informative and inspiring session on the sacredness and sanctity of marriage, I noticed a sign on the room locater at the hotel that said, **"Miss Gay America."** I could not help but ponder the stark contrast involved with these two groups meeting at the same place and at the same time. It reminded me of the widening, worsening moral crisis that is threatening our society. Not only have we witnessed the demise of conscience but the bankruptcy of shame as well. What was previously whispered in the closet is now being shouted on the rooftop for all to hear and see.

The truth as revealed categorically and doctrinally in the Word of God and ultimately in the incarnation of the Lord Jesus Christ is suffering not only the persistent attack of its enemies but the pernicious neglect of its friends as well. God has spoken authoritatively and with finality on the essence of true and genuine sexuality and the nature of the marital union. Homosexuality or any other form of deviant sexual behavior is a clear violation of the clear teachings of the Bible. The Apostle Paul writing to the Roman church said, "For this cause God gave them up unto vile affections: for even their women did change the natural use into that which is against nature: And likewise also the men, leaving the natural use of the woman, burned in their lust one toward another; men with men working that which is unseemly, and receiving in themselves that recompence of their error which was meet" Romans 1:26-27.

The idol most valued and in vogue today is the idol called "Self". Oswald Chambers in his classic <u>My Utmost for His Highest</u> confronts this issue very insightfully when he writes, "The nature of sin is not immorality and wrongdoing, but the nature of self-realization which leads us to say, 'I am my own god.' This nature may exhibit itself in proper morality or in improper immorality, but it always has a common basis - my claim to my right to myself." It is true, left to our own devices, we can only plummet and plunge into the disabling, distorting grasp of a dark, deadly and demonic hell.

For this reason and so many others, the church has a grave and urgent responsibility to confront the moral evil and ills of our day with biblical truth and rationale that lead people from self to the Savior. Nowhere is this need more pressing and pervasive than clear teaching and instruction about sex, singleness and marriage.

The Compelling Constant

"Jesus Christ the same yesterday, and today, and forever."
(Hebrews 13:8)

Henry Ward Beecher, the famous 19th century American preacher, once said, "Every artist dips his brush in his own soul, and paints his own nature into his pictures." Every single creation, whether a work of art, a music score, a chapter of literature or even the children that God blesses us with, mirror who we are. The colors of Fall are breathtaking during this season of the year. As I view this panoramic portrait, my faith tells me that God, the Supreme Artist, has taken his paint brush, dipped it into the creative and compelling palette of his incomparable essence, and splattered the landscapes with colorful hues that hint to all who truly observe and wonder that God stands within the shadows keeping watch over His own. Indeed, in the marvelous march of this majestic mosaic of colors, the words of the Apostle Paul to the Romans ring true: "For the invisible things of Him from the creation of the world are clearly seen, being understood by the things that are made, even His eternal power and godhead" (Romans 1:20a).

From another perspective, Fall marks the end of summer and the approaching advent of winter. The colors soon fade; deterioration levies its inevitable toll and the once pleasing and proud plumage falls to the earth in a timely death. This is a reminder to all of us that life is transient and transitory and that true happiness and joy cannot be found in the seasonal or the sensory, but in Him who is the Compelling Constant of life. The times and the seasons are in our Creator's hands and He knows what is best for us. Our lives, while constantly subject to the ravages of change and transition, are not arbitrary. God made us in His image and then saved us through the offering of His only Son for our sins. In Him, we are designer men and women vested with dignity and destiny. Jeremiah the prophet encountered this wondrous truth when God said to him, "For I know the thoughts that I think toward you, saith the Lord, thoughts of peace, and not of evil, to give you an expected end" (Jeremiah 29:11).

For the child of God, like the seasons of the year, endings and beginnings are intertwined and interlaced. Celebrate with me today the constancy of the One whose love is here to stay! Oscar Wilde once said that "life imitates art and art imitates life." Therefore, I am encouraged by the words of the popular song by Dru Hill titled "So Special" that describes superbly well the constancy of a lover's care:

"Winter spring Summer fall These four seasons tell it all Each has a special way Of saying my love is here to stay."

The Treasure in Trial

"My brethren,
count it all joy when ye fall into divers temptations;
Knowing this, that the trying of your faith worketh patience."
(James 1:2-3)

The Apostle Paul said, "My brethren, count it all joy when ye fall into divers temptations; Knowing this, that the trying of your faith worketh patience" (James 1:2-3). The Greek word translated "patience" is **hupomeno** and means to "abide under". It is a reference to the unique quality of life that emerges only during seasons of trial and testing; in essence, the treasure we discover when facing adversity.

The Lord allows the believer to experience suffering in order to perfect (literally complete) and mature our faith. Therefore, suffering for blessing is part and parcel of the believer's advance to maturity. When facing difficulty and trial, we have the confidence of knowing that God will use discomfiting circumstances to deepen our faith, energize our witness and stimulate our joy. One songwriter said it well: "If I never had a problem, I wouldn't know God could solve them; I wouldn't know what faith in God can do!" (Andre Crouch).

Christian Commitment

"Even so faith, if it hath not works, is dead, being alone."

(James 2:17)

Commitment is a residue and non-negotiable consequence of the Christian life. Commitment is the compelling recognition on the part of the believer that God has made us completely for God's Self, and that our greatest treasure is to know Him, and our greatest pleasure is to serve and please Him. After eleven chapters of didactic (abstract teaching of biblical principles), the Apostle Paul challenges Christians at Rome to put their performance and practice where their profession and praise were. He said, "I beseech you therefore brethren, by the mercies of God, that ye present your bodies a living sacrifice, holy, acceptable unto God which is your reasonable service" (Romans 12: 1).

There are some significant principles related to the great Apostle's appeal and exhortation that are relevant to us today. First, by implication, knowledge alone is not the sole criterion for a productive Christian life. We must apply what we know. Bible doctrine circulating in the mentality of the soul of the believer must be placed on the launching pad of commitment and applied vertically (our priesthood) and horizontally (our ambassadorship) in life. Application of doctrine that has been received into the human spirit by faith becomes the basis of deploying the problem solving devices needed for abundant Christian living. This passage also suggests that God wants living sacrifices. Jesus condemned the church at Sardis for having "a name that thou livest, and art dead" (Revelation 3:1). He condemned the Pharisees for being whitened sepulchers, full of dead men's bones. (See Matthew 23:27.) We can only be living sacrifices when the Spirit of God is alive in our hearts and we yield submissively to the Spirit's leadership, establishing our candidacy for spiritual production.

The Apostle Paul accentuates the sacredness and separateness of the Christian life. We are living and holy sacrifices. We have been set apart. We are called to live Godly lives. Committed Christians are different from the world. In the subsequent verse he said, "And be not conformed to this world but be ye transformed by the renewing of your mind, that ye may prove what is that good, and acceptable and perfect will of God" (Romans 12:2). We are not to be pressed into the world's mold. This mold is a way of thinking before it is a way of being or a way of doing. The battle line is our viewpoint. Committed Christians will exude in all things the Divine viewpoint that is recorded in the Word of God. That is why the apostle said that committed service is "reasonable" or (literally) logical Word-oriented and Word-delineated service or ministry.

This passage is relevant when in our churches 20% of the people still do 80% of the work and provide 80% of the resources of time, talent, temple, tithe and treasure. This passage is relevant to the loss of passion for evangelism and missions. The song says, "Lord prepare me to be a sanctuary, pure and holy, tried and true." If we are not careful, what God intended to be a sanctuary (our lives) could become a dead and unfruitful thing in the spiritual realm. James, the Lord's brother, said it best: "Even so faith, if it hath not works, is dead, being alone" (James 2:17).

Departure Time

**"Whereas ye know not what shall be on the morrow.
For what is your life? It is even a vapour,
that appeareth for a little time,
and then vanisheth away."**

(James 4:14)

When preparing to take a trip, the packing process is influenced by a number of factors including duration of the trip, destination, climate, departure and arrival times, as well as any special activities one anticipates participating in. With very sobering terms, the writer of Hebrews reminded his readers, "And as it is appointed unto men once to die, but after this the judgment" (Hebrews 9:27). There is a trip each of us must take. Our departure time is totally a matter of God's sovereignty. No matter what is going on in our lives, we cannot change this appointment. However, the preparations we make here have much to do with our ultimate destination.

Because life is "even a vapour, that appeareth for a little time, and then vanisheth away"(James 4:14b), we must make careful plans and provision here and now to spend eternity with God. The alternative of course is hell, which is a place of everlasting torment where there is weeping and gnashing of teeth. Our preparation must include laying up treasures such as faith, love, joy, peace, hope, and endurance. These are the riches that stand the test of time which do not wither or corrode. Are you ready to take this trip?

Graced Out!

*"Forasmuch as ye know that ye were not redeemed
with corruptible things, as silver and gold,
from your vain conversation
received by tradition from your fathers;
But with the precious blood of Christ,
as of a lamb without blemish and without spot."*
(I Peter 1:18-19)

The plan of God for the salvation of the human race is characterized by a provision, by protocol and by a policy. The provision is God's Own Self in the person of the Lord Jesus Christ who is the Good Shepherd that "giveth his life for the sheep" (John 10:11). We are redeemed (ransomed from the slave market of sin) by the precious blood of Christ as a lamb without blemish and without spot. (See I Peter 1:19). The protocol in the Plan of God involves proper authority orientation (humility), submission to (and subsequent filling of) the Holy Spirit as the basis of the energizing and stabilizing inhale and exhale of the Word of God. This develops in the believer in Phase 2 of the Plan of Salvation (the believer in time) cohesiveness and strength of soul so that he or she will not fragment (implode) when exposed to the outside pressures of life (adversity). The believer will be able to maintain a grace orientation, master the details of life, experience a relaxed mental attitude, and express personal love to God and impersonal (virtue-dependent) love to one's spouse, family, friends and others.

The policy of God's plan of salvation throughout the ages has always been grace. I teach new members that Grace is <u>G</u>od's <u>R</u>econciliation <u>a</u>t <u>C</u>hrist's <u>E</u>xpense. We are saved by grace, sustained by grace, and will one day be eternally changed and transformed by grace. John Newton, the former slave trader who became a Christian, once said, "When I get to heaven I shall see three wonders there. The first wonder will be to see many people there whom I did not expect to see; the second wonder will be to miss many people whom I did expect to see; and the third and greatest wonder of all will be to find myself there." Grace is the basis of my and your experience of a life of perpetual wonder and unmerited favor in the Lord Jesus Christ. While so many are living without Christ in this world and are "spaced-out" by the unrelenting pressures of a contingent and uncertain existence, the believer in union with Christ is truly "graced-out" and confident that God can and God will take care of you. Hallelujah!

Victorious Surrender

"Humble yourselves therefore
under the mighty hand of God,
that he may exalt you in due time:
Casting all your care upon him;
for he careth for you."

(I Peter 5:6-7)

Surrender? You must be kidding! In this victory vexed, achievement acclaimed, success saturated, and win weary society of ours, "surrender" is not a word that is viewed in a positive way. It is associated with defeat, quitting, losing or coming up short. Never give up and never give in is the mantra that drives so many sometimes to the brink of madness and misery. Marriages have been mangled, families fractured, businesses bankrupted and congregations convoluted and conflicted because of the refusal to surrender or submit. "I'm right and you're wrong" and "I'm doing it my way" are sure formulas for failure and frustration. It occurred to me that one place where surrender can be sweetened with victory is in our relationship with God. Here and only here can we in an ultimate sense experience "victorious surrender". We do so when we let go and LET GOD! This is what the Apostle Peter had in mind when he wrote in his epistle, "Humble yourselves therefore under the mighty hand of God, that he may exalt you in due time; casting all your care upon him, for he careth for you" (I Peter 5:6-7). Wow! Peter is reminding us that descent precedes ascent (God's way up is down) and that surrender is the nonnegotiable condition for success in the spiritual realm.

On a sunny day in December 2008, our missions team arrived at the airport terminal in Durban, South Africa after a long flight from the U.S. We were asked to surrender our passport for examination as we entered the country. Of course, either the lack of a valid passport or refusal to surrender it to the examining official would have preempted and prevented entrance into the country and participation in a life-changing and memorable experience. I'm afraid we forfeit so many blessings when we fail to surrender our cares and concerns to God. Joseph Scriven, the hymn writer, said it well when he wrote:

"What a Friend we have in Jesus, all our sins and griefs to bear! What a privilege to carry everything to God in prayer! O what peace we often forfeit, O what needless pains we bear, All because we do not carry, everything to God in prayer!

Our mothers exude and exemplify this type of victorious surrender, for every mother willingly goes to death's door to give birth to her child. This sacrifice is extraordinary and merits our highest praise and commendation. But more important to all of us is the victorious surrender of our Savior and Lord who willingly submitted His life to the plan of God and died on Calvary so that we might be saved from our sins and given the right to the Tree of Life. He died so that we might live, and He lives today so that we will not die! His surrender is our victory!

Cultivating Capacity

"Grace and peace be multiplied unto you
through the knowledge of God, and of Jesus our Lord,
According as his divine power hath given unto us
all things that pertain unto life and godliness,
through the knowledge of him
that hath called us to glory and virtue."
(II Peter 1:2-3)

The promise of financial prosperity and stability is one aspect of the awesome portfolio of blessings the believer receives from God. According to Ephesians 1:3, these blessings have their origin in God and are *spiritual blessings* used to advance the believer-priest in the Plan of God. (See II Peter 1:2-3.)

Ultimately, God is the sole arbiter of our condition in life. God knows what is best for us. God can see further than we can see and knows the end from the beginning. While the world defines financial prosperity in quantifiable terms, the Word of God reveals that we can experience prosperity even in the midst of scarcity. This is because God delights in expressing God's mightiness in the midst of our meagerness.

Over and over again, the Bible reminds us that blessing is directly related to (1) our obedience and (2) capacity. God blesses us consistent with God's righteousness. In other words, God would never bless us in a way that would compromise His own righteousness or violate our free will. God also blesses us in response to our *capacity for blessing*. Our failure to receive is related to both lack of faith (perception) and lack of capacity. (See James 1:3.) We increase our capacity for blessing as we yield to the leadership of the Holy Spirit, humble ourselves in prayer, and increase our spiritual density through the consistent inhale and exhale of the Word of God. (See Isaiah 26:1- 4.)

What a Fellowship!

"That which was from the beginning,
which we have heard,
which we have seen with our eyes,
which we have looked upon,
and our hands have handled,
of the Word of life;
(For the life was manifested, and we have seen it,
and bear witness, and shew unto you that eternal life,
which was with the Father, and was manifested unto us;)
That which we have seen and heard declare we unto you,
that ye also may have fellowship with us:
and truly our fellowship is with the Father,
and with his Son Jesus Christ.
And these things write we unto you,
that your joy may be full."

(I John 1:1-4)

Fellowship is one of the five fundamental functions of the New Testament Church. The others are evangelism, worship, discipleship, and ministry. The church grows warmer through fellowship, larger through evangelism, stronger through worship, deeper through discipleship, and broader through ministry and missions. Fellowship is therefore fundamental to the Christian community. It is significant that the church was born on the Day of Pentecost when all the members were "with one accord in one place." (See Acts 2:1.)

Fellowship is an ambassadorship function and involves horizontal relationships in the body of Christ. Our ability to function effectively in this domain is predicated on and interdependent with our relationship with God in a vertical dimension – the believer's priesthood. This is clearly the teaching of I John 1:3. "That which we have seen and heard declare we unto you, that ye also may have fellowship with us: and truly our fellowship is with the Father, and with his Son Jesus Christ." God's love for us and our love and obedience to God is the basis of true fellowship with others.

The word fellowship in the Bible translates the Greek word that means "to have in common". Fellowship is energizing and Spirit-directed interaction around the common and shared realities that shape the Christian life. This is the "unity of the Spirit" that we must endeavor to keep. (See Ephesians 4:1-6.)

Our fellowship extends not only to our interrelationships in the local church but also to our relationship to others in the larger body of Christ. Always, that fellowship is predicated on the common ground of our shared faith in the Lordship of Jesus Christ and the professed faith once delivered to the saints.

Salvation as Position, Pedigree, Progression and Prospect

"Beloved, now are we the sons of God, and it doth not yet appear what we shall be: but we know that, when he shall appear, we shall be like him; for we shall see him as he is."

(I John 3:2)

Salvation is simultaneously position, pedigree, progression and prospect. One way to think about this reality is to understand that all three members of the Godhead (Trinity) are involved in the salvation project. The Father planned it, the Son executes it and the Holy Spirit reveals it. This is the clear teaching of Hebrews 9:4: "How much more shall the blood of Christ, who through the eternal Spirit offered himself without spot to God, purge your conscience from dead works to serve the living God? "

One can also reflect on salvation in terms of the believer's actual experience. The moment we accept the Lord as our personal Savior, we enter into a relationship that can never be severed. We experience not only pardon, but a privileged position and priceless pedigree. As the guarantor and seal of our new position, the Holy Spirit indwells every believer, setting us apart (sanctifying us), but also working in us to conform us to the very image of Christ. (See I Corinthians 6:19.) This progressive pattern and process is the focus of the Apostle Paul's teaching in II Corinthians 3:18: "But we all, with open face beholding as in a glass the glory of the Lord, are changed into the same image from glory to glory, even as by the Spirit of God."

Finally, every believer should be energized and encouraged by the hope that looming on the horizon of this world is the promising prospect that we will one day be and live in the presence of God and our transformation will be complete. The Apostle John reminds the church of this in his first epistle, "Dear friends, now we are children of God, and what we will be has not yet been made known. But we know that when he appears, we shall be like him, for we shall see him as he is" (I John 3:2).

A Biblical Perspective of Faith

"Beloved, when I gave all diligence to write unto you of the
common salvation, it was needful for me to write unto you,
and exhort you that ye should earnestly contend for the faith
which was once delivered unto the saints."

(Jude 1:3)

The doctrinal category of faith in the Word of God consists of
two primary dimensions. First of all, there is the body or tradition
of faith that is passed down from one generation of believers to
another. This is the focus of Jude 3. "Beloved, when I gave all
diligence to write unto you of the common salvation, it was
needful for me to write unto you, and exhort you that ye should
earnestly contend for the faith once delivered unto the saints."
As New Testament believers, we inherit a wonderful legacy
of doctrinal truth, divine revelation that has been preserved
supernaturally and constitutes the canons of the Old and New
Testament (the sixty-six books of our Bible). The Greek word
translated "contend" in Jude 3 means to "fight about a thing as a
combatant." We live in a world where the very notion of absolute
truth is met with great suspicion and even outright hostility.
Therefore, we have a responsibility not only to proclaim the truth,
but to protect and preserve the truth as it has been ultimately
revealed in the Lord Jesus Christ. (See John 14:6.)

The other dimension of the word "faith" in the Scripture
focuses on non- meritorious perception that has as its object the
Word of God and the Person of God. The rationalist uses the
intellect; the empiricist uses the scientific method which is based
on sensory perception and evaluation. But the believer walks by
faith and not by sight. The Word of God teaches that "faith is the
substance of things hoped for, the evidence of things not seen"
(Hebrews 11:1b). Furthermore, "without faith, it is impossible to
please Him [God]" (Hebrews 11:6a). While the operation of faith
is a constant characteristic of every member of the human race,
it is the OBJECT of faith that makes Christianity distinctive and

unique. As the songwriter says, "I dare not trust in the sweetest frame but wholly lean on Jesus name." Who or what are you trusting today? If it's not Jesus, all other ground is sinking sand.

Vigilance

"Beloved, when I gave all diligence to write unto you of the common salvation, it was needful for me to write unto you, and exhort you that ye should earnestly contend for the faith which was once delivered unto the saints."

(Jude 1:3)

The church must remain vigilant and steadfast while guarding the doctrinal purity and biblical consistency of her teaching. Forces are at work in society as well as in the contemporary church which, if succumbed to, will undermine the authority of the Word of God in matters of faith and practice. A few days ago, I overheard two well-known television preachers say essentially that the imputation of the righteousness of God means that at a point in time we can become *equal* to *God*. How damnable and heretical is such an assertion! It only accentuated to me how urgent and imperative it is that pastors feed their flock with true knowledge and understanding.

Vigilance in this area begins with the faithful and committed ministry of the pastor-teacher who is responsible for giving spiritual oversight to the congregation. Three principles in the New Testament support the crucial work of this communicator of doctrine. The **Concentration Principle** recorded in Acts 6:1-7 emphasizes the importance of pastors giving themselves to prayer and the ministry of the Word. Opportunities for distraction and diffusion abound. The office of deacon was established in the early church for this very reason. The **Consecration Principle** recorded in I Timothy 4:11-15 underscores the centrality of the Word of God and ethical living in the cultivation of the pastor's personal piety and the spiritual health and wealth of the congregation. Finally, the **Continuity Principle** outlined in II Timothy 2:1-2 recognizes the importance and the imperative of the pastor's role in equipping others to participate in the teaching ministry of the church. Those who serve faithfully and effectively as teachers in the local church must submit consistently to the teaching authority of the pastor.

Silence in Heaven

"And when he had opened the seventh seal,
there was silence in heaven about the space of half an hour."
(Revelation 8:1)

On the island of Patmos, John the Apostle saw in a vision a great multitude of saints that no man could number. He was informed, "These are they which came out of great tribulation, and have washed their robes, and made them white in the blood of the Lamb" (Revelation 7:14). This chapter ends on a triumphant note with the tribulation saints in the presence of God and comforted by the promises of God's unceasing care.

However, the Eighth Chapter of Revelation begins with the opening of the seventh seal and the troubling, haunting notice, "There was silence in heaven." Can you imagine silence in the place of perpetual praise? My thoughts are stretched and strained while weighing the gravity of these words - silence in the sanctuary of the Beloved where billions of angels sing "Alleluia" when one sinner is saved by grace. The context of this passage only exacerbates its difficulty. These words are spoken at a time when the prayers of the saints of all ages are laid upon the golden altar. (See Revelation 8:3)

Upon further reflection, however, you must agree with me that there are times when our prayers, pleas and petitions seem to be greeted only with God's silence. These can be challenging and unsettling seasons for the believer who is trying to find faith and resolve to hold on and hold out in a difficult situation. Satan uses these times to tempt us to question the wisdom, goodness and purposes of God for you and me.

A further examination of this chapter of Revelation reveals that the silence in glory was only a magnificent prologue and prelude to the eruption of an all out assault by God upon the forces of sin, evil, death and destruction on earth. It was literally, the "calm before the storm". Don't confuse God's silence in your situation for lack of compassion or concern. God answers every prayer with either a "yes," a "no," or "wait a while". Remember, while you and I are waiting, God is still working on our behalf.